Modern Philosopher Kings

Edinburgh Studies in Comparative Political Theory & Intellectual History
Series Editor: Vasileios Syros

Edinburgh Studies in Comparative Political Theory & Intellectual History welcomes scholars interested in the comparative study of intellectual history/political ideas in diverse cultural contexts and periods of human history and Comparative Political Theory (CPT).

The series addresses the core concerns of CPT by placing texts from various political, cultural and geographical contexts in conversation. It calls for substantial reflection on the methodological principles of comparative intellectual history in order to rethink of some of the conceptual categories and tools used in the comparative exploration of political ideas. The series seeks original, high-quality monographs and edited volumes that challenge and expand the canon of readings used in teaching intellectual history and CPT in Western universities. It will showcase innovative and interdisciplinary work focusing on the comparative examination of sources, political ideas and concepts from diverse traditions.

Available Titles:
Simon Kennedy, *Reforming the Law of Nature: The Secularisation of Political Thought, 1532–1689*
Lee Ward, *Recovering Classical Liberal Political Economy: Natural Rights and the Harmony of Interests*
Evert van der Zweerde, *Russian Political Philosophy: Anarchy, Authority, Autocracy*
Haig Patapan, *Modern Philosopher Kings: Wisdom and Power in Politics*

Forthcoming:
Leandro Losada, *Machiavelli in Argentina and Hispanic America, 1880–1940: Liberal and Anti-Liberal Political Thought in Comparative Perspective*
Filippo Marsili & Eugenio Menegon, *Translation as Practice: Intercultural Encounters between Europe and China and the Creation of Global Modernities*
Vassilis Molos, *The Russian Mediterranean: Shaping Sovereignty and Selfhood on the Island of Paros, 1768–1789*
Miguel Vatter, *Machiavelli and the Religion of the Ancients: Platonism and Radical Republicanism*

Modern Philosopher Kings

Wisdom and Power in Politics

HAIG PATAPAN

EDINBURGH
University Press

Edinburgh University Press is one of the leading university presses in the UK. We publish academic books and journals in our selected subject areas across the humanities and social sciences, combining cutting-edge scholarship with high editorial and production values to produce academic works of lasting importance. For more information visit our website: edinburghuniversitypress .com

Edinburgh University Press Ltd
13 Infirmary Street
Edinburgh EH1 1LT

First published in hardback by Edinburgh University Press 2023

Typeset in 11/13pt Sabon LT Pro
by Cheshire Typesetting Ltd, Cuddington, Cheshire

A CIP record for this book is available from the British Library

ISBN 978-1-3995-0877-3 (hardback)
ISBN 978-1-3995-0878-0 (paperback)
ISBN 978-1-3995-0879-7 (webready PDF)
ISBN 978-1-3995-0880-3 (epub)

Contents

Introduction: Between Wisdom and Power   1

1. Paradox of the Philosopher King   9

2. Prophets, Popes and Princes   35

3. The Public Intellectual   57

4. The Artist as Creator   77

5. The Hidden Philosopher King   104

6. The Scientist as Modern Benefactor   134

7. The Wise and Sovereign People   152

Conclusion: Modern Philosopher Kings   171

Bibliography   191
Index   219

διὸ δὴ πᾶς ἀνὴρ σπουδαῖος τῶν ὄντων σπουδαίων πέρι πολλοῦ δεῖ μὴ γράψας

Plato, *Seventh Letter*

Introduction:
Between Wisdom and Power

In the Kurukshetra battlefield, soon after blowing the conch of war, Pandava prince Arjuna instructs his charioteer Krishna to drive to the centre of the battle between the armies of the Pandavas and the Kauravas to see who is eager for war. When he does, he is dismayed to see his own relatives, beloved friends and revered teachers among the enemy. Filled with doubt and despair, he wonders if it is more noble to fight or renounce and leave the war. Overwhelmed with sorrow he drops his bow and turns to his charioteer and guide Krishna for advice on what to do. In the subsequent conversation as recorded in the *Bhaghavad Gita* or Song of God, Krishna, who reveals himself to be an incarnation of Vishnu, counsels Arjuna on his duty as a prince, a warrior and a righteous man, allowing him to enter battle and win the war for the Pandavas. The insight that we have an all-too-human need for wisdom in wielding power, and that such a union is made possible by divine intervention, is not unique to the Vedas. *Prajna*, wisdom or discernment and the Four Noble Truths – the truth of suffering, the truth of the cause of suffering, the truth of the end of suffering and the truth of the path that leads to the end of suffering – required the enlightenment of Siddhartha Gautama and instruction of the Buddha. King Solomon's wisdom, preserved in the Song of Songs, Proverbs, Ecclesiastes, Psalms and Odes had its source in the Lord, who 'giveth wisdom: out of his mouth cometh knowledge and understanding' (Prov. 2: 6). Jesus in the Sermon on the Mount (Matt. 5: 3–11) reveals the new foundations for blessedness and happiness where he declares that the poor in spirit, those that mourn, the meek, those that thirst for justice, the merciful, the pure of heart, the peacemakers and those who are persecuted will receive their reward in heaven. The *Qu'ran* is the written record of the laws and commandments of the All-Knowing and All-Wise Allah as revealed to the Prophet Muhammad by the angel Gabriel.

These diverse and distinct manifestations of divine wisdom, counsel and command confirm our ubiquitous and powerful longing to have wisdom guide our thoughts, words and deeds. They also reveal the difficulty of uniting wisdom and power in the absence of such divine intercession. The Hundred Schools of Thought was a great flourishing of philosophers and schools with Confucian, Legalist, Daoist as well as other scholars vying with each other to advise warlords and generals on good government during the disunity and violence of the Spring and Autumn period (770 to 476 BCE) and Warring States periods (453–221 BCE) in China. During the later stages of Warring States period King Zhang of Qin was so impressed by the Legalist Han Fei that he implemented a series of reforms based on his writings, subduing his six rivals and unifying China in 221 BCE. Soon after, however, the new Emperor Qin, the founder of the China's first dynasty, had Han Fei imprisoned, forcing him to take his own life, after which he is said to have burned books and executed scholars by burying them alive. Why is it difficult to unite wisdom and power, philosophy and politics?

In Aesop's famous tale of the wolf and the lamb, the wolf accuses the lamb of a series of transgressions that the lamb gently repudiates and disproves – he could not have insulted him last year as he was not born then; he did not feed on the wolf's pastures since he has yet to taste grass; and he never sullied the waters of the creek because he is still nursed by his mother. Despite these indisputable arguments and the justice of the cause, the wolf devours the lamb. Aesop's tale suggests that reason, however compelling, is frequently exploited by the cunning, and justice has little purchase in the world of the powerful. Wolves and lambs of course do not speak or argue, and hungry wolves must perforce eat lambs. Perhaps Aesop is mistaken, and reason and wisdom are much more influential in human affairs? Sadly, the bleak insights of ancient poets are too readily verified and substantiated by the testimony of history. Indeed, recent experience seems to go further, suggesting that not only is politics at best indifferent, at worst hostile to wisdom, but philosophy may be politically corrosive, exacerbating the demands of justice. Cambodian Saloth Sar went to Paris in 1949 on a scholarship to study radio electronics but instead became involved with the French Communist Party and joined a group of young left-wing Cambodian nationalists who later became his fellow leaders in the Khmer Rouge. With his new revolutionary pseudonym Pol Pot or Brother No. 1, he led the Cambodian Communist Party and became prime minister of the new Khmer Rouge government from 1976 to its overthrow in 1979. During this time, the *Angkar* or Organisation and later the Communist Party of Kampuchea initiated 'Year Zero', a revolutionary society that implemented a programme of radical social and agricultural reforms that resulted in the deaths of more than one million people from forced labour, starvation, disease, torture or execution. Confronting the inhuman cruelty of the attempts to 'purify' the country, Pol Pot refused to blame the revolution, redoubling his efforts to remove 'enemies', who were starved or tortured to death. Even on his deathbed, he remained unremorseful, blaming others while acknowledging mistakes had been made.[1]

The prospect of a world ruled by force and fraud understandably fills us with dismay. When Shakespeare's Hamlet declares,

O God! God!
How weary, stale, flat and unprofitable
Seem to me all the uses of this world!
Fie on't! ah, fie! 'tis an unweeded garden
That grows to seed; things rank and gross in nature
Possess it merely[2]

we hear the plaintive and heartfelt despair of someone repulsed by the duplicitous and deadly intrigue in the 'unweeded garden' of Elsinore, longing to return to Wittenberg University where the purity of reason and learning is unsullied by power and politics. For those such as Hamlet, the life of action or the political life, with its volatility, feverish perfidy and cold cruelty, is so incommensurate to the clarity, unalloyed joys and collegiality of the contemplative life that it compels all good people to seek its sanctuary. Such a tragic view of politics leads to the conclusion that philosophy can be nothing more than a palliative and curative refuge.

Others, confronted by the fear that politics is a world removed from reason, philosophy and justice, at best indifferent, at worst hostile to wisdom, will seek succour and solace in the divine. In his *Peloponnesian War*,[3] Thucydides recounts the war between the Athenians and the Spartans and in particular the famous dialogue between the Athenians and the Melians where the Athenians demand the Melians join the Delian League and pay tribute. In attempting to persuade the Melians, the Athenians declare 'since you know as well as we do that right, as the world goes, is only in question between equals in power, while the strong do what they can and the weak suffer what they must'. Seeking to preserve their freedom and neutrality, the Melians respond,

> You may be sure that we are as well aware as you of the difficulty of contending against your power and fortune, unless the terms be equal. But we trust that the gods may grant us fortune as good as yours, since we are just men fighting against unjust, and that what we want in power will be made up by the alliance of the Lacedaemonians, who are bound, if only for very shame, to come to the aid of their kindred. Our confidence, therefore, after all is not so utterly irrational.[4]

The Melians therefore remain unpersuaded by the Athenian arguments and dismiss the Athenian Envoy, with the result that the Athenians lay siege to Melos and in due course kill all Melian men of military age, enslave all the women and children, and turn Melos into an Athenian colony.[5]

The painful lesson to be derived from these reflections on the seemingly enduring tension, even animosity, between wisdom and power therefore seems to be the extreme alternatives of a life of tragic resignation or of hopeful piety. But is this tension and the contrary dispositions it engenders inevitable? Is it possible to combine wisdom and power without sacrificing one to the other, so that wisdom is empowered, and politics ennobled? This question was first posed by Socrates in Plato's *Republic* when he proposed philosophers rule as kings or rulers becoming philosophic.[6] As his most radical reform in founding *kallipolis* or the beautiful and just city, Socrates conceded it was a ridiculous suggestion, even a paradox, a puzzling or counterintuitive proposition. Ever since the idea of the philosopher king has mesmerised and tantalised, the force of its elusive and epigrammatic formulation has invited and provoked an examination of the interrelationship of philosophy and politics. But its allure and appeal can be traced above all to Socrates' extraordinary observation that unless political power and philosophy coincide, 'there is no rest from ills for the cities'.[7] It is this remedial and ennobling aspect of the philosopher king that has driven the hopes and ambitions of those who reject a humanity tragically disfigured and fundamentally riven, destined to suffer injustice. Moved by the promise that justice is within the province and discretion of humanity and not at the unpredictable whim of force and chance or a matter of divine supplication or dispensation, they have sought to implement the promise of the philosopher king. The philosopher king is therefore not only a profound theoretical puzzle that invites us to meditate and explore the relationship between wisdom and power, but also the alluring practical prospect that the union of wisdom and power is feasible and will yield progress and human perfectibility.

In this book I explore this paradox and promise of the philosopher king. The engagement with the paradox will shed new light on wisdom and power, philosophy and politics, revealing the interrelationship between them. The investigation of the promise will allow us to evaluate the success of the ever-present and indefatigable human ambition to secure justice. Together they promise a meditation on the nature of humanity, the beneficence of nature and the role of providence in accommodating our place within a cosmological whole.

The ambition to unite wisdom and power has manifested itself philosophically in works that directly engage with Socrates and his successors, and more generally in various attempts to examine the theoretical possibility of such a union. It is also evident in diverse political initiatives that have endeavoured to secure such a combination in multiple cultural, historical and institutional contexts. The complex and manifold channels and streams through which this ambition courses explain the wide reach of this book. Wisdom manifests itself in diverse ways, and is distinct from art, science, prudence and the intellect.[8] Thus, philosophers can be said to be those who long for a wisdom that remains out of reach or those who possess it. Equally, power is a complex notion that alludes to and may comprehend necessity, compulsion, consent, legitimacy and authority. Acknowledging these subtleties, the varied nature of these modern experiments in actualising the philosopher king is the reason we will adopt the broadest understanding and conceptions of philosophy and politics, wisdom and power, eschewing precise definitions that may foreclose or preclude revealing aspects of these modern experiments. The diversity of these experiments also accounts for the breadth, range and varied terrain we will traverse and navigate to explore the intersection and confluence of the various attempts to combine wisdom and power. We will thus interrogate and assay pious kings, intellectuals, artists, advisors, scientists and 'The People' as various expressions of the modern ambition to realise the promise of the philosopher king. In each case we will explore the nature of such attempts and how they are informed and shaped by their unique contexts and domains to discern what new insights they yield into the paradox, evaluate the extent of their success and assess the obstacles they confront in seeking to unite wisdom and power.

As we will see, our examination of the variety of modern attempts to fulfil the promise of the philosopher king shows the elusiveness or limited success of such initiatives at uniting wisdom and power. Politics, constituted by a diversity in our abilities, limited by our inability to discern or defer to wisdom, the brief span of our lives that constrains its influence and reach, and *fortuna*, with its unpredictability that constantly mocks our vain attempts to cage and tame it, account for the limited success of various modern experiments in the modern philosopher kings. But a different picture emerges when we examine the alternative formulation of the paradox of the philosopher king, the possibility of rulers becoming philosophical. From this perspective we see that the transformative influence of philosophical writings on rulers allows philosophers to rule, albeit indirectly and in complex and unpredictable ways. Thus, the writings of philosophers allow wisdom and philosophy to have a much greater influence in the world, permitting a form of the philosopher king that is superior because it overcomes the limitations of politics, nature and *fortuna* that limit the actual rule of philosopher kings. But it also issues new challenges, ranging from novel limitations on prudence to a new politics and agonism of books and philosophers.

The book examines the paradox and promise of modern philosopher kings by taking up and exploring in each chapter prominent yet diverse attempts to combine wisdom and power. The 'Paradox of the Philosopher King' (Chapter 1) details the paradoxical nature of Socrates' claim, how it was intended to counter the blandishments of the Sophists and the basis for its subsequent longevity and influence. 'Prophets, Popes and Princes' (Chapter 2) examines the way the *munus triplex Christi*, or threefold functions or offices of Christ in his earthly ministry as prophet, priest and king, initiated three distinct forms of the modern philosopher king. How the prophet soon gave way to the pope and pious king, who in turn contested political authority, shows the promising yet politically fraught nature of the pious philosopher king. We then turn to one of the most well-known modern versions of the philosopher king, the 'The Public Intellectual' (Chapter 3), who as a child of progress, both heroic and tragic, and threatened by the transformation of the public sphere, reveals the potential and limits to this modern experiment in combining wisdom and power. 'The Artist as Creator' (Chapter 4) examines the role of the artist as genius and creator, a *Künstler-Philosoph* who promulgates tablets of values and transforms politics by mythmaking. The rarity of such artists, and the difficulty of distinguishing between them and the false prophet and ideologue, reveal the limits modernity imposes on the artist as the philosopher king. 'The Hidden Philosopher King' (Chapter 5) explores the philosopher as counsellor to rulers as another modern initiative of combining wisdom and power. Machiavelli's reservations concerning such a solution, contrasted with Confucius's endorsement, reveals the limitations of such a resolution of the paradox of the philosopher king, which is to some extent replicated in Hegelian and Weberian contests regarding the role of modern bureaucracies as counsellors to democratic sovereigns. The theme of our next chapter, 'The Scientist as Modern Benefactor' (Chapter 6) is the influential contemporary example of the scientist as philosopher king. The Baconian innovation of science as philosophy resulted in the technocrat as the modern philosopher king who is increasingly facing new challenges that question the truth, benevolence and morality of modern science and scientists. As these chapters reveal, in its critique of elitism and inclination to favour the dispersal of offices and power, democracy appears as the most formidable obstacle to all modern attempts to secure philosopher kings. But is democracy itself, in the form of the sovereign people, the preeminent modern form of the philosopher king? In 'The Wise and Sovereign People' (Chapter 7) we take up the possibility that 'the people', combining deliberative judgement and sovereignty, provide the conclusive modern answer to the paradox and promise of the philosopher king. Who 'the people' are, as well as epistemic and deliberative aspects of such rule, reveal the limits of this form of philosopher king. Finally, in 'Modern Philosopher Kings', the concluding chapter, we reflect on the reach and limits of modern philosopher kings as noble attempts to civilise power and to empower wisdom. Though politics is open to wisdom and philosophy, there are also powerful elements within it resistant to such a union. As we will see, the limited success of these modern philosopher kings reveals the constraints on human ambition to realise progress and justice. Yet as we conclude, it may still be possible to achieve the aspirations of philosopher kings but in its alternative form of kings as philosophers. To the extent that rulers are disciples and advocates of philosophers, such a possibility effectively means the philosophers' attenuated rule through writing, both as philosophical reflection and education, and through law and constitutionalism. The brief, rare and fortuitous coincidence of wisdom and power therefore points to writing as a form of political rule that either in foundational philosophical works or in the enactment of laws and constitutions that defend and accommodate wisdom becomes the surest and perhaps only means for securing the rule of the wise.

The limited success of the modern philosopher kings questions our hope and ambitions that progress and perfectibility will secure justice. Yet our examination of the elusiveness of the union of wisdom and power also confirms the influence of wisdom in politics, even if its reach and potency is not as extensive or comprehensive as the spirit of modernity presumed or anticipated. Whether wisdom can be powerful, and politics wise, is an enduring and profound question that can lead to the extremes of tragic despair or pious resignation. It can also, however, give rise to a spirit of self-sufficiency to surmount these alternatives by willing the union of wisdom and power in the hope of securing justice. Our hopes and longings for justice therefore reveal themselves as either admirable and justifiable endeavours to secure our dignity or overvaulting desires that immoderately and hubristically deny all limits to human ambition. Our close study of the paradox and promise of modern philosopher kings therefore seeks to discover whether and how successfully wisdom and power can be united and in doing so provide a clearer understanding that will limn the contours of this common ground, revealing the true dominion and reign of the philosopher king where it may be possible to empower wisdom and ennoble politics.

Notes

1. Mydans (1998).
2. *Hamlet* (I, ii, 136–41).
3. Thucydides (1982: 351).
4. Ibid. 353.
5. On why the Athenian argument cannot persuade the Melians and the consequence of this for Athens see Orwin (1997).
6. *Republic* (473c9–e). References to the *Republic* are to Plato (1991a).
7. Ibid. 473d4.
8. See, for example, Aristotle's *Nicomachean Ethics* (1138b–1145a10), his *Metaphysics* (980a–993a25) and the discussion of the divided line and the distinctions between intellection, thought, trust and imagination in Plato's *Republic* (509c ff.). References to *Nicomachean Ethics* are to Aristotle (2012) and to *Metaphysics* are to Aristotle (1979).

Chapter 1

Paradox of the Philosopher King

'Xi Jinping Thought on Socialism with Chinese Characteristics in the New Era', or more simply 'Xi Jinping Thought' was incorporated in the Constitution of the Chinese Communist Party in 2017 and in the People's Republic of China Constitution in 2018. As one of the only two leaders with a 'Thought' (the other is Mao Zedong, the founder of the People's Republic of China), Xi Jinping rises above his two most recent predecessors – Hu Jintao with his 'scientific development perspective' and Jiang Zemin with his 'important thought of the Three Represents', and even Deng Xiaoping who only had a 'theory'. Though the precise meaning of 'Xi Jinping Thought' remains elusive, what is more intriguing is why Xi took such pains to alter the Party and state constitutions to announce its existence. Politics is of course one possible reason – the legal entrenchment of Xi Jinping Thought provides him with a constitutional fortification and bulwark against opportunistic domestic challenges to his leadership. Yet the means chosen to secure his position, focusing on Xi as 'thinker' and his thought and ideas as his most distinguishing and meritorious contribution, suggests that it is not sufficient to occupy the highest office and wield the greatest power to be an outstanding leader; to be truly exceptional a leader also needs a unique 'Thought' and therefore needs to be thinker or philosopher. Philosophy or wisdom if not superior, at the very least complements and completes political authority or power. Xi Jinping and Xi Jinping Thought therefore confirms the centrality of the idea of the 'philosopher king' in modern China. Xi Jinping and China are not unique in this respect. Modern founders of states and revolutionary leaders have also tended to provide a philosophical or theoretical justification for their actions. Consider, for example, the famous writings or books that accompanied, justified or defended new states: Lenin's *What is to Be Done* (1902); *Mein Kampf* (1926), Hitler's notorious justification for the Third Reich; Mussolini's *The Doctrine of Fascism* (1932); Stalin's *Marxism and the National Question* (1935); Nasser's *The Philosophy of the Revolution* (1956); Mao's *The Little Red Book* (1964); Mahathir's *Malay Dilemma* (1970); Qaddafi's *The Green Book* (1975); Khomeini's *Islamic Government* (1979); Kim Il-sung's *Jeojakjip* (1979); Niyazov's *The Rukhnama* (2001). Irrespective of their political leanings and whatever their political affiliations, these leaders consider themselves, or feel compelled, to claim the title of philosophers as much as founders of states.[1]

That an exceptional leader needs to be both philosopher and ruler can be traced to its most famous formulation by Socrates in Plato's *Republic*:

> 'Unless', I said, 'the philosophers rule as kings or those now called kings and chiefs genuinely and adequately philosophize, and political power and philosophy coincide in the same place, while the many natures now making their way to either apart from the other are by necessity excluded, there is no rest from ills for the cities, my dear Glaucon, nor I think for human beings, nor will the regime we have now described in speech ever come forth from nature, insofar as possible, and see the light of the sun.'[2]

As perhaps the best known of Plato's formulations and an enduring and influential idea in political thought, the philosopher king is a Pole Star, an inspiration and aspiration for good leadership and an uncompromising indictment of the ever-present perfidy and corruption of venal and incompetent officeholders.[3] But our high regard for the idea of the philosopher king obscures and perhaps conceals its dubiousness when first proposed by Socrates. Socrates introduces the philosopher king in Plato's *Republic* after much hesitation, in his attempt to show the feasibility of *kallipolis* or the just or beautiful city that he, Plato's brothers Glaucon and Adeimantus and others have founded in speech. When he does introduce it, he calls it a 'paradox', a view that runs *para* (counter to), a particular *doxa* (belief or opinion).[4] Socrates fears that the philosopher king as the third 'wave' of reform would 'drown' him in 'laughter and ill repute', even more so than the other 'waves' of common education of men and women, and the community of women and men he had proposed.[5] Indeed, as Glaucon notes when he declares an alliance with Socrates to defend him, rule by philosophers is not only seen as absurd but even dangerous, with 'very many men, and not ordinary ones' willing to attack Socrates.[6] The philosopher king in its first seminal formulation was therefore considered a ridiculous and dangerous innovation.[7]

In this chapter we examine why the philosopher king was considered a paradox when first proposed and how this paradox subsequently became a promise, a modern goal or ambition to secure justice. Both as paradox and a promise, our engagement with the original debates regarding the merits and limitations of the philosopher king will allow us to discern more clearly the nature of philosophy and politics and how each can accommodate and benefit from the other. Beyond this, however, to the extent that the philosopher king promises a solution to the 'ills' of cities and humanity more generally, it allows us to reflect on the extent to which human endeavour is warranted to repair or even ameliorate natural and divine bounty and providence, and therefore whether the cosmos favours and accommodates humanity. To understand the paradoxical nature of the philosopher king, we first need to examine who is a philosopher and what is the nature of politics according to Socrates, before we turn to the variety of attempts to resolve the paradox, especially the Sophists' reliance on wisdom to overcome the problems of politics. In our concluding discussion we explore the extent to which the paradox of the philosopher king resulted in the promise of the philosopher king – modern attempts to combine philosophy and politics in a variety of forms, ranging from pious kings to intellectuals, artists, advisors, scientists and 'the people' to attain justice.

Philosophy and Politics

In Plato's *Republic*, Socrates, along with Plato's brothers Glaucon, Adeimantus and others, discuss the nature of justice, first in the individual and later 'writ larger' in the just city that they found. The entire discussion is shaped in large measure by Glaucon's political ambitions, and his confrontation with Sophists and teachers of rhetoric such as Thrasymachus, who question the goodness of justice and in doing so advocate the tyrannical life for exceptionally talented individuals. The proposal of the philosopher king, which emerges as a necessary means for founding the noble or just city, is therefore a consequence of both immediate political ambition and more theoretical debates concerning the meaning of the good life for both individuals and cities. To understand why Socrates calls the philosopher king a paradox, we first need to explore his conception of the philosopher. The philosopher, according to Socrates, is a lover, a 'desirer of wisdom, not of one part and not another, but all of it'.[8] Unlike the lovers of hearing, of sights and of the practical arts, philosophers are the 'lovers of the sight of truth'.[9] Philosophers are therefore those who have the capacity to not only delight in what is fair, but in the 'nature of fair itself'.[10] These people are rare, according to Socrates, yet it is these few who base their thoughts on knowledge who are 'awake' and 'healthy', unlike the majority who relying only on opinion can be said to be asleep or dreaming.[11] Because opinion lies between what 'is' and knowable and what is not, which is unknowable, philosophers are defined as those who 'delight in each thing that is itself', and those 'who are able to grasp what is always the same in all respects'.[12] Philosophers are 'always in love with that learning which discloses to them something of the being that *is* always and does not wander about, driven by generation and decay'.[13] They therefore love all learning and are not limited by what some may consider trivial or shameful. In addition, because they love wisdom, they have 'No taste for falsehood; that is, they are completely unwilling to admit what is false but hate it, while cherishing the truth.'[14] Desiring learning, they will therefore be concerned 'with the pleasure of the soul itself with respect to itself and would forsake those pleasures that come through the body', which means they will be moderate and not lovers of money.[15] More than this, however, to someone who contemplates 'all time and all being', human life will not seem to be anything great, so that such a person will not think death is a terrible thing.[16] The philosopher is therefore said to be 'a rememberer, a good learner, magnificent, charming, and a friend and kinsmen of truth, justice, courage and moderation'.[17] What is notable about this summary is the emphasis on intellectual ability and the observation that the virtues of philosophers are a consequence of the dominance of philosophical desire that 'like a stream that has been channelled off in that other direction' deprives the other desires of their force – the desire to know and its related virtues distract and divert philosophers from conventional vices.[18]

It is this approbatory account of philosophers that prompts Adeimantus to challenge Socrates with the observation that those who persist with philosophy beyond childhood become 'quite queer, not to say completely vicious', while the decent become 'useless to the cities'.[19] Socrates does not reject this general view but instead attempts to explain it through the use of 'images', resulting in the famous accounts of the 'Ship of State' and later, the Cave.[20] These images and the subsequent discussions adopt the philosopher's perspective to understand the relationship between the philosopher and the city, and in doing so dramatically portray the distance that separates the two. The famous Ship of State simile has the owner of the ship as strong but deaf, short-sighted and unable to navigate the seas, while the role of pilot is fought over by those who deny there is such an art, or reduce it to the skills necessary to persuade or intoxicate the owner to gain rule in order to drink and feast. Though the philosopher is the only true pilot according to Socrates, he will be dismissed as a 'stargazer, a prater and useless'.[21] That the philosopher does not seek to rule is justified by Socrates on the grounds that it is wrong for the wise to go to the door of the rich, and proper for the sick to seek out a doctor.[22]

This explanation of why philosophers do not rule and are indeed seen as useless is augmented and complicated in the subsequent depiction of the Cave, where Socrates famously tells of the ascent of the philosopher out of a dark cave to see the sun. With this account Socrates will explain why the philosopher will appear ridiculous, graceless and even dangerous, since the journey to the contemplation of what *is* will be distressing and blinding, both when escaping the cave and upon the return, after having seen the sun.[23] In doing so, however, Socrates reveals that having seen what *is*, the philosopher will consider himself happy and pity others, will have contempt for conventional honours and authority, be prepared do anything rather than live that life, and be unwilling to 'mind the business of human beings' because he believes to have 'emigrated to a colony on the Isles of the Blessed while they are still alive'.[24] From this Cave image we realise that the political neglect of philosophers has another source – the philosophers themselves, who in experiencing the pleasures of the philosophic life have no desire to be pilots, doctors or rulers and take an active role in political life. Indeed, in a later observation regarding the very small number who become philosophers Socrates notes,

> Now the men who have become members of this small band have tasted how sweet and blessed a possession it is. At the same time, they have seen sufficiently the madness of the many, and that no one who minds the business of the cities does virtually anything sound, and there is no ally with whom one could go to the aid of justice and be preserved.[25]

Neither willing to join in injustice, nor able to resist, such a person

> keeps quiet and minds his own business – as a man in a storm, when dust and rain blown about by the wind, stands aside under a little wall. Seeing others filled full of lawlessness, he is content if somehow he himself can live his life here pure of injustice and unholy deeds, and take his leave graciously and cheerfully with fair hope.[26]

These poetic images help to explain the nature of philosophers, their loves and desires, and how they find their complete satisfaction in a life outside politics. In doing so, however, they also provide insights into the distinguishing features of politics. The Ship of State shows the life of cities to be dominated by contests over rule for the benefit of the victors. It is a world defined by persuasion, deception and force, with the overriding objective of gaining political power. This world is characterised by faction and stasis, which is replicated internationally, so that war is not only a means of preserving gains from predatory nations, but indeed another source of aggrandisement. Disunity, conflict and war are therefore the distinguishing features of politics, both domestically and in foreign affairs. But why does war, which celebrates greed, duplicity and cruelty, exercise such a powerful influence in politics? In Socrates' explanation of why philosophers are considered not just useless but vicious, he traces this influence to the cities and their education of the young. In doing so, he shows that politics not only neglects philosophy, but by its very nature is inhospitable to it, even at its own cost.[27]

The influence of politics on the life of the mind can be seen from the image of the Cave, which depicts politics as a world of shadows where citizens are enchained and therefore imprisoned by opinions devised by a few. These opinions are so pervasive and powerful that they make the *periagoges* or turning around necessary for philosophical liberation rare. What makes these opinions so potent? Socrates' explanation of how the most talented, the potential philosophers, are corrupted and made vicious by what the city praises and criticises, reveals the desires that predominate in politics. His discussion starts with the reminder that potential philosophers are 'few and born rarely among human beings', and that those with the most abilities who have the potential to benefit the city will also have the potential to do most harm.[28] The power of politics to shape and influence these promising young manifests itself in manifold ways according to Socrates. It is very difficult for the young to resist what the public praise and blame in 'assemblies, courts, theatres, army camps' and other places.[29] Moreover, the public have the ability to enforce their views through deeds, with 'dishonor, fines and death'.[30] This education is reinforced by sophists who practice other arts but are attracted to the reputation of philosophy. Regarding wisdom to be nothing more than the knowledge of the desires of the many and how to approach, provoke and tame it, sophists pander to the multitude, thereby anticipating and teaching the convictions of the many.[31] Consequently, unless endowed with a divine nature, the young will not escape such an education.[32] What, then, is the substance of this education? Most people do not have the abilities of the talented few so that the 'multitude' cannot philosophise, rejecting what they consider to be 'useless studies' that do not promise immediate and practical advantages.[33] The concerns of the body and therefore wealth and power will predominate, directing the most able to political careers that promise both. Consequently, the talented few will be assailed by family, friends and colleagues who will 'lie at his feet begging and honouring him, taking possession of and flattering beforehand the power that is going to be his'.[34] As a result, the most able and potential philosopher but especially those fortunate to be from a big city, well born, wealthy and handsome, will be 'overflowing with unbounded hope, believing he will be competent to mind the business of Greeks and barbarians, and won't he, as result, exalt himself to the heights, mindlessly full of pretension and empty conceit?'[35]

This account of the way cities corrupt potential philosophers is intended to show how the prevailing view of the viciousness of philosophers can be traced not to the influence of philosophy but to the way cities miseducate their most talented citizens. In doing so, it also shows how this political education corrupts politics by encouraging the glorious ambitions of the few and thereby exacerbating struggles over wealth and power. Politics, longing for unity and harmony, is driven and riven by its prevailing passions towards dissensus, conflict and war. These conditions are accentuated by the way it educates its citizens, and indeed, this education provided by laws and facilitated by sophists reinforces and accelerates these tendencies with no immediate or obvious political resource or means to impede or stop such tendency and trajectory.

Philosophers as Kings

Our examination of Socrates' understanding of who is a philosopher and therefore what is distinctive about philosophy and politics reveals with greater clarity what Socrates meant when he described the philosopher king as a paradox.[36] As we have seen, philosophers have exceptional facility in clarity of thought and recollection and the moderation and courage to seek all knowledge, whether honourable or not. They love truth and wisdom above all and are moved by the pleasures of the soul; their focus is on what *is* so that their examination of the 'good' absorbs and satisfies them more than any other endeavour. This love and disposition make them depreciate all those things concerning the body that seem to move most people, such as wealth, honour and authority, and they are especially unconcerned with death. Though most qualified to rule, philosophers will not seek office and will indeed see it as a duty or burden rather than something desirable for its own sake. Consequently, philosophers who are least eager to rule because they find satisfaction and contentment in their life in the sun, must be compelled to return to the 'dark things' and the labours of the city. But who will compel the philosophers if the city ignores or disdains them? The philosopher's disinterest in politics and therefore reluctance to rule is matched and reciprocated by an equal indifference or even antagonism towards philosophers by those in politics who will dismiss them as useless or indulgent 'stargazers'. Concerned above all with those pleasures attending the body, politics favours an instrumental education that corrupts the most able who have the potential to be philosophers, making them indistinguishable from the sophists who claim wisdom to be nothing more than the ability to gain and keep rule. Importantly, even if such compulsion is possible, is it just? The city may need those who do not desire to rule and therefore will rule for the benefit of others, but in forcing them to rule they will be denied the life they value above all.[37] The happiness of the city therefore seems to justify the sacrifice of its foremost citizens.[38] There would therefore seem to be an unbridgeable gulf between philosophy and the demands of politics, raising the question of the feasibility and justice of philosophic rule.[39]

Even if philosophers could gain office, there is the equally challenging question of whether they would be good rulers. It is not clear if philosophers actually possess the wisdom essential for rule, or are rather erotic lovers of wisdom who claim to know little.[40] It is also not clear whether contemplation yields the practical judgement required for the urgent demands of political rule. Wisdom may give the right to rule, but whether it comprehends the skills or disposition required for the practice of politics is not evident. The astronomer Thales was said to have fallen into a well while gazing at the stars, prompting the Thracian servant girl to remark that in his eagerness to know the things in the sky he could not see what was at his feet.[41] The struggle for limited goods means that deception and force predominate in politics making stasis and war inevitable. As a consequence, politics celebrates above all the virtues of the victorious warriors who are admired for their courage and resoluteness in acquiring and distributing wealth. But these are the skills and abilities philosophers lack or are constitutionally incapable of implementing. Moreover, the philosopher loves the truth above all and hates falsehoods, but as the *Republic* shows, even in the best city the rulers will need to tell noble lies and of course guile and mendacity are the currency of foreign relations.[42] Philosophy may be a blessed life, but politics demands sacrifice – we should not forget that philosophers will be compelled to serve the city for the benefit of all. And even cruelty – consider the grim suggestion that the quickest way to found the best city is by removing the influence of parents by sending everyone more than ten years old to the country.[43] Finally, philosophy relies on dialectic while politics is the domain of rhetoric and poetry that guide and enchant rather than enlighten the soul.

These reflections bring to light the different elements that constitute the paradox of the philosopher king. In its most obvious sense the paradox of the philosopher king is premised on the general reluctance, even hostility, of politics towards philosophers because, as Adeimantus observes, they are seen as useless or pernicious. But this *doxa* or general belief or opinion reflects and articulates a deeper puzzle regarding the happiness for the individual and the city and the extent to which nature and the cosmos accommodates human flourishing and happiness. The discussion above appears to support the view that nature makes possible cities whose telos and perfection is realised in the philosopher who is outstanding in faculties of the mind and in the perfection of virtues that distinguish humanity. Indeed, not only are philosophers the culmination or fruit of political life, but their skills, abilities and character complete and enrich cities, establishing justice and happiness in public and private lives. The concept of the philosopher king with its promise of philosophical and political excellence, seems to provide the answer to profound questions concerning humanity, nature and the divine. It implicitly defends the beneficence of nature in accommodating and nurturing individuals and communities, confirming the favoured place of humanity in the cosmos and hinting at the divine providence that made this possible. A closer examination, however, reveals a competing, more complicated and darker picture. The philosopher is the best human, enjoying a blessed life in contemplation and therefore uninterested in ruling. Politics founded predominantly on the needs of the body elevates the active life above the contemplative, regards philosophers as useless or vicious, teaching its most able to seek another life and in doing so corrupting their outstanding virtues. Such neglect and even disdain exacerbates the deception, violence and cruelty that predominate in political life with no immediate political remedy for this destructive impulse. The solution lies with the rule of the philosopher, but they do not want to rule and politics is unwilling to acknowledge or defer to such a ruler. Even if it did it would amount to injustice against them. In this sense, the paradox of the philosopher king points to the perplexing role of nature, chance and therefore providence that makes possible both the philosopher and politics, and shows how their combination leads to justice and happiness for individuals and for cities, but crucially, does not seem assure their union. Indeed, given the character of each it almost seems that nature makes such union difficult, so that not nature but human intervention is required to combine philosophy and politics to ensure justice. It therefore presents in stark terms profound and puzzling questions concerning the cosmos and whether it accommodates humanity by favouring its prosperity and happiness. In sum, the paradox of the philosopher king is that it simultaneously says the philosopher king is possible and it is not, that philosophy and politics can be combined and they cannot and, more generally, that justice in this life is both possible and it is not.[44]

Paradox as Contemplation and Action

How should we engage with the paradox of the philosopher king? Perhaps the most famous examples of paradoxes are those by Zeno of Elea, a student of Parmenides who sought to deny plurality and change. Zeno's Arrow Paradox, for example, states that if motion is infinitely divisible then nothing moves. All Cretans are liars, declared by a Cretan, is the Epimenides Paradox attributed to Stoic logician Chrysippos, with a more contemporary iteration in Bertrand Russell's Liar Paradox. The immediate effect of a paradox is to make us think, trying to understand the puzzle posed. Paradoxes thereby arrest and divert us from our own course, even if briefly and in doing so show the power of thought and reflection.[45] But before too long contemplation and perplexity yields to the desire to solve the paradox. Why do we feel compelled to solve paradoxes? Put somewhat differently, why does a paradox in a sense force us into action, directing us to resolve the tension or contradiction? Certainly, for some it is the amusement of the puzzler, who enjoys the challenge of solving riddles. For others it may have its source in profound unease because the paradox may question something we hold dear, such as the power of wisdom, the tractability of power and the possibility of justice. Whatever the reason, the shift from contemplation to attempted resolution appears to confirm that all paradoxes have an internal movement between thought and action, philosophy and politics, mimicking or reflecting the paradox of the philosopher king. Of course, the initial contemplation or confrontation with a paradox is not readily apparent but attempts at resolution appear more visible – Diogenes the Cynic claimed to refute Zeno's Paradox that motion is impossible by standing and walking.[46] Paradoxes therefore provoke thought and incite action. And the more serious the questions addressed by the paradox, the more profound and far-reaching will be the effect of the paradox.

Socrates' acknowledged radical proposal of the paradoxical philosopher king is therefore a revealing formulation to provoke us into asking the true relationship between philosophy and politics, and importantly, the relative merits of the two ways of life. It prompts a profound meditation on the extent to which the individual longing for happiness will coincide or find satisfaction in the best regime, or put somewhat differently, whether the best city can replicate the excellence of the most outstanding individual. But beyond an invitation to meditate on these grave questions, the paradox of the philosopher king focuses attention on the practical consequences of the paradox, directing our attention to those who sought to resolve its tensions through political action and innovation. Socrates thought the just city and regime were 'not in every way prayers; that they are hard but in a way possible'.[47] But it seemed to require a 'coincidence', 'chance' or even 'divine happenstance'.[48] Others, however, seemed more sanguine about these prospects. To see how the philosopher king nicely captured, clarified and revealed the powerful ambitions of the sophists, anticipating the hopes and aspirations of modern philosopher kings, we need to recall the three foundational yet contending views on how to reconcile philosophy and politics that were manifest from the beginning, when philosophy became increasingly influential, and have continued to be prominent since.

The first approach was to deny the possibility of any conciliation between philosophy and politics, seeking to preserve philosophy as an essentially private concern by removing it from the political forum. The major motive for this was clearly to ensure the safety of philosophers, whose insights and discoveries concerning, for example, the origins of the cosmos, would challenge the morality and piety of cities. But a more profound philosophical reason for such seclusion was the view that since few could philosophise, it was important to secure philosophical insights and the welfare of the public by philosophising only with those with ability. Practically, this separation could mean the simple expedient of seclusion to allow private conversation, as in the case of Epicurus who established his famous 'Garden' that allowed him to live and converse with friends.[49] For others, the form or appearance of various cults, with disciples, rituals and secrets, were the useful pious garbs to endow legitimacy and conceal philosophical speculation, as we can see from the Pythagoreans, who seemed to adopt the forms of Orphic rituals to ensure disciples preserved the hidden insights into the nature of the 'One'.[50] Such seclusion had the additional benefit of addressing the enduring problem of how to preserve insights and instruct future students and philosophers. Writing was considered a questionable innovation because it was accessible to everyone and unlike personal conversations could not respond to questions.[51] Thus, some of the most profound philosophers – Thales, Pythagoras and Socrates – never wrote. Those who did write, such as Heraclitus and Parmenides, concealed their thoughts in elusive or enigmatic poetry or, like Plato, invented a new dialogic form that approximated conversations with philosophers in a form that seemed to combine poetry and plays. Conversations with individuals or small groups were therefore considered the only reliable form of philosophical speculation and instruction.[52]

Such separation was ironically also the approach adopted by those who wanted to protect politics from philosophy. That philosophers are useless or vicious was, as we have seen, a widely shared view. Not distinguishing between natural scientists, sophists and political philosophers, most people regarded philosophers as impious in questioning the divine origins of the city and as politically dangerous in corrupting the ambitious young with their teachings on how to gain power. The seriousness of these concerns justified the political response not only to disregard philosophy as something intrusive and foreign to politics, but to actively stop its perceived corruption of politics. In some cases this meant censorship, which in Athens took the form of *asebeia* or criminal charges for various acts of irreverence and impiety.[53] In others the response was more serious, culminating in capital punishment. Aristotle, it is claimed, fled Athens 'lest the Athenians sin twice against philosophy' alluding, of course, to the most infamous instance of the city repudiating philosophy, the trial and execution of Socrates.[54] Thus both the philosophical and political approaches resorted to similar remedies to what they considered the dissonance between philosophy and politics – for philosophers the dangers of politics were to be avoided by private speculation and political seclusion, while for politics the threat of philosophy was also to be resolved by neglect at best, though given the superior resources possessed by the city, the more forceful remedies of shame, censorship, ostracism or even capital punishment were also to hand. This consensus that it was necessary to isolate philosophy and politics for the sake of each, even as they deployed different means, presumed the infeasibility of the philosopher king. It would soon confront the prospect of a novel third alternative from the Sophists.

Sophistēs or the 'wise men' was the assumed title by their most famous and wealthiest representative Protagoras of Abdera, who attempted to associate himself with the earlier designation for poets, musicians, rhapsodes, seers and diviners and especially the Seven Wise Men. Other sophists included Gorgias of Leontini who taught the art of rhetoric or how to make the weaker argument stronger, Prodicus of Ceos who was famous for his work on language, Hippias of Ellis who prided himself as a polymath, and Thrasymachus of Chalcedon who was teacher of rhetoric.[55] Unlike their predecessors, however, these itinerant sophists were willing to teach for pay, charging large sums of money to instruct in wisdom and virtue. Notably, as Protagoras advertised, they promised the ability to become politically powerful. Though patronised by foremost leaders such as Pericles as well as tyrants and the wealthiest individuals and families in the cities, sophists had a questionable reputation. They were suspect because by being willing to sell their services they seemed mercenary, and as itinerants and foreigners their patriotism was questionable. There were also lingering doubts concerning what they taught and the extent to which this teaching corrupted the young of the city, especially in questioning their civic loyalties and commitments to the city's gods. Their teachings seemed to undermine morality, as evident in Protagoras's famous claim that 'Man is the measure of all things, of things that are as to how they are, and of things that are not as to how they are not'.[56] And piety, as we can see from his statement, 'About the gods, I am not able to know whether they are or are not, given the obscurity of the matter and the brevity of human life.'[57] There were also lingering questions concerning the political character of their instruction, with the suspicion that their lessons in rhetoric and making the weaker argument stronger empowered the wealthy young to undermine democracy, fuelling their ambition to seek tyrannical rule. The success – and precariousness – of the sophists is acknowledged by Protagoras who claims he has only survived by his use of a new rhetoric.[58]

What is distinctive about the sophists was therefore their rejection of the view that philosophy and politics be kept separate and their claim that philosophy could make a significant contribution to politics. To understand why the sophists took this approach and the substance of their contribution, it is necessary to focus on their distinctive insight – their turn to *phusis* or 'nature' to evaluate and transform politics. The mythical, poetic and ancestral accounts of the gods and heroes, especially of Homer and Hesiod, were in due course challenged by *physiologoi* or 'inquirers into nature'.[59] Their focus on *phusis* or nature included an investigation into what was the permanent and primary substance that constituted all things, as well as laws or processes of change, causality and motion. They were therefore especially interested in the questions of what is the cosmos or the whole, how it is constituted, and how it came about and changed.[60] The discovery of nature gave rise to profound speculations and contending views regarding its meaning and substance.[61] Thales of Miletus, considered the first to inquire into nature and founder of what was later called the Milesian School, proposed water as the cause of all things and the source of their subsequent change.[62] His successor Anaximander who claimed nature guides and steers, proposed the enigmatic *aperion* or indefinite as the principle and element of all things, while his student Anaximenes proposed air with condensation and rarefaction the source of change. Other philosophers offered alternative contending conceptions of nature. Heraclitus of Ephesus, for example, speaks of an eternally valid *Logos*, claiming that 'everything flows and nothing abides', and 'war is both father and king of all', yet also that 'Opposition brings concord. Out of concord comes the fairest harmony.'[63] To the contrary Parmenides of Elea argued that being is one, ungenerable, imperishable and unchangeable, so that the world of change and appearance is not real. Challenging both were pluralists such as Empedocles of Acragas who claimed the four 'roots' of earth, water, air and fire were moved by Love and Strife, and Anaxagoras of Clazomenae who stated all things were set into motion by a cosmic *nous* or Mind. More generally, Democritus of Abdera thought the world constituted by an infinite number of solid, uncuttable (*atomon*) units of matter that differed only in shape, position and arrangement in a void, while others, such as Pythagoras, proposed that 'All is Number'.

Though employing familiar or political expressions, such as love, war and harmony, the *physiologoi* focus on nature tended to ignore ethics and politics. Nevertheless, their insights inevitably had wider political implications. The concept of nature, with its implicit view of an ordered cosmos whose principles were accessible to unaided human reason necessarily questioned the authority and providence of the gods. Iris was therefore not god's messenger but a coloured cloud according to Xenophanes, and Thales is said to have predicted a solar eclipse in 585 BCE, suggesting that the sun and planets were not divine.[64] Their insights also brought into sharp relief the differences between what was natural, and what was artificial or made by humans, distinguishing between *techne* or those things that could be learned and taught such as the medical arts, and *nomos* or laws, customs and conventions. Did nature provide consistent and superior guidance to the arts as well as the diverse and contradictory ancestral laws and norms that Herodotus had recounted in his Persian Wars?[65] Importantly, the discovery of nature raised questions concerning its purposes or principles, and the extent to which it accommodated human flourishing. Did Anaxagoras's Mind with its account of Socrates' 'bones and sinews' provide an adequate account of the goodness of Socrates' decision not to flee jail on the day of his execution?[66]

It was the sophists who began to explore these political implications of the discovery of nature. Their particular focus was the 'naturalness' of 'nomos' or laws, conventions and therefore justice. Were norms divine? Or were they merely human artefact, a necessary artful response to our forsaken original condition?[67] If norms were an artefact or by convention, did they assure individual happiness or were they rather an obstacle to the best life? In Protagoras's mythic account of the origin of humanity in Plato's *Protagoras* we see how the discovery of nature shaped the theological, metaphysical and philosophical insights of the sophists.[68] According to Protagoras, it is the improvidence of Zeus and the poor judgement of Epimetheus who in distributing benefits to all the other animals leaves humans naked and cold that compelled Prometheus to provide fire, necessitating human ingenuity and self-reliance to devise technical innovations to improve our parlous condition. But what implications did this have regarding the laws and justice? In Plato's *Gorgias* Callicles, a student of Gorgias, claims that the good life is being able to fully satisfy one's desires, unhindered by others.[69] In nature the strongest take what they want while the weak, who are in the majority, desire but are unable to do so. Laws and justice may provide for security and peace, but they also limit the strongest. Similarly, justice according to Thrasymachus in Plato's *Republic* is the 'advantage of the stronger', so that the powerful set down laws to their advantage and enforce them by calling them just and even divine. The partiality of all laws shows the ambiguous character of all regimes and raises questions concerning the status of the virtues and of the origins and providence of the gods. In practice, this means democracies are founded by the many weak, who unable to pursue what they desire but fearful of being dominated compromise by agreeing to legislate and promote equality. Flattering the wealthy and ambitious young as naturally superior, the sophists counselled them on how to realise and fulfil their natural excellence by gaining political power. In a democracy this meant above all the mastery of the art of persuasive speech, or how to make the weaker argument stronger. The best life or the life of unrestrained satisfaction of natural desires therefore ultimately pointed to the natural superiority of tyranny.[70] For the sophist, then, philosophy introduces a new clarity to politics. It shows how human endeavour can correct the deficiencies of nature and the improvidence of the divine through the artifice of norms and justice. In doing so, however, it also shows the conventional nature of these remedies and points to the natural superiority of the tyrannical life.

The sophists' proposal to combine philosophy and politics in the person of the philosophical tyrant helps us to understand why Socrates proposes the philosopher king. The moral drama of *Republic* consists of its young and ambitious interlocutors desiring to rule justly, yet fearing that Thrasymachus, the sophists and even the great poets may be right about the nature of justice and the merits of the tyrannical life. For Glaucon and the others, whose desires are the motive force of the dialogue, the philosopher king appears to take up the promise of the sophists but ennobles it, by showing how the satisfactions of the powerful political desires through the instrumental use of philosophy need not terminate in tyranny but is consistent with justice and welfare of all. But this proposal does not merely adopt and alter sophists' insights into nature and norms. Socrates takes the sophists seriously because of their discovery of nature yet he was also at pains to distinguish himself from them, not only because of their suspect reputation, but especially since Socratic dialectic questioned major aspects of their approach. Metaphysically and epistemologically Socrates interrogated the theory of flux with its implicit materialism evident in Protagoras's claim that 'Man is the measure of all things.' Morally he questioned Callicles and Gorgias on whether pleasure is the greatest good. Above all, however, he challenged Thrasymachus's repudiation of justice and its endorsement of tyranny as the best life. If the concept of nature questioned whether individual happiness had its complete fulfilment in the city, Socrates rejected that this happiness culminated in tyranny as the sophists suggested due to their materialism, hedonism and relativism. Socrates' ennoblement of the sophistic potential for a philosophical politics is therefore accompanied by serious reservations regarding their ambition to combine the two. It does so by raising profound questions regarding philosophy's ability to master nature, chance and the divine that dominate politics. We have noted Socrates' reluctance in introducing the innovation of the philosopher king. Indeed, the philosopher king does not appear in any other Platonic dialogue.[71] There are also complex questions concerning its relationship to the just city outlined in the *Republic*, and whether the entire discussion of the just city and the philosopher king represents a meditation on the political limits of justice, or is indeed intended as a comprehensive template for political reform.[72] Socrates' philosopher king therefore speaks to Glaucon and others like him, persuading them that philosophy is a necessary first step for satisfying their political ambitions, thereby diverting and moderating their desires, even if provisionally. Yet beyond its specific charm for the ambitious young, Socrates also presents the philosopher king as a paradox, challenging the sophistic claims regarding the character of nature and the ability of humanity to overcome its deficiencies. This is evident in the conditional form of the proposal – which can be read as a promise of 'rest' through the human solution to the 'ills of the city' or alternatively as the recognition of the unavoidable and intractable problems that assail all political life. It can also be seen in the ambiguous terms used by Socrates to claim that the philosopher king is possible, with references to prayers as well as coincidence, chance and the divine.[73]

The philosopher king remains a paradox, an invitation to meditate on the limits of wisdom in political life, to examine the tractability of nature, the force of chance and the providence of the divine. For others, the allure of the philosopher king lies in its promise of progress and perfectibility. It is a call to action, an enticing opportunity to see if humanity can finally gain 'rest from the ills of the city', securing peace, justice and happiness both for individuals and the larger community by combining wisdom and power.

Modern Philosopher Kings

The philosopher king is therefore both a paradox and a promise, an ambitious project that seeks to combine philosophy and politics to secure justice. The paradox of the philosopher king – the tensions between philosophy and politics and distinctive ways of reconciling them – continues to shape politics, even if coloured by specific contexts. The Athenian debates were repeated in Rome, with Cato the Elder attacking in the name of *mos majorum* or ancestral custom the Athenian philosophers and ambassadors Carneades, Diogenes and Critolaus who visited Rome in 155 BCE. Though Hadrian, as well as the emperors Nero, Julian the Apostate and Marcus Aurelius, favoured philosophy, Vespasian banished all philosophers from Rome. Comparable debates would reappear throughout history. Philosophically, the paradox of the philosopher king, framed in terms of the competing claims of the *vita contemplativa* and *vita activa*, continued to pose an intriguing and challenging puzzle regarding the best life, the relationship between wisdom and power and the place of humanity within the whole. Indeed, all great philosophers will inevitably reflect on and seek to resolve the paradox, either proposing a radical separation of the two in the interests of both or by claiming the primacy of the political by collapsing the distinction and asserting all is political because disinterested knowledge is not possible. Works as diverse as Boethius's *The Consolation of Philosophy*, Marcus Aurelius's *Meditations*, Bertrand Russell's *The Problems of Philosophy*, Arendt's *The Human Condition*, de Botton's *Consolation of Philosophy* and Hadot's *Philosophy as Way of Life* are well-known representatives of the approach that defends the virtues of the philosophical life. At the same time, much of modern political philosophy can be seen as attempts to shield and safeguard the vigour and grandeur of politics from the debilitating prejudices and corrosive idleness of philosophy. These range from works that demarcate the limits of human reason, such as Descartes's *Meditations*, Locke's *Essay Concerning Human Understanding* and Kant's *Critiques*, to Rousseau's *First and Second Discourses* that charge philosophers with immorality and Nietzsche's *Zarathustra* that accuses them of destructive nihilism. The dangers of philosopher kings continue to be a theme in contemporary thought, as we can see with Michael Oakeshott's *Rationality in Politics and Other Essays*, Richard Wolin's *Seduction of Unreason*, Mark Lilla's *The Reckless Mind*, Czeslaw Milosz's *Captive Mind* and Ronald Beiner's *Dangerous Minds*.

There were, however, important political and theoretical innovations that complicated the relationship between philosophy and politics and in doing so strengthened the prospect of the philosopher king as an enterprise for pursing justice. The increasing theological reach and political influence of the Abrahamic religions posed a new challenge to both philosophy and politics. In asserting the primacy and sufficiency of faith and piety, religion repudiated philosophy, as we can see from Tertullian's Latin apologetics challenging believers by asking 'What has Athens to do with Jerusalem?', the Islamic theologian al-Ghazali's 'Destruction of Philosophy' and the Jewish philosopher and poet Halevi's *Kuzari* that rejects Aristotle. At the same time, however, there was an attempt to appropriate philosophical insights, albeit on pious terms. St Thomas's adoption of Aristotelian philosophy as a handmaiden to theology, the scholarship of Islamic philosophers Farabi and Averroes, and the influential Jewish philosopher Maimonides's *Guide to the Perplexed* showed how philosophy could persist in new theological vestments.[74] Just as piety challenged philosophy, it confronted and altered the demands of politics. And as in the case of philosophy, the pious response took a variety of forms, influenced significantly by the foundations of each faith. On the one hand a powerful current of spiritualism encouraged a radical removal from worldly concerns, ranging from the stylites and monastic orders in Christianity, to the spiritualism of Sufism, and the Jewish sects such as the Essenes and Therapeutae. But the more dominant approach was to confront and alter politics, shaped by the unique features of each religion. Thus both Judaism and Islam, with extensive legal codes, directly challenged secular rule by combining the prophet and the king, while the absence of orthopraxy in Christianity made its political responses more complex, ranging from separation of Church and state to the divine right of kings. Importantly, to the extent that piety and revelation introduced a more dogmatic formulation of what constituted wisdom and justice, they strengthened the feasibility of the philosopher king as an ambition and a goal.

The promise of the philosopher king was also aided by the transformation in the public reception of philosophy. Certainly the philosopher king has to some extent lost its paradoxical aspect, no longer seeming as absurd or ridiculous as it did to a nonplussed Glaucon, Adeimantus and colleagues when it was first tentatively proposed by Socrates. This new-found legitimacy and authority explains in part the ready recourse by political leaders to the title of philosopher, declaiming their philosophical credentials as authors or initiators of new concepts or comprehensive 'thoughts' or ideologies to defend their legitimacy. This transformation from a paradox or a puzzle to a hope and an ambition can be traced to a number of sources but perhaps the most influential was the success of the Platonic defence of philosophy and the philosopher.[75] The Platonic dialogues taken as a whole could be seen as a defence of the philosophical life, and an attempt to replace the Homeric heroes with the philosopher Socrates distinguished by his bravery (*Laches*; *Phaedo*), moderation (*Charmides*; *Symposium*), prudence (*Phaedrus*) and justice (*Crito*; *Republic*). Combined with the powerful influence of new comprehensive philosophies or what Marx termed 'ideologies', these new ways of conceptualising philosophy and politics promoted the realisation of the philosopher king in practice. Consequently, we find public declarations of the project of the philosopher king, most famously Machiavelli's *The Prince*, that offer a new modern settlement between the wise and the powerful, and Marx's defiant declaration in his Eleventh Thesis of the *Thesis on Feuerbach* (1988) that 'Philosophers have hitherto only interpreted the world in various ways; the point is to change it.'

These changes complicated and in an important sense obscured the paradox of the philosopher king just as they strengthened its promise. In doing so they presented in even more compelling terms the larger questions and deeper concerns that the philosopher king articulated regarding the role of nature, chance and the gods in promoting human progress. Whether nature and the cosmos were beneficent or humanity was compelled to rely on its own means to obtain happiness became not only a powerful philosophical puzzle but also a compelling political question for those who wanted to secure a heretofore elusive justice and happiness. Consequently, the disparate and powerful impulses borne of fear, pride and piety encouraged some to instantiate the philosopher king. They attempted, in other words, to implement the aspirations of sophists refined and ennobled as the philosopher king. The promise of the philosopher king as the mutual accommodation and fruitful coexistence of wisdom and power became a test of human independence, ambition, even dignity.

How successful have been these ambitious modern attempts to combine wisdom and power, philosophy and politics to overcome the 'ills of the world'? For some, the philosopher king has been a siren call for dangerous utopianism and holistic social engineering. The philosopher king is the key to the *Republic*, according to Karl Popper's (2012) influential *Open Society and its Enemies*, and is nothing other than 'Plato himself, and the *Republic* is Plato's own claim for kingly power'.[76] As a form of '*sophocracy*' or rule by the wise, the *Republic* is a 'political manifesto', a 'quest for power' and therefore a 'monument to human smallness'.[77] Popper therefore sees Plato as a 'totalitarian party politician, unsuccessful in his immediate political undertakings, but in the long run only too successful in his propaganda for the arrest and overthrow of the civilization which he hated'.[78] Plato's political programme is for Popper totalitarian and anti-humanitarian so that the roots of modern totalitarianism can be traced to Platonism, and specifically the idea of the philosopher king. Far from being a solution to the ills of the world, Popper thus saw the philosopher king and attempts to combine wisdom and power as fatal to 'open society'. Whatever the theoretical merits of Popper's attempts to discern Hegelian and Marxist historicism in Plato (and Aristotle) he reminds us of the enduring influence and power of the idea of the philosopher king and importantly the challenge it presents to modern democracy. He therefore provides a provocative invitation to examine the force of the philosopher king, not just in its extreme expressions and manifestations of grim totalitarian experiments, but in the way its impulse and drive manifests itself in manifold ways.

The ambition to combine wisdom and power is a powerful expression of the indefatigable desire for justice. In this book we explore these subtle, complex and diverse expressions of the powerful ambition and resolute commitment to secure justice by making politics philosophical and philosophy political. We do so to see the extent to which wisdom and power can be conjoined, to assess the insights they yield into the nature of philosophy and politics, and more comprehensively, to examine the subtle and complex questions they entail regarding nature's providence and our place within the whole. We therefore examine the most prominent expressions of this desire to see the potential and limits to empowering wisdom and ennobling power for securing justice.

As we will see, our examination of prophets, intellectuals, artists, advisors, scientists and 'the people' confirms that politics is open to wisdom. Yet it also shows a reluctance or resistance, even intractability due to the transience of time, adventitious chance, and the distinctive admixture of rarity of wisdom and ubiquitous primacy of the body that characterises humanity and therefore all politics. Consequently, the understandable ambitions of those who long for justice and will endeavour to realise it by means of the philosopher king will always have to be tempered by present contingency and future uncertainty. The perilous trip between the Scylla of tragic resignation and the Charybdis of pious hope therefore lies in the seemingly modest yet much more enterprising and arduous solution of writing, which is the combination of wisdom and power that overcomes time, chance and humanity. Writing first as philosophy and later as law therefore represent the most enduring and successful expression of the modern philosopher king.

Notes

1. See Kalder (2018) who documents the variety of books written by dictators, evaluating their relevance and influence.
2. *Republic* (473d–e).
3. For its continuing influence see, for example, the titles of the books by Schofield (1999); Reeve (1988); and more generally Popper (2012).
4. *Republic* (472a). For a different understanding of paradox see Weiss (2006: 5), who regards 'no one does wrong willingly', 'virtue is knowledge' and 'all the virtues are one' as Socratic paradoxes. Accordingly, 'What will make Socrates' paradoxes, then, will not be that they are counterintuitive but rather that they oppose *doxai* that Socrates regards as moral hazards' (2006: 6).
5. *Republic* (473c, 457a–d).
6. Ibid. 474c.
7. There is of course an extensive scholarship on the philosopher king, generally in the context of the reforms necessary for the founding of the just city. Guthrie (1969) sees the *Republic* generally as the 'dreams of an impractical theorist'. Rosen (2005: 228) states 'the philosopher king personifies the conflict between theory and practice'. For the so-called 'ironic' account see Strauss (1978); Bloom (1968); Lampert

(2010); and the discussion in Morrison (2007). For Annas, 'The just state remains more effective as an ideal to stimulate virtue in individuals than as a blueprint for any real society' (1981: 187). Pappas calls it the *Republic*'s most radical political idea (1995: 110) and 'The union of theoretical and practical knowledge remains a problem for Plato' (1995: 119). For Yunis it is 'a feeling, or perhaps an intuition that philosopher kings are simply preposterous', resulting in Plato's task to convey not just a counterargument but a 'counterfeeling' (2007: 22). O'Connor contrasts between 'brute resistance of the highest political goals to human control' and 'grip of the escapist mood' (2007: 70). White notes the tension between ruling the city and the pleasures of philosophising (1979: 22–3). This may seem an obstacle to the notion of philosopher ruler, 'on the ground that the motivations for ruling and philosophizing seem to pull in opposite directions, so that the tasks of the ruler and philosopher could not be combined in one person' (ibid.).

8. *Republic* (475b).
9. Ibid. 475d–476a.
10. Ibid. 476b.
11. Ibid. 476b, 476c, 476d.
12. Ibid. 480a, 484b.
13. Ibid. 485b.
14. Ibid. 485c.
15. Ibid. 485e.
16. Ibid. 486b.
17. Ibid. 487a, see also 490b.
18. Ibid. 485d.
19. Ibid. 487d.
20. Ibid. 488a *et seq.*, 514a *et seq.* As Socrates states, Adeimantus is to 'teach the image' to those who may wonder why the cities do not honour philosophers (*Republic* 489), implying that their poetic or painterly nature is designed to appeal to the broadest audience.
21. *Republic* (489a).
22. Ibid. 489b.
23. Ibid. 517a–d.
24. Ibid. 516c, 518b, 516c, 518b, 517d, 519c.
25. Ibid. 496c.
26. Ibid. 496d.
27. Ibid. 489d *et seq.*
28. Ibid. 491b, 495a–b, 492b.
29. Ibid.
30. Ibid. 492d.
31. Ibid. 495d, 493b.
32. Ibid. 492e. Circumstances, such as exile or a small city may assist. Other examples include Theages who was limited by ill health and

Socrates whose *daimonion* stopped him from becoming political (*Republic* 496a).

33. *Republic* (494a, 527d).
34. Ibid. 494c.
35. Ibid.
36. For specific discussion of the philosopher king see Schofield (1999); Nichols (1984); Steinberger (1989); Duncan and Steinberger (1990).
37. *Republic* (342c, 346e, 347d, 517c7–d1).
38. Ibid. 519d.
39. On the question of justice see, for example, the contending views of Cooper (1977), who argues that philosophers will be willing to give up a flourishing life to benefit the city to 'advance the reign of rational order' and Mahoney (1992) who contends that it is just for philosophers to rule, though doing so seems to deny a potential tension between private and public good. For White (1979: 49–51) justice seems to require sacrifice for the common good but there is no evidence as to why the 'good' would motivate one to desire to rule (1979: 49).
40. For Morrison (2007: 236–7) the 'utopian' character of the philosopher king needs to acknowledge the two different senses of the meaning of 'philosopher': as lover of wisdom or as the wise. Socrates shifts from one to the other: for example, in Book 5 the philosopher is a lover (*Republic* 479e–480a, cf 376b), while in Book 6, they are those who know (*Republic* 484b–d). Thus, 'In tacitly moving from one conception of philosopher to another, Plato makes the happy city seem more possible than it is' (Morrison 2007: 239).
41. Plato (*Theaetetus* 174a). References to *Theaetetus* are to Plato (1984b). Thus, the Roman poet Ennius summary, *Quod est ante pedes nemo spectat, caeli scrutantur plagas* ('No one regards what is before his feet when searching out the regions of the sky') was later cited by Cicero (*Republic* I: 25) and Thomas Aquinas' *Commentary on Aristotle*. Note, however, that Aristotle (*Politics*, Book 1, 1259a) recounts how Thales' knowledge of the stars predicted a bumper olive crop, allowing him to profit from renting all the olive presses in Miletus and Chios. References to *Politics* are to Aristotle (1984).
42. On the need for a noble lie even in the just city see *Republic* (414d ff.). On the lies regarding the rigged marriage lottery see *Republic* (459e–460a). On the lies of rulers see the discussion in Reeve (1988: 208–13).
43. *Republic* (540e).
44. See Steinberger (1989) who makes a comparable argument but the distinction between philosophy and politics I have outlined is elaborated by him in terms of the difference between guardians and philosopher kings.

45. For example, the philosopher king paradox for Steinberger (1989) makes us ask if ruling is a *techne* as per the guardians or something more, while for Rosen (1965), it reveals how our longing or 'rage' for justice, unlike our longing for wisdom, is not moderated and has no limit.

46. See Simplicius (2022) and Huggett (2019).

47. *Republic* (540d, 499b–c).

48. Ibid. 473d, 499b–c.

49. On the garden of Epicurus see Wycherley (1959).

50. On the life and thought of Pythagoras see Riedweg (2005).

51. Consider generally Plato's *Phaedrus*, and the discussion in the concluding chapter of this book. References to the *Phaedrus* are to Plato (1998a).

52. Comparable examples would include the absence of writing by Christ or the Buddha. Thus, the earliest Gospels were written forty years after Christ's death and the words of Buddha initially transmitted orally were only written down in Pali in the Theravadan communities of Sri Lanka hundreds of years after his death.

53. As Kerferd (1981: 20–1) notes, its victims included Anaxagoras, Socrates, Aspasia, Protagoras and Euripides.

54. For a detailed account see Plato's *Apology of Socrates*. References to *Apology* are to Plato (1984a).

55. For an overview see Kerferd (1981: 42–58).

56. *Theaetetus* (152a6–9).

57. Freeman (1983: 126).

58. See Plato's *Protagoras*. References to *Protagoras* are to Plato (2004). See also Bartlett (2016).

59. Of the 'whole of nature and of being', as Aristotle puts it in *Metaphysics I* (see also his *Physics I*, *De Anima I*) and 'nature and the universe' as per Plato's *Lysis* (214b). References to *Lysis* are to Plato (1979). See also his *Protagoras* (315c).

60. For the importance of nature for the so-called 'pre-Socratics' see Heidel (1910); McCoy (2013); Wheelwright (1997); Harry and Habash (2020).

61. For the diversity in the meanings of 'nature', from core principle to causative power, subsisting foundation for the cosmos, essential form and the 'natural world' see Close (1969).

62. 'Nature' makes its first appearance in Homer's *Odyssey* where Hermes gives Odysseus 'Moley' to protect him against the wizardry of Circe, in the process explaining its distinctive characteristics. See Homer (1991: x.287–8).

63. For references see Wheelwright (1997: 69–79).

64. See Curd (2021: 3).

65. Herodotus (1988: Book III, Chapter 38).

66. *Phaedo* (96a6ff). References to *Phaedo* are to Plato (2009).

67. On the nature of this debate see Kerferd (1981: 111–30) and Burnet (1950: 105–6).
68. *Protagoras* (320c8–322d5).
69. *Gorgias* (486d1, 488e–499e). References to *Gorgias* are to Plato (1998b).
70. On pleasure as the only natural standard, see Plato's *Gorgias*, and *Protagoras* and Bartlett (2013).
71. Aristotle does not mention it in his critique of Plato in the *Politics*. Schofield (1999: 28 ff., Chapter 2) explores the absence of the philosopher king in subsequent dialogues including *Timaeus*, *Statesman* and *Laws*, suggesting that it is nevertheless an implicit theme in them.
72. It is not clear, for example, whether the philosopher king forms part of the city or is intended to found it. As Steinberger (1989) argues, the philosopher king is not part of *kallipolis* but a means to implement it in practice. Moreover, as Strauss (1978) notes, the philosopher king seems to make the preceding discussion of *kallipolis* redundant.
73. *Republic* (473d, 499b–c, 540d).
74. For an examination of the philosopher king in Jewish thought see Melamed (2003).
75. On the contemporary democratic reception of Plato see Lisi (2013: 83–4); on 'postmodern' Plato see Zuckert (1996); and for modern engagements with the challenge posed by Platonic political philosophy see Strauss (1985) and Ward (2020).
76. Popper (2012: 144).
77. Ibid. 136, 143, 146.
78. Ibid. 162.

Chapter 2

Prophets, Popes and Princes

Solomon the Wise, Ashoka the Great and Suleiman the Magnificent were all powerful rulers who were especially esteemed and celebrated because they were wise. All three were also distinguished by their piety, Solomon as the builder of the First Temple in Jerusalem, Suleiman as Kanuni or 'Law Giver' who harmonised *kanun* or sultanic law with Sharia, and Ashoka whose Edicts promoted *dharma* and Buddhism. The importance of faith and religion for these wise kings prompts us to ask to what extent does piety reconceive and resolve the paradox of the philosopher king, reconciling wisdom and power, philosophy and politics? Classical political philosophy inevitably had to confront the gods as sacred founders, dangerous demons, hearth and boundary deities.[1] And of course each great religion with its unique conception of the sacred adopted a diverse range of responses in its engagement with philosophy and politics. As we have seen, the religions of the book, or the Abrahamic revealed religions, with their conception of a monotheistic, all powerful and providential god that promised immortality of the soul, fundamentally challenged and redefined both philosophy and politics, reconceiving the relationship between wisdom and power and thereby redefining the promise of the philosopher king. The orthopraxy of Judaism and Islam, where Moses who revealed the Torah and Mohammed who received the Qur'an were both regarded as prophets and lawgivers, meant that the prophet–lawgiver resembled in important respects the philosopher king. Thus Islamic philosophers such as Al-Farabi could introduce and reconcile the Platonic conception of virtuous rule and the philosopher king with the Qur'an, and in doing so, their ideas were adopted, subject to halakhic modifications, into Jewish thought, beginning with Philo of Alexandria, reaching its zenith with Maimonides and ending with Spinoza.[2] By contrast, the philosopher king was more theologically problematic for Christianity as a religion of orthodoxy that distinguished between faith and law. In this chapter we will focus on the way Christianity reconceived and transformed the philosopher king, not only because these innovations had far-reaching political implications, but because the ambiguous place of the philosopher king in Christian thought allows us to see more clearly the philosophical and political promise and limitations of the 'pious king' as the modern philosopher king.[3]

According to Christian doctrine, the *munus triplex Christi* or threefold functions or offices of Christ in his earthly ministry are those of prophet (Christ declares the will of God), priest (by which he makes sacrifice for sin) and king (by which he rules with authority over people). Prophetic, priestly and kingly therefore represent the three contending ways the paradox and the promise of the philosopher king was addressed and transformed by piety. The prophet, inspired by the Holy Spirit, rebuked the pious and the powerful to mend their ways, as well as foretelling the Second Coming. As the wise and pure voices of the divine who admonished rulers, prophets therefore occupied a new and ambiguous place between knowledge and authority. Priests and Christian princes, on the other hand, represented the two new solutions to the philosopher king. Our examination of the pope as the spiritual and secular leader, and emperors as kings and priests shows how these two versions of the pious king were at tension, how philosophy in the form of apologetics and theology intervened in these debates, and finally the limitations of both just as they exercised a decisive influence in shaping European and world politics.

A New Conception of Philosophy and Politics

To see how the philosopher king was reconceived as the prophet, the Christian prince and the pope, it necessary to examine the way Christianity transformed the classical understanding of philosophy and politics. Jesus did not write, which meant his teachings were conveyed by word of mouth so that as the initial anticipation of the imminent *parousia* or the promised return of Christ to Earth at the Last Judgement – 'the night is far gone, the day is near' – slowly receded, there began the movement to record his thoughts and sayings.[4] The Gospels or 'good news', the Acts of the Apostles, various

Letters and the Apocalypse or the 'unveiling' constitute some of these works. Soon, however, there were disagreements regarding the validity of these various accounts, resulting in the need to establish a canon (based on the Greek *kanon* as straight rod) or authoritative texts, which were finally settled in 367 CE with the selection of the present twenty-sevne canonical books of the New Testament.[5] These written works and their teachings soon confronted Greek and Roman philosophical and political works, especially Plato, but in time also Aristotle, Cicero and others. Stoic and Epicurean thought was familiar to the Apostles.[6] Plato's *Timaeus* became a major influence for St Augustine, his other dialogues becoming available only when translated by Marsilio Ficino (1433–1499).[7] Subsequently, Cicero and other Roman thinkers became influential in Christian theology so that in addition to an education in the Roman trivium (grammar, logic and rhetoric) that drew on Horace, Quintilian and Sallust, the curriculum was later dominated by law and theology. Politics was seen as a practical philosophy concerned with virtue and distinguished from theoretical philosophy. From the fifth century, Latin translations of Aristotle's logical writings *Categories* and *De interpretation* by Boethius were called *logica vetus* (old logic) until *logica nova* or new translations from Greek were made of his *Prior* and *Posterior Analytics*. To these were added the natural philosophy writings *De anima* and *Physics*. Influential other works included Boethius's commentary on Porphyry's *Isagoge*, and Cicero's *De Inventiones* and *Moralia*. Subsequently, from the end of the eleventh century to the thirteenth century, Arabic and Jewish thinkers introduced works of Plato, Aristotle and Greek medical science to Latin West. In addition to Al-Farabi (870–950) who wrote commentaries on Plato's *Republic* and *Laws*, Ibn Sina or Avicenna (980–1037) discussed the ideal state in his *The Healing* where Plato's philosopher king and lawgiver was equated with the Muslim prophet in a state that did not distinguish between religion and politics. The Jewish thinker Maimonides (1138–1204) in his *Guide for the Perplexed* drew on Plato and Al-Farabi to argue that scripture and Talmud correctly interpreted conformed with the ethical and metaphysical teachings of Aristotle. Averroes (1126–1198) wrote commentaries on Plato's *Republic* and Aristotle's *Nicomachean Ethics*, with his ideal state based on Plato. The complete Latin translation of Aristotle's *Nicomachean Ethics* and *Politics* was by William of Moerbeke in 1265, when Aristotle's teachings on ethics, politics and rhetoric came to dominate, with *scientia politica* regarded as the sovereign of the practical sciences.

The confrontation between sacred and philosophical works took a variety of forms, ranging from repudiation to accommodation. Some rejected altogether the role of reasoning, with the theologian, polemicist and moralist Tertullian (155–240) from Carthage arguing that philosophers were 'patriarchs of heretics' who obscured and opposed the 'maxims of heavenly wisdom' revealed by the Lord:

> What indeed has Athens to do with Jerusalem? What concord is there between the Academy and the Church? What between heretics and Christians? Our instruction comes from 'the porch of Solomon', who had himself taught that 'the Lord should be sought in simplicity of heart'. Away with all attempts to produce a mottled Christianity of Stoic, Platonic, and dialectic composition! We want no curious disputation after possessing Christ Jesus, no inquisition after enjoying the gospel! With our faith, we desire no further belief. For this is our palmary faith, that there is nothing which we ought to believe besides.[8]

This approach persisted, as we can see from the *Condemnations* of 1210–1270 of heretical works by the University of Paris, and the writings of Melanchthon and Luther that led to the Reformation. 'Virtually the entire *Ethics* of Aristotle', according to Luther, 'is the worst enemy of grace.'[9]

Others attempted to reconcile and accommodate classical insights into theology. Justin Martyr (100–165) defended philosophy and Christianity with his idea of *logos spermatikos*, where Christianity was the final goal of all philosophies. Similarly, Clement (150–215) saw Greek thought as part of God's plan for human destiny. Augustine (354–430) argued that the gold and silver dug out of the mines of providence of God by philosophers and especially Platonists could be put to their proper use, a view endorsed by the French theologian and poet Peter Abelard (1079–1143) and his English student John of Salisbury (1115/20–1180).[10] Perhaps the most famous example of this *ancilla theologiae* was Thomas Aquinas's (1225–74) magisterial *Summa Theologiae* where reason is presented as a 'hand-maiden' to theology.[11]

Implicit in both these approaches was the view that philosophy now had to justify itself before piety, resulting in a fundamental transformation in the meaning of philosophy. Rather than a zetetic endeavour exploring human nature and the cosmos, philosophy now had to accept that the truth had been revealed through the Old and New Testaments, the Gospels, and the Letters of the

Apostles. Christianity now taught the theological virtues, faith, hope and charity, that were infused by God into one's soul, and since piety was now wisdom, philosophy's primary responsibility was now apologetics, the reasoned defence and justification of the Christian faith against its critics. This new role for philosophy inevitably introduced novel metaphysical dilemmas unfamiliar to classical political thought, as well as new fora for deliberating on these questions in the form of Synods and Ecumenical Councils, and unique neoteric rhetorical forms such as sermons and encyclicals. Philosophy was now deployed to adjudicate novel theological debates to determine what was orthodox or heretical. For example, it now had to attend to soteriology, Christology and the nature of the Godhead in adjudicating the Arian controversy and Apollinarian debate regarding the humanity of Christ, leading to the Council of Nicaea's (325) affirmation that Christ was *homoousios*, 'of one substance with the Father', a view subsequently endorsed by the Council of Chalcedon (451). Similarly, disputes between Augustine and the Cappadocian Fathers (Basil and the two Gregories) regarding Trinitarian Doctrine and the divinity of the Spirit was confirmed with the Nicaea's Christology of Father and Son. Other theological contests concerned Ecclesiology or the debates regarding the Donatist controversy over the holiness of the Church (whether it was made up of saints or 'mixed bodies') or the Pelagian controversy on the priority of Grace of God in all parts of human life and whether humans could take the initiative in their salvation.

Revealed religion also transformed the nature of politics, which now had to be reinterpreted and revalued according to piety. The resurrection of Christ and therefore the promise of the immortality of the soul, eternal salvation and damnation, necessarily refashioned and reordered all politics. There were now two kingdoms, that of God and that of Caesar, yet as Jesus said, 'My kingdom is not of this world.'[12] If Heaven was infinitely superior to Earth, how were quotidian political demands to be reconciled with these transcendent hopes and fears? If all earthly kingdoms were nothing more than 'great bands of robbers' as Augustine suggested, should one remove oneself entirely from politics or take an active role ruling, proselyting and spreading the good news?[13] Similarly, the injunction to love one's enemies introduced profound challenges to political life.[14] If justice was nothing more than helping friends and harming enemies, as Polemarchus suggested in Plato's *Republic*, then the new understanding of love turned this notion on its head: 'You have heard that it was said, "Love your neigh-bour and hate your enemy". But I tell you, love your enemies and pray for those who persecute you, that you may be children of your Father in heaven.'[15] This revaluation of love, friendship and justice proposed new standards for the exercise of political judge-ment, and in doing so it gave rise to a series of puzzling political questions that demanded theological explication. Should rulers be obeyed or was there a right of rebellion? Obedience to God's com-mands meant obeying rulers as God's ministers, though there was the suggestion of 'passive obedience' and in some cases arguments for disobedience and rebellion.[16] What was the status of private property? 'Thou shalt not steal', the eighth Commandment, pre-sumed private property, yet Jesus and early Christians seemed to endorse poverty and communism of property.[17] Was a slave prop-erty? 'There is neither Jew nor Greek, there is neither bond nor free, there is neither male nor female: for ye are all one in Christ Jesus' may have denied slavery but equally it could mean that slav-ery was a matter of indifference and was not condemned, with Paul returning a fugitive slave seemingly endorsing this view.[18] How should heretics and unbelievers be treated? While the general view that belief could not be compelled imposed limits on coer-cion of heretics, subsequent arguments suggested both compulsion and confiscation of property could be justified.[19] On the important question of whether war was ever justified, the tension between the Old Testament and Christian love of neighbour were reconciled with different versions of just war theory. Augustine, who initiated the phrase 'just war', claimed killing in such circumstances did not violate the Fifth Commandment, while Aquinas in developing his three criteria for just war argued it should only be used as a last resort.[20]

In addition to these immediate political concerns, there was the question of the Church itself and how its authority was to be reconciled with that of secular rulers. How was papal and lay spiritual authority to be justified? Papal authority or apos-tolic Petrine secession of the papacy was founded on Christ's com-mission to St Peter.[21] There was also Christ's command to 'Feed my sheep.'[22] This view was at tension, however, with the alterna-tive perspective that accorded these powers to bind and loose to all disciples, without distinction, raising questions regarding the authority of laity as well as the independence of bishops who could trace their authority to other apostles.[23] Finally, how were papal and secular powers to be reconciled? The 'Two Swords' theory showed the scriptural ambiguity of the problem. On the one hand there was Christ's injunction to Peter, 'put away the sword', 'for all they that take the sword shall perish with the sword. Thinkest thou that I cannot now pray to my Father, and he shall presently give me more than twelve legions of angels?'[24] But there was also his advice to use swords as needed: 'And they said, Lord, behold, here *are* two swords. And he said unto them, It is enough.'[25] This brief overview, which indicates the profound and diverse ways revealed religion recast the nature and relationship of philosophy and politics, allows us to better understand the three new pious conceptions of the philosopher king.

Prophets

The first innovation in philosopher kings made possible by religion is the prophet. The early Christians responded in diverse ways to their new faith and calling. For some, piety demanded 'quietism', a removal from worldly temptations and entanglements. St Antony (251–356), a Coptic peasant, was the model of an ascetic who lived a solitary life in remote places but perhaps the best known of these *eremitic* or solitary monastic ascetics was St Simeon Stylites the Elder (390–459), a Syriac saint who lived for thirty-seven years on top of a pillar near Aleppo, Syria.[26] Though an earlier ascetic named Macarius had created a number of proto-monasteries called *lavra* or cells, where holy men who were physically or mentally unable to achieve the rigours of Anthony's solitary life would live in a community setting, the first *cenobitic* or communal monastics was founded by St Pachomius (292–348), a follower of St Antony, who created a community of monastics living together led by an abbot or abbess. These communities became the model for the Benedictines (520) and the more severe Cistercian order (1098). Though resembling the Epicurean 'Garden' of philosophic contemplation, these orders were devoted to a solitary life of prayer, silence and labour. But these monasteries were not always successful in avoiding society and political life, their insights and innovations making significant contributions to agriculture, hospitals and scholarship. They also became influential in deciding future bishops and popes, thereby shaping Church dogma and practice. St Basil and his brother St Gregory of Nyssa and Sts Gregory Nazianzen and John Chrysostom all came from the monastic tradition. Some of the greatest theological minds were monks, including Giles of Rome and Thomas of Strasbourg who were Augustinians; Albert the Great, Thomas Aquinas and Peter of Trantaise who were Black Friars or Dominicans (established in 1221); while Bonaventura, Duns Scotus and William of Ockham were Gray Friars or Franciscans (1126). Their influence would continue until the rise of universities in the thirteenth century, founded by kings and emperors to educate future 'clerks' or administrators as well as advisors.[27]

In contrast to this monastic quietism we find others who took a much more active role. Jesus promised to send after him 'prophets, sages and teachers'.[28] According to Paul, the 'body of Christ' had many members, 'And God hath set some in the church, first apostles, secondarily prophets, thirdly teachers, after that miracles, then gifts of healings, helps, governments, diversities of tongues'.[29] The early twelve apostles were relatives of Jesus such as James his brother or had been chosen by him from his disciples, such as Peter. After the death of Judas his replacement Matthias was elected by lot. Paul was not chosen by Jesus but claimed he was commissioned as 'apostle to the Gentiles' by post-ascension Jesus.[30] Apostles were appointed and authorised by Jesus to heal the sick and drive out demons and later to preach the Gospel to all nations.[31] They were therefore distinctive in their proselytising, bringing the 'good news' to the whole world, both Jewish and gentile. The apostles travelled extensively and the churches they founded were known as apostolic sees, with bishops claiming apostolic succession from the twelve. The distinction between an apostle and a prophet was more difficult to discern. Jesus was called a prophet and after his Resurrection was considered the Messiah, the final prophet.[32] *The gift of* prophecy', according to Paul, was spiritual gift, an understanding of 'all mysteries, and all knowledge'.[33] Yet, as the early Church began to assume a more formal structure, prophets were increasingly seen as potential sources of instability, as is evidenced by 'Montanist enthusiasm'. Montanus, who began prophesying in Phyrgia in Asia Minor around 156 CE, and his early followers Prica and Maximilla described by the later convert Tertullian as *pneumatic* or spirit filled, claimed the Spirit used their voices to deliver oracles, predicting the imminence of the Apocalypse. For these reasons the early Church began to counter the power of prophecy by confining it solely to *episkopos* or bishops.[34] Pious and wise, as well as politically influential, prophets as pious kings seemed to represent a modern version of the philosopher king.

The art of prophecy, or the ability to foretell the future has ancient origins, drawing on astrology, hepatoscopy, necromancy, cleromancy, *hostieae consultatoriae* and dream interpretations.[35] The most famous Greek prophet was the Pythia, whose trance-like sounds were interpreted by priests as Delphi. The prophet resembled but was distinct from classical sophists and rhetoricians, itinerant teachers who charged large sums to teach the ambitious young how to gain and keep political power. Perhaps the closest classical approximation of the prophet was Socrates counselled by his *daimonion*, exhorting the Athenians to be virtuous.[36] The Christian prophet had as its proximate model the Jewish prophets.[37] Amos, Jeremiah and Isaiah, prophets of the Old Testament, were deeply moral, demanding justice. One of the most famous was Joseph who had interpreted Pharaoh's dream of the seven fat and lean cows.[38] Another foremost prophet was Elijah, who proclaimed Yahweh while rejecting Baal as a false god, as well as rebuking King Ahab's judicial killing of Naboth.[39] Nathan the prophet admonished King David for committing adultery with Bathsheba and arranging the death of her husband, Uriah the Hittite.[40] John the Baptist, who preached that the kingdom of heaven was at hand, was beheaded by Herod Antipas for rebuking him for divorcing his wife and unlawfully taking the wife of his brother.[41] As these examples show, the Jewish prophets were primarily admonitory, prophesying the perilous consequences if the word of God was disregarded.[42] Prophets were wise but inspired by God and therefore were not 'philosophers' who relied on their own wisdom. Having no formal office and often living alone in the wild, they were ostensibly powerless, yet in criticising and prophesying they became politically influential.

Christian prophets were comparable to the Jewish prophets in castigating sinful and immoral thoughts and deeds, but they were especially concerned with prophesying the *parousia*. They were 'filled with the spirit of God', with *charism* manifest in the gift of wisdom.[43] John had been inspired to write the Apocalypse.[44] Paul was distinctive in being converted by a blinding vision while also claiming to be 'apostle to the gentiles'.[45] Their prophesies ranged from apocalyptic and parentic predictions to prophetic prayer. Yet to the extent that they demanded fundamental moral and legal change they inevitably confronted and challenged political and legal orders that saw their preaching as dangerous. They were therefore tested and sometimes martyred for their faith. The prophet therefore represented a unique Christian version of the philosopher king. As a knower the prophet resembled the philosopher but as witness and believer was distinguishable from those who relied on their own means to pursue knowledge. Often alone and removed from society, the prophet seemed politically powerless, yet in speaking and testifying the truth before the politically powerful, and performing miracles as proof of their holiness, the prophet became a politically influential individual who changed lives and confronted the powerful. This view of the prophet as a pious philosopher king inevitably raised a series of formidable questions. Foremost was how to distinguish a prophet from the 'False Prophets' who would exploit believers for personal advantage.[46] Jesus had advised that prophets could be judged by the 'fruit they bear'.[47] The most compelling evidence was the performance of miracles, though intelligibility of the prophecy, the absence of personal gain, and fortitude in suffering were also signs of holiness. Moreover, there was the heavy burden of being chosen as a prophet, requiring sacrifice in the name of God. Prophets were often prosecuted and, in many cases, suffered grim deaths through crucifixion, stoning and burning for their testimony of Jesus, making them martyrs (from the Greek 'witness'). Jesus Christ as faithful witness was therefore the first martyr, soon followed by others, such as St Stephen, who was stoned to death.[48] This unique combination of philosophy and politics was therefore especially fraught, a radical and distinctive combination of faith and politics that demanded the greatest sacrifice from the prophet and was by its very nature a specific, limited and unpredictable solution to the problem of wisdom and untrammelled power.[49] In any case the feasibility of this solution was soon undermined, as we have seen, by the establishment of the Church as *Corpus Christi* or the 'body of Christ'.

Pious Princes and the Papacy

In addition to the prophet, revealed religion gave rise to two other versions of the philosopher king – the Christian prince and the pope. The nature of these new combinations of piety and power, and how they contended with each other, requires an understanding of the way Christianity evolved from a minority faith to a state religion, and how the subsequent development of the Christian church, especially the increased influence of the Bishop of Rome, gave rise to the pope as the new spiritual and secular authority. Though this account is frequently presented as the contest between church and state, our focus is much more specific, examining how the Christian prince and the pope represented unique solutions to the tensions between knowledge and power, philosophy and politics.

After the crucifixion of Jesus and the spread of the Gospel of Christ's resurrection by the Apostles, Christianity began to reach a wider population of both Jews and Gentiles. In addition to charismatic prophets, miracle workers and those who spoke in tongues, communities also had *episkopoi* or supervisors, *diakonos* or servants and *presbuteror* or elders who became influential in the development of the Church.[50] These changes were accompanied by widespread and sporadic persecution due a range of reasons, from suspicions regarding the nature of the Eucharist, to their unwillingness to sacrifice to Roman gods. As Tacitus notes in his *Annals*, to avoid the blame of having started a fire in 64 CE, Emperor Nero 'fastened the guilt and inflicted the most exquisite tortures on a class hated for their abominations, called Christians by the populace'.[51] The *Diocletianic* or Great Persecution initiated by Diocletian in 303 CE was the last and most severe persecution of Christians in the Roman Empire. This treatment of Christians was to change fundamentally when at the Battle of Milvian Bridge in 312 CE, Constantine the Great saw a great cross (the Christogram Chi-Rho) in the sky with 'In this sign, conquer' written below it. After his victory when he claimed emperorship in the west, Constantine authorised the Edict of Milan (313 CE), granting to everyone in the Roman Empire the freedom to worship any god of their choice.[52] After his conversion, Constantine became the first Christian Roman Emperor, while retaining the title of *pontifex maximus* or the chief priest of the Roman religion, unifying the offices of emperor and priest.[53] Having founded in 330 CE his new imperial capital in Byzantium, renamed Constantinople, Constantine as the head of church and empire convened the various 'Ecumenical' or general councils to determine dogmas and deal with heresies. It was by this authority, for example, that Constantine convened the First Council of Nicaea (325 CE) where the Arian controversy was resolved with the profession of the Nicene Creed.[54] That the emperor was head of both church and state was publicly acknowledged in Emperor Justinian's subsequent commission of the church of St Sophia (Hagia Sophia or Holy Wisdom) in 537 CE as the largest building in the Christian world. The emperor was not a chief priest but dominated the subtle interdependence between church and state, an arrangement that would continue until the

Schism between the churches of east and west in 1054, the attack of western crusaders on Constantinople 1204–61 and finally the fall of Constantinople to the Ottoman Turks in 1453, ending the Byzantine Empire.

Such a union of piety and political authority would be reasserted in the west when Charlemagne (Charles I) united Europe restoring much of the old Roman Empire. When Charlemagne was crowned by Pope Leo III to the acclamation 'Emperor of the Romans' in 800 CE, he was announcing himself as the theocratic king–priest of the west, and implicitly conceding power to the papacy to anoint emperors. The 'Carolingian Renaissance' that followed led to far-reaching political, economic, educational and religious reforms. The Carolingian version of Constantine's union of the emperor and Pontifex Maximus was *rex et sacredos*, king and priest, founded on the divine right of monarchy and the notion of the king's two bodies, derived from the fact that the king was vicar and vice-regent of God and king by God's grace (*rex dei gratia*) as well as a human individual.[55] God–man by grace and ecclesiastical consecration and a specific mortal king therefore became a new modern version of the philosopher king. This new pious king allowed Charlemagne to discipline clerics, control ecclesiastical property and define orthodox doctrine.[56]

The other modern pious version of the philosopher king that coexisted with the first and was at tension with it was a distinctive understanding of the papacy that fundamentally questioned the authority of the emperor. As we have seen, Constantine's founding of Constantinople and the subsequent councils convened by him to determine orthodoxy asserted the dominance of the emperor over the Bishop of Rome. After Theodosius I convened the Second Ecumenical Council in Constantinople in 381 CE, Damasus, the Bishop of Rome called a rival council in Rome and his successor Siricius proclaimed the right and duty of the Bishop of Rome to rule over Christendom. The Christian Church had begun to see itself as a spiritual empire, with Christendom or dominion of Christ overseen by successors of Peter. This transformation was aided by the reorganisation of the Church on the model of the Roman Empire.[57] The doctrine of apostolic Petrine secession of the papacy was founded on Christ's command to 'Feed my sheep' and his commission to St Peter:

> And I say also unto thee, That thou art Peter, and upon this rock I will build my church; and the gates of hell shall not prevail against

it. And I will give unto thee the keys of the kingdom of heaven: and whatsoever thou shalt bind on earth shall be bound in heaven, and whatsoever thou shalt loose on earth shall be loosed in heaven.[58]

The Bishop of Rome was according to this view the *principatus* or head of the Church that was the Body of Christ. The claim of papal authority therefore meant that in addition to the prophet and the Christian prince, the pope represented the other new way to combine piety and politics as the modern philosopher king.

But this papal claim appeared to challenge the Christian prince, so that in effect the two forms represented contending versions of the union of piety and politics or modern philosopher kings. We can see this in the subsequent contestation between the pope and princes as to who had primacy and sovereignty. Later 'Successors of Peter' became more insistent that they rather than Constantinople would be arbiters of all Church affairs. Pope Leo I (440–61 CE) called himself 'Vicar of Peter' and Pope Gelasius (492–496 CE) advanced the Gelasian doctrine, the claim that apostolic Petrine succession of the papacy gave the pope undisputed ecclesiastical authority in the Church, an authority extended to all matters spiritual.[59] Gelasius accepted that the emperor had temporal power, but because the priesthood bore the greater burden in rendering an account to God for men and kings, the clergy superseded the temporal.[60] The doctrine was subsequently taken to mean a separation of the spiritual from the secular and denial of the possibility of uniting the headship of Church and 'state'. Supported by the *Donation of Constantine*, the forged ninth-century monastic document that purported to show Constantine donating the entire Western Roman Empire to Pope Sylvester and his successors, this doctrine in time became the theory of papal supremacy over church and state, with temporal authority graciously conceded to kings, leading to the potential for popes to depose kings. Thus, Pope Gregory I (590–604) in his *Regula Pastoralis* emphasised that the just ruler was under God's law and therefore owed obedience to the Church.

These doctrinal contests were shaped by the specific political circumstances of the Bishop of Rome, who after the establishment of Constantinople and the sacking of Rome by Goths in 410 CE, became the representative and eventually its 'pope' or father of the city and its people. This political role and therefore authority of the pope were magnified when King Pippin II, Charlemagne's father, gave Pope Stephen II (752–7) the Bishop of Rome extensive Lombard territories ranging from the north-east of Rome to

Ravenna and bestowed on him the title *Patricius Romanorum*, making the Bishop of Rome king over these 'papal states'. Combined with the decline of the other Apostolic Sees of Jerusalem, Antioch and Ephesus evangelised by the Apostles but now under Islamic control, the pope as Bishop of Rome assumed unprecedented authority. Nevertheless, for the next 200 years, from John VII (872–82) to John XII (955–64), the papacy would become a tool in Italian factional struggles, until Germany as the new seat of the Holy Roman Empire took over and dominated it. The East–West Schism of 1054, with the mutual excommunication of the Pope Leo IX of the Western Church and the Patriarch Michael Cerularius of Constantinople, and the dominance of the German emperors led to reassertion by the cardinals in Rome of papal supremacy, resulting in a series of doctrinal and political struggles between the papacy and emperors. The major contests were those between Pope Gregory VII (1073–85) and Emperor Henry IV (1050–1106),[61] between Pope Innocent III (1198–1216) and Emperor Frederick II (1197–1250), and between Pope Boniface VIII (1294–1303) and Philip IV, King of France (1268–1314).[62] These contests would continue with the 'Captivity' of the Papacy in Avignon (1303–78), the Schism between two and later three popes (1378–1417) and in the Conciliar Movement (1417–50) which asserted that ultimate authority in the Church rests with the bishops in council rather than the pope.

These contests gave rise to extensive debates among theologians. In the struggle between Philip V, King of France (1293–1322) and Pope Boniface VIII (1294–1303) and Pope Clement V (1305–14), Giles of Rome's (1302) *De ecclesiastica potestate* (On Ecclesiastical Power) asserted hierocratic claim for supreme papal power on the basis that the pope is God's deputy on earth, who delegates power to governments and supervises their activities. The alternative position was advanced by John of Paris (1306), who argued that the pope cannot have supreme temporal power because the sources of these powers are different and therefore they should be held by different persons. This debate was revisited during the papacy of John XXII (1316–34), who rejected the elector's choice of Ludwig of Bavaria as Roman Emperor and countered with new arguments to defend the independence of secular rulers. Marsilius of Padua's *Defensor pacis* (1324) refutes the doctrine of papal fullness of power by locating sovereignty in the people, arguing the supreme ruler cannot be a cleric since Christ has forbidden such involvement in temporal affairs, and in the Church the pope has no more authority than any other cleric. Marsilius also sides with the Franciscans in defending the poverty of the clergy so that the pope and clergy are denied lordship in either coercive jurisdiction or in ownership of property. Another Franciscan, William of Ockham (1285/7–1347) went further, arguing in a series of books and letters that Pope John XXII and his successor Benedict XII should be deposed because they were heretics. He did not reject papal fullness of power in every case, defending the pope's supreme power in the Church. But secular involvement could only take place in exceptional circumstances when no layperson is able or willing to take the lead. Yet Ockham also rejected Marsilius's endorsement of fullness of power for the emperor, arguing that the emperor is not *legibus solutus* or 'released from the laws' but bound by natural and divine laws as well as law of nations.[63]

The struggle between emperors and popes escalated when Pope Boniface VIII deposed Philip IV of France, who in retaliation invaded the papal palace and threatened to kill the pope if he did not abdicate. After this incident, the French King transferred the papacy from Rome to Avignon, Southern France, so that the next seven popes would be French. This 'Babylonian Captivity' (1305–78) ended when Pope Gregory XI (1370–8) returned the papacy to Rome in 1377. After his death in the next year, a Roman mob forced the cardinals to choose an Italian pope, who after safely leaving Rome appointed a rival, so that for the next forty years there were two popes, one in Rome and the other in Avignon, with France, Spain and Scotland favouring Avignon, while Italy, Germany and the Catholic states of central Europe supported Rome. When a council in Pisa in 1409 attempted a reconciliation, neither pope attended, so that the Council deposed both and appointed a third, Benedict XIII. This curious situation of three popes was only resolved in 1417 when German Holy Roman Emperor Sigismund deposed all three claimants and appointed a new pope. In ending this Schism, the remaining authority of the pope was undermined by the Conciliar Movement that vested supreme authority in the Council. Thus the papacy lost its authority over kings and emperors.

Prince and Pope as New Philosopher Kings

As this complex history and theology shows, the prophet as the modern philosopher king was soon displaced by the Christian prince and the pope, who became new models of the pious philosopher king. How successful were these modern philosopher kings in combining wisdom and power? In attempting to answer this question, we cannot avoid the overarching fact that we are now confronted by two modern philosopher kings who were inextricably related and therefore inevitably at tension with each other. Consequently, there was a core and foundational instability in these modern philosopher kings and therefore in their attempts to combine wisdom and power. This instability and tension manifested itself in both philosophy and in politics.

The union of wisdom and power in the form of the Christian prince and the pope transformed philosophy into theology, a combination of philosophy and piety, and entangled it in politics. As we have seen, philosophy as theology was now focused on apologetics and the determination of orthodoxy and dogma and the repudiation of heresy. The precise and subtle logical and philosophical insights of classical philosophy were now enlisted in the examination of subtle questions of piety, for example the nature of Christ, the meaning of the Eucharist, the purity of Mary and the role of faith in salvation. Drawing on seemingly contending statements in the Bible, these debates gave rise to continuing and grave conflicts within the Church and determinations of heretical views with serious religious implications for the pious, such as the declarations of *anathema* – a curse by a council or pope excommunicating someone or denouncing a doctrine.

These new forms of philosopher king meant philosophy as theology, and Church dogmatics inevitably became a political weapon, and conversely, politics was entangled and shaped by dogmatics so that the struggle between these modern philosopher kings was fought on the plane of both theology and politics. Theologically, the doctrinal contests within the Church between Franciscan and Dominican theologians regarding the nature of poverty inevitably arose and were coloured by the contests between secular and religious power. This entanglement is nowhere more evident than in the Protestant Reformation. Initially an attempt to reform the church and the office of the papacy, the Ninety-five Theses written by German theologian Martin Luther in 1517 attacked corruption in the Church by tracing it to a perversion in the Church's doctrine of redemption and grace. Luther challenged the pope's authority to issue indulgences, and in doing so opened the path to the Reformation's original three *Solae* or Latin phrases that summarised the Reformers' theological convictions: *sola scriptura* (scripture alone is authoritative), *sola fide* (justification is by faith and not by works) and *sola gratia* (salvation through divine grace and not merit).[64] Luther was excommunicated in 1521 but the reform movement expanded, notably adopted by a French lawyer John Calvin who became influential through his *Institutes of the Christian Religion* (1536) as a model for the community he established in Geneva. Soon Lutheranism dominated northern Europe, Socianism in Poland, Anglicanism in England and Presbyterianism in Scotland, with counter-reformation movements in Spain and Italy.[65]

The other distinctive feature of these modern philosopher kings was the way politics was transformed by philosophy as theology. The Christian prince or the pope now saw the world in terms of both political expediency and theological purity, so that each new prince or pope, depending on their character, disposition and piety, relied on one or both in their deliberations. But because the transcendent was mysterious and infinite, the secular and spiritual became incommensurable, exacerbating the challenge of prudence and sound political judgement. It was this combination that would result in domestic and international politics that were historically unprecedented. The examples from domestic politics are extensive but a few are notorious. The Fourth Lateran Council had made it the duty of bishops to identify and punish heretics. Soon the papacy established inquisitors, condoning torture and authorising secular authorities to execute the guilty. The Inquisitions spread through Europe and in Spain became a secular initiative to test 'converso' or converted Jews who had been baptised, using torture and auto-de-fé or public punishments of the guilty, culminating in the 1492 edict by Spanish King Ferdinand and Queen Isabella I of Castile to expel from Spain Jews who did not convert to Christianity. There is also the notorious St Bartholomew's Day Massacre in 1572 planned by Queen Catherine de Medici and carried out by Roman Catholic nobles and other citizens resulting in the deaths of more than 10,000 French Huguenot. Internationally, there were eight Crusades, from 1095 to 1291. The First Crusade in response to the 1095 call by Pope Urban II to aid the Byzantines and recapture the Holy Land from Muslim control resulted in the conquest of Jerusalem in 1099 and the slaughter of 60,000 of its inhabitants. The infamous Fourth Crusade (1202–4) culminated in the sack of Constantinople itself in 1204, where thousands were killed, great scholarly and artistic works stolen or destroyed, and the Byzantine Empire divided between Venice and the Crusade's leaders.[66] But the most protracted and destructive were the European religious wars of the sixteenth, seventeenth and early eighteenth centuries, where religion and national interests contributed to continuing conflict. The wars began with the minor Knight Revolt (1522) and included the protracted and deadly Thirty Years' War (1618–48) which ended with the Peace of Westphalia (1648), though subsequent conflicts were to continue into the 1700s.[67]

Pious Philosopher Kings

In 1929 the Lateran Treaty, a component of the Lateran Pacts of 1929 between the Kingdom of Italy under King Victor Emanuel III and the Holy See under Pope Pius XI, declared Roman Catholicism the state religion of Italy and recognised the new state, 'Vatican City', as fully sovereign and independent.[68] The papacy had regained some of its authority, but the limited terms of the Treaty showed how much the authority of the Church had contracted in modernity, revealing the restrictions on the prophet, the Christian prince and the pope as pious innovations in reconciling wisdom and power. These modern philosopher kings were made possible by reinterpreting the meaning of philosophy as theology, where insights of philosophy, especially those that presented a challenge to revealed religion, continued to play an important role in theology. But the overriding new concerns were apologetics, dogmatics, defence of orthodoxy and doctrinal purity, giving rise to a new politics that needed to comprehend the numinous, and the 'City of God' that gave meaning to, and therefore revalued radically, all earthly politics. Secular and spiritual were therefore now mutually constitutive, and the pious ruler was now an altogether new solution to the problem of transvalued politics. There were, however, inherent limitations to these innovations. The most important for prophets was the ambiguous place they occupied between piety and politics, and the difficulty of distinguishing the false prophet from the true. For the prince and the pope, the political entanglement of politics with faith, and the necessary coexistence and tension between the two new versions of the philosopher king, meant a pious politics distinctive in its zeal, contestation and immoderation.

The inherent instability of these new versions of philosopher kings would soon confront a much more formidable external challenge – a radical questioning of piety in the name of human reasoning and science. Machiavelli's rejection of pious cruelty, Galileo's repudiation of the centrality of the earth, Spinoza's questioning of the provenance of the Bible and the status of miracles,

Descartes's defence of radical doubt as foundation for science, Newton's mathematical nature, the Baconian innovation in scientific method and the Hobbesian social contract that endorsed individual rights led to a fundamental questioning of revealed religion. The Enlightenment and modernity therefore represented a formidable attack on the very origins of prophetology, the papacy and the Christian prince. Combined with modern empiricism, theories of evolution and the primacy accorded to economic and historical forces, perhaps it was inevitable that the claim 'God is dead' now seemed plausible, undermining the feasibility of rule by prophets and Christian princes and popes. Though prophets still proclaimed their truth, the Vatican had the pope, and leaders proclaimed their faith, the claim that these new leaders were pious philosopher kings seemed less compelling.

Notes

1. For an examination of religion and laws in Greece and Rome see Fustel de Coulanges (1980).
2. See generally Melamed (2003), who demonstrates the significant mutual influence of Islamic and Jewish thinkers in the adoption and dissemination of the concept of the philosopher king. On the limits of the concept in Jewish thought see the division of functions of *ketarim* or 'Three Crowns' of prophet–lawgiver–king as opposed to the single philosopher king, and the more ambiguous role of the monarchy in Jewish thought (Melamed 2003: 10).
3. On the openness of Christianity to philosophical speculation and the importance of Islam in the rediscovery of political philosophy see Fortin (2002).
4. Rom. (13: 11–12).
5. The Gnostic challenge was countered with the claim that revelation was to be found in Scripture and not in 'secret' teachings: see Herring (2006: 33–7).
6. See, for example, Paul's use of Stoicism in his 'Areopagus Address' (Acts 17: 22–31).
7. For a reception of Plato in the renaissance see Hankins (1990).
8. *Prescription Against Heretics*, VII. See Tertullian (1985).
9. Thesis 41. See also Thesis 50: 'Briefly, the whole of Aristotle is to theology as darkness is to light': Luther, *Disputation Against Scholastic Theology* (1517) in Lull (2012, 3–7).
10. This view can be discerned in the modern conciliatory approach adopted by John Paul II's (1920–2005) *Fides et Ratio* (1998) that sees philosophy as indispensable help for faith and communication of the Gospel (McFarland et al. 2011: 154).

11. For a general overview of the relationship between philosophy and theology see de Mowbray (2004).
12. Matt. (22: 21); John (18: 36).
13. *City of God* (IV 4: 147–8). References to *City of God* are to Augustine (1994).
14. Matt. (5: 43–8).
15. *Republic* (332d); Matt. (5: 43–8). See also: 'But I say unto you which hear, Love your enemies, do good to them which hate you, Bless them that curse you, and pray for them which despitefully use you. And unto him that smiteth thee on the *one* cheek offer also the other; and him that taketh away thy cloke forbid not *to take thy* coat also. Give to every man that asketh of thee; and of him that taketh away thy goods ask *them* not again. And as ye would that men should do to you, do ye also to them likewise. For if ye love them which love you, what thank have ye? For sinners also love those that love them' (Luke 6: 27–3; see also Matt. 5: 39).
16. Rom. (13: 1–5); 2 Sam. (1: 14–16).
17. Ex. (20: 2–17); Matt. (19: 21–4); Acts (4: 32–5).
18. Gal. (3: 28); 1 Cor. (7: 20–2); Eph. (6: 5); Philem. (1: 12).
19. Augustine, *Tractates on the Gospel of John* (XXVI 2 cf. VI 25), available at <https://www.newadvent.org/fathers/1701.htm> (last accessed 5 July 2022).
20. Augustine, *City of God*; *Summa* (II, II, Q 40) on the contending views. References to *Summa* are to Aquinas (1920).
21. Matt. (16: 18–19).
22. John (21: 15–17).
23. See Matt. (18: 18); John (20: 23).
24. Matt (26: 49–53).
25. Luke (22: 35–8).
26. Monasticism may have originated independently from Egypt among the Syrians in Mesopotamia and Persia, see Vööbus (1951: 30).
27. Plato's Academy was suppressed in 529 CE when the Monte Cassino monastery was established. Charlemagne established with imperial decree monastic schools and cathedral schools as seats of learning and centres of theological research and education until the rise of universities in the thirteenth century. On the history of universities see Perkin (2007) and Scott (2006).
28. Matt. (23: 34).
29. 1 Cor. (12: 27).
30. Rom. (11: 13).
31. Mark (6: 7–13); Matt. (28: 19).
32. Matt. (21: 10–11); Acts (3: 19–21).
33. 1 Cor (13: 12).
34. See generally Kyrtatas (1988); Ash (1976). As Horrell (1997: 322) notes, the Canonical Pauline corpus shows a shift from itinerant

apostles, such as Paul and others, to male heads of households who were leaders in Christian communities.

35. See Wewinshon (1958); Aune (1983).
36. See Plato's *Apology* (30e). Note, however, that this view of Socrates as 'gadfly' is contradicted by his perennial claim of ignorance and that he is nothing more than a 'midwife' (Plato's *Theaetetus*). On the gadfly see Nussbaum (1997: 10) who views it as 'waking democracy up so that it could conduct its business in a more reflective and reasonable way'.
37. On the origins and history of Jewish prophecy see Redditt (2008).
38. Gen. (41 1–57).
39. 1 Kings (17–19); 2 Kings (1–2).
40. 2 Sam. (12: 7–14).
41. Mark (6: 17–29).
42. See Cook (2009: 270).
43. Gen. (41: 38–9).
44. Rev. (1: 10–11).
45. Rom. (11: 13).
46. See Acts on the resemblance of prophets to Cynics. Prophets were admonished for seeking personal gain – they were not to seek food or lodging beyond three days (Horrell 1997: 330).
47. Matt. (7: 15–23).
48. Acts (6: 11–13). Pope Gregory I, in *Homilia in Evangelia*, wrote of three modes of martyrdom, designated by the colours, red, blue (or green), and white, referring to those who suffered violence, those who denied desires and desert ascetics. See generally Hoel (2020).
49. See Ash (1976) on the decline of ecstatic prophecy.
50. 1 Cor. (12: 27).
51. Tacitus, Book XV, 44, <https://www.perseus.tufts.edu/hopper/text?doc=Perseus%3Atext%3A1999.02.0078%3Abook%3D15%3Achapter%3D44> (last accessed 6 July 2022).
52. There is no consensus on the conversion of Constantine. Accounts vary from those of Lactantius, tutor to Constantine's son, and Eusebius, who suggests the bishops who travelled with Constantine may have interpreted the sign as Jesus's triumph over death. Another possible interpretation emphasises the political aspects of the decision to convert, especially the character of the new religion with its uncertain dogma and a politically less influential priesthood as a useful new civic religion for the new founding in Constantinople.
53. Augustus adopted the title Pontifex Maximus in 12 BCE and this title continued until its rejection by Emperor Gratian (375–383 CE). Not long after Gratian laid it aside the popes took up the title, with the head of the Roman Catholic Church to this day often being associated with the term.

54. Subsequent councils included those of Ephesus (431 CE) and Chalcedon (451 CE).
55. 1 Cor. (15: 10); John (3: 27).
56. See generally Kantorowicz (1957).
57. Especially after the establishment of the Christian Church and the suppression of all pagan religions by emperor Theodosius I in 380 CE. Theodosius had been a Spanish monk and his extreme view of what it means to be 'vindicator of orthodoxy' can be seen in his order to kill 7,000 citizens in Thessalonika in revenge for the death of an imperial officer.
58. John (21: 15–17); Matt. (16: 18–19).
59. Based on Christ's commission to St Peter (Matt. 16: 18–19), his command to Peter to 'Feed my sheep' (John 21: 15–17) and the notion of hierarchy derived from St Paul's disciple Dionysius the Areopagite who was in fact the Christian Neo-Platonist Pseudo-Dionysius whose theory of 'infusion of differentials of power' traced all authority to the head (Coleman 2000: 23). Note that there was dispute as to whether the popes or bishops had such authority (as all disciples were accorded the authority to bind and loose: Matt. 18: 18; John 20: 23). St Ambrose had in the fourth century argued clergy were superior to the laity.
60. See generally Coleman (2000); McGrath (2017).
61. In the 'Investiture Contest', the eleventh-century conflict between Pope Gregory VII and Emperor Henry IV of Germany, Pope Gregory would pronounce that kings and emperors were no more than lay members of the Church so that even the king was placed beneath the lowest of the order of the clergy.
62. Pope Boniface refined the theory of *plenitude potestatis* derived from a letter of Pope Leo I (440–61 CE) to claim that it derived from Christ's unlimited earthly lordship (*dominium*). His bull *Unam sanctum* of 1302 is considered the most extreme of all claims to papal power (Woodhead 2004: 115).
63. See generally Hawkins (1947: 136–42).
64. The original three solas now include *Solus Christus* (Jesus Christ alone is our Lord, Saviour and King) and *Soli Deo Gloria* (We live for the glory of God alone).
65. On the history of the reformation see MacCulloch (2005).
66. For an overview of the crusades see France (2005).
67. See generally, MacCulloch (2010).
68. For the terms of the Treaty, which include political, financial and a concordat, see <https://vatican.com/The-Lateran-Treaty> (last accessed 20 June 2022).

Chapter 3

The Public Intellectual

'The intellectual', according to the first Czech President, playwright and dissident, Václav Havel,

> should constantly disturb, should bear witness to the misery of the world, should be provocative by being independent, should rebel against all hidden and open pressure and manipulations, should be the chief doubter of systems, of power and its incantations, should be a witness to their mendacity.[1]

According to Christopher Hitchens (2008) who claimed the role, the intellectual is someone 'who makes his or her living through the battle of ideas'. Implicit in this view is the notion of the intellectual as outsider to the powerful. Thus, in his 1993 Reith Lectures, Edward Said observed,

> At bottom, the intellectual, in my sense of the word, is neither a pacifier nor a consensus-builder, but someone whose whole being is staked on a critical sense, a sense of being unwilling to accept easy formulas, or ready-made clichés, or the smooth, ever-so-accommodating confirmations of what the powerful or conventional have to say, and what they do. Not just passively unwillingly, but actively willing to say so in public.[2]

Or, as he would put it later, 'the intellectual's provisional house is the domain of an exigent, resistant, intransigent art into which alas, one can neither retreat nor search for solutions'.[3] Similarly, 'It is the responsibility of intellectuals', according to Noam Chomsky, 'to speak the truth and to expose lies'.[4] 'The intellectual', according to Foucault, 'spoke the truth to those who had yet to see it, in the name of those who were forbidden to speak the truth: he was conscience, consciousness and eloquence.'[5] In short, intellectuals are admirable, even heroic figures who 'speak truth to power', counselling on the proper use of power without possessing it and in doing so risking themselves for the public good.[6] They may be a uniquely modern attempt to ennoble politics, but lacking power, they cannot be described as modern philosopher kings who possess and command both.

A different, more complex understanding of the character, ambition and power of intellectuals emerges when we locate them as agents of progress within the larger context of the Enlightenment. From this perspective, far from being powerless, intellectuals derive their authority not only from their wisdom but also from their moral integrity gained from their distance from political power. It is their ability to be critical of power and avoid its temptations that empowers them and therefore allows them to combine wisdom and a power independent of politics, making them a new distinctive form of the philosopher king. If a modern philosopher king in this sense, how successfully has the intellectual resolved the paradox of the philosopher king? In this chapter we will explore the distinctive challenges faced by intellectuals in pursing the promise of the philosopher king. As we will see, the new source of power they wield gives rise to a novel form of the paradox of the philosopher king where the more their advice and counsel is heeded and even adopted and the closer they come to political power, the more vulnerable they become to losing the distance that sustained their moral and political legitimacy and therefore authority. That is, the more they succeed in changing politics, the less politically powerful they become. This is a precarious, high-wire act for intellectuals who want to reform politics yet with their success risk compromising their independence, moral integrity and authority. Such a delicate balancing act reveals how the intellectual is a modern philosopher king, albeit one who confronts a unique modern challenge in combining wisdom and power. In this chapter we explore how intellectuals negotiate the new paradox of wisdom and power by starting with a definition of an intellectual. We then examine if the proposed separation or distance of the intellectual from politics is possible, before evaluating its merits from the perspective of both the intellectuals and politics. In our concluding remarks we consider the claim that intellectuals are in decline, presenting a core challenge to the feasibility of the intellectual as a modern philosopher king.

Who is an Intellectual?

Who is an intellectual?[7] Each year invariably produces a new survey of eligible candidates, with each nation boasting its own list, though a few leading intellectuals can claim to have an international standing.[8] Yet the precise meaning of the intellectual remains elusive, attempts to answer the question complicated by the fact that it has been intellectuals themselves who have proposed the definitions.[9] The idea of a 'public' intellectual, for example, was introduced by C. Wright Mill and was taken up by Jacoby in the American context due to academic specialisation and new communication technologies.[10]

The term 'intellectual' itself has been traced to a number of sources.[11] *Intelligentsia* referred to nineteenth-century educated Russian advocates of modernisation and social emancipation, as well as Polish nationalists opposed to occupying powers.[12] The role of *die Intelligenzen* was debated by Marx, Engels and especially Karl Kautsky, author of *Der Socialismus und die Intelligenz*.[13] Though the term was previously in use in France, Émile Zola's famous 'J'Accuse . . .!' open letter to President of the Republic Felix Faure in *L'Aurore Litéraire* on 13 January 1898 protesting the mistrial of Colonel Dreyfus and the subsequent publication of the *Manifest des Intellectuels* on the Dreyfus affair by scholars, artists and scientists gave the term greater social prominence.[14] It came into general use in the first decades of the twentieth century and became commonplace from the 1950s.[15]

As we have seen, an important aspect of being an intellectual has been the view that they had a transcendent moral mission of countering power by giving public voice to the silenced and vulnerable. This moral dimension of the intellectual has an older source in the Enlightenment (*siècle des Lumières; Aufklärung*), an intellectual movement of the seventeenth and eighteenth centuries that emphasised the use of reason as the means to advance human freedom and secure happiness.[16] Early modern thinkers distinguished between scientific and philosophical insights and the common or 'vulgar' perspective.[17] Unlike classical thinkers, who drew on common opinions to refine their philosophical reflections, modern philosophers attempted to overturn what they thought was an inherent confusion in the popular view. Drawing on mathematical principles, politics was now to be an exact science, reshaped on a new, more rational basis.[18] Their ambition was therefore nothing less than the transformation of everyday life, founded above all on the idea of progress where advances in knowledge disseminated to the public would yield social, material and moral advancement. The intellectual was therefore a distinctive individual but also part of a larger movement with the essential role of permanently transforming society. More than a scientist or technician, the intellectual was a moral defender of humanity who challenged all contemporary politics. This conception of the intellectual as an agent of progress can be seen clearly in the French *philosophs*, writers, poets and scientists such as Diderot, d'Alembert, Voltaire and Condorcet who defended individualism and freedom from the corrupting force of church, army, aristocracy and royalty. Diderot and d'Alembert's (1751) *Encyclopédie, ou dictionnaire raisonné des sciences, des arts et des métiers*, is an ambitious and compendious work in this tradition, with its avowed intention to gather all the knowledge contained in the world, to examine it critically and rationally, and to use it for social advancement. Yet as the notion of progress evolved, and sources of resistance and political corruption changed, the intellectual too was transformed, challenged by critiques of the Enlightenment that drew on nature, history, materialism and even radical historicism. Thus these foundational critiques of the notion of progress itself suggested new conceptions of intellectuals whose duty became to question radically the very role of the intellectual, accounting for the diversity of intellectuals, the ideas they advocate and the politics they oppose.[19] Nevertheless, certain core elements can be said to define all intellectuals. Intellectuals are thinkers who deal with 'non-material' factors or symbols but not in a technical sense, distinguishing them from scientists and technicians.[20] As such, intellectuals are concerned with ideas, themes and things that transcend any specific or particular interest or class. They therefore adopt an overarching or conspectus view rather than a partial and interested one.[21] Intellectuals are not private thinkers like scholars or academics who pursue their research without engaging the public; they are 'public' in the sense that they take an active or prominent role in politics. But such involvement is not from the centre of power; it is from a vantage point that resides outside the prevailing economic and political sources of power and authority. It is this distance that secures their autonomy and empowers intellectuals to counter, correct and remedy the vagaries of power in the name of universal principles of morality and justice.[22] Intellectuals therefore always feel apart from everyone, yet from their perspective are compelled to serve the greater good, sacrificing their welfare for the public. There is therefore something of the oracular prophet in intellectuals, their abilities shining only in times of darkness and need.

Separation of Truth and Power

This account of the complex and multifaceted nature of intellectuals appears to show why they cannot be considered to be philosopher kings. The philosopher king aspires to combine or unify wisdom and power, philosophy and politics to secure justice. Yet the intellectual, as we have seen, presumes and even advocates the separation of judgement and authority. 'Speaking truth to power' encapsulates both the distance and tension between wisdom and power, revealing the unique new role of the intellectual who is political but not of politics. What exactly is the nature of this puzzling relationship, and does it repudiate the possibility of the philosopher king? Does the intellectual represent a radical separation of wisdom and power, or a more complex, subtle, even fragile relationship between the two, initiating a novel modern version of the philosopher king?

The question of whether the intellectual was a disinterested champion of truth or was inevitably entangled in partisan politics was addressed indirectly in the examination of the sociology of the intellectual, where it was posed as the question of 'class' – are intellectuals 'class-less' or do they form a distinctive sub-class of the ruling powers? The leading view that intellectuals do not belong to any class implies that it is possible to separate truth from power, philosophy from politics. Karl Mannheim argued that education allowed intellectuals to choose their affiliation, whether as theorists for conservatives, proletariat or bourgeoisie.[23] Interested in seeing the whole rather than a part, intellectuals had a 'mission' to encourage mutual understanding among classes, and were therefore 'unanchored, relatively class-less stratum'. For Talcott Parsons intellectuals were 'people concerned with the meaning of symbolic systems' and were not necessarily the 'primary holders of political power or controllers of economic resources'.[24] Intellectuals, according to Edward Shils, had universalistic ideals that were different from society's mundane concerns.[25] Though they had frequent access to 'courts of glory', he thought their true role was of responsible critic.[26] Intellectuals were therefore autonomous and indeed there was even a rivalry and conflict within intellectual networks.[27]

This view was countered by others who argued that intellectuals were incapable of keeping their distance from power either because they inevitably formed a separate and independent class that wielded power, or from a Marxist approach that they always represented and advocated the views and interests of the dominant or ruling class. The origin of the first view that intellectuals form a distinctive class is Julien Benda's (1969) *The Treason of the Intellectuals*, who defined intellectuals as those who 'seek their joy in the practice of an art or a science or metaphysical speculation' so that they looked to the interests of society as a whole. Because they were duty-bound to avoid defending nation, class and race, intellectuals had common interests that set them apart and determined how they would organise, making them a class of their own. The political ascendency of this class was regarded by some as a dangerous development, resulting in the 'reign of scientific intelligence, the most aristocratic, despotic, arrogant, and contemptuous of regimes'.[28] Others saw it as 'elites' or a 'new class' of critical intellectuals and technical intelligentsia that pursued their own rather than the public interest, or an 'intellectual field', constituted by hierarchies, divisions and conflicts, but which nevertheless revealed a shared interest by intellectuals in the form of 'cultural capital'.[29]

The other approach that claimed intellectuals were always entangled with power drew on Marxism, yet in doing so had to confront a theoretical puzzle in Marxist theory itself. The Marxist tradition has 'struggled with the contradiction between a theoretical identity rooted in the vision of proletarian self-emancipation and the political reality of a movement dominated by intellectuals'.[30] The initial 'vanguardist' role for intellectuals advocated by Kautsky was later taken up by Lenin who proposed the 'cadre-intellectuals' in a party apparatus that is repository of theory, strategy and political vision, a view that dominated the actual history of Marxist movements and revolutions. The alternative view by anarchists such as Bernstein, Luxemburg and Lukács saw revolutionary consciousness emerge from proletarian culture. Gramsci attempted to bridge this divide with his notion of the 'organic' intellectual. Drawing on Marx, Gramsci argued every social group produced its own intellectuals, so that 'traditional' intellectuals that claimed autonomy and independence were delusional. But there was an 'organic' relationship between intellectuals and the 'world of production', so that just as bourgeoisie produced intellectuals, so did the proletariat. It was these 'organic' intellectuals that would allow revolutionary movements to escape bourgeois hegemony and bureaucratic deformation.[31] Such a class-bound approach to sociology of intellectuals therefore saw intellectuals as speakers for the power elite.[32]

As this brief overview suggests, whether it is possible for intellectuals to keep their distance from power is a complicated question shaped by the specific assumptions and concerns of those who have sought to answer it. It has, as we have seen, been informed by the sociology of the intellectual, as well as the unique problem the intellectual has presented to Marxist thought where attempts at understanding the independence of intellectuals have invariably been entangled in intermural contests over the revolutionary nature of the proletariat. What both approaches make clear, however, is an intricate and complex relationship between intellectuals and the powerful, where intellectuals seek to wield power while its centripetal force compels them to resist its attractions and temptations. To see whether this relationship is characterised by a separation of wisdom and power, representing a repudiation of the philosopher king, or indeed evinces a more complex relationship between the two so that the intellectual represents a unique modern philosopher king it is necessary to take a closer look at the subtle relationship between the intellectual and power.

Our starting point for this examination is the idea of progress that justified a wholly new conception of the philosopher and politics.[33] The intellectual differs from the classical philosopher in being a perplexing combination of someone who is detached and removed from politics and power, while at the same time being essentially concerned with public welfare and reforming political orders.[34] The classical philosophers who pursued the *vita comptemplativa* were political to the extent that politics provided them essential *entrée* into philosophical questions, disclosing ideas and concepts that facilitated philosophical reflections that were informed by the particular civic duties and obligations they necessarily confronted as citizens. Yet in a profound sense philosophical reflection also required a critical approach to politics, in Socratic terms the *periagoge*, to gain greater clarity about both the political and heavenly matters. Socrates was always in the marketplace and unlike the sophists never left Athens, yet he did not pursue political office nor was he ambitious for political rule. From this perspective, politics was essential for philosophical contemplation, but there were serious reservations regarding the extent to which philosophy could transform politics. The philosopher returned to the cave to liberate specific individuals, rather than illuminating and therefore transforming the cave for everyone. By contrast, modernity understood the relationship between philosophy and politics in a fundamentally new way. Hard-won philosophical insights gained by dispelling the darkness of prejudice, tradition and religion could be disseminated to the many, assuring unlimited material improvement and political progress. The role of the modern philosopher – the intellectual – was therefore to permanently transform politics by challenging contemporary practices through the reform of people's thoughts and perceptions. The intellectual as an agent of progress and educator ameliorating public opinion and consciousness was therefore required to be in the public eye. It is in this sense that intellectuals had an enduring attachment to politics and public life and sought out these forums to fulfil their mission. Yet, as we have seen, the intellectual was not a politician, advisor to political office holders or even a bureaucrat or public servant who pursued the public good by implementing desirable policies. To the contrary, the intellectual was necessarily detached, alienated, a misfit, desperate to avoid the offices and trappings of power. Why did the intellectual who wanted to reform politics choose such detachment and distance from political power?

This detachment was not a matter of the individual character or personal disposition of the intellectual, for example the notorious misanthropy of a Heraclitus. Rather, it was the other face of the intellectual as agent of progress, mandated by the way progress conceived the character of politics itself. Intellectuals had a complex and contradictory view of politics, reflected in their role and responsibilities. 'Suspicion and dissent', according to Bauman,

> constantly alternate with a powerful attraction – nay, fascination – with the power of the state. Sometimes, they succeed each other with a breath-taking speed. Most of the time, they cohabit uneasily within the same intellectual community; often inside the same 'split personality'; of a single intellectual – even if many an intellectual does not like to be reminded of it'.[35]

The intellectual admired and even envied the power and potential of politics to pursue genuine innovation and secure steady progress. Yet these sanguine views coexisted with a dark alternative, a fundamentally jaundiced view of politics that denied it nobility or grandeur. Politics is powerful yet also occlusive or corrosive of judgement and integrity. The political permits the pursuit of the good but because it lacks a larger vision it is selective, tending towards partiality and corruption. Politics was at best incompetent, invariably corrupt, a venal forum for endless and brutal power seeking by specific or partisan interests that exploited the public good. Consequently, it was essential for the intellectual to avoid the temptation of power, as it subtly and unavoidably corrupted all those who came within its seemingly irresistible orbit.

To keep a distance from power seemed to be a high price to pay, depriving the intellectual of the resources to achieve genuine change and promote progress. Yet ironically it was this distance from direct power that empowered the intellectual. Standing outside or away from political power preserved the intellectual's clarity of vision, judgement. It permitted the uniquely panoptic vision of intellectuals, allowing them to see beyond the specific or partial political context and interests to comprehend the drama and panorama of historical progress. Perhaps more importantly, just like priests and prophets whose vows of poverty and celibacy gave them moral authority, the public rejection of office, wealth and influence by intellectuals gave them the moral authority and legitimacy to be heard by the public, to speak on behalf of great causes and in doing so to be believed by the public who long admired such selfless commitment and dedication to the common weal.[36] It also allowed intellectuals to display their virtue and to exercise the courage needed in speaking truth to power, risking personal benefit and advantages for the public good. The distance between the intellectual and power was therefore essential for the integrity, authority and the unique new power of the intellectual for pursuing progress.

In speaking truth to power the intellectual seemed to reject combining both, seemingly denying the role of a modern philosopher king. But the intellectual as a child of progressive modernity reveals a more complex picture, a philosopher suspended and defined by the flux between wisdom and power, philosophy and politics. Intellectuals in seeking to reform politics will necessarily distance themselves from its corrupting power. Yet ironically it is this very distance that empowers them, both in terms of clarity of vision and perhaps more importantly, in moral rectitude and thereby public legitimacy. Intellectuals therefore are modern philosopher kings who combine wisdom and power, but on wholly modern terms, with their wisdom and power derived from the integrity and authority of a herald and advocate at the vanguard of progressive innovation.

Intellectual as Tragic Hero

To what extent did intellectuals, as modern philosopher kings, overcome or resolve the paradox of the philosopher king? In other words, how efficacious is this modern union of wisdom and power, both for the intellectual and for politics more generally? Certainly, the intellectual seems to have an enviable life. Lauded for one's wisdom and insights, praised for moral integrity in standing up to power, admired for one's writings and speeches, the life of the intellectual appears to have it all. International invitations to give keynote addresses, prestigious prizes and university posts, and the ability to command the attention of the public make the intellectual the deserved celebrity of the modern era. The heady cocktail of flattery, fame and fortune is undeniably intoxicating. Yet not all intellectuals enjoy this life. From the very beginning the *philosophes* had to write anonymously, concealing their true thoughts and intentions and even avoiding certain themes and topics altogether to avoid state censure. Elsewhere intellectuals have been penalised, incarcerated, expelled and in some cases faced capital punishment.[37] These two disparate lives therefore depend on the causes intellectuals pursue and their personal circumstances, though some combination of both will arguably confront all intellectuals. There is therefore something heroic about the intellectual, bravely challenging powerful vested interests and sacrificing for the welfare of others.

There is, however, also something tragic about intellectuals that has its source in the curious combination of detachment and commitment that defines their lives. The problem for those intellectuals who have a comprehensive initiative they want to pursue and implement is that the more they succeed by having their views adopted and endorsed by the public and political authorities, the more they appear to lose their integrity and moral and political authority that is founded on the distance between what they want to promote and their success in achieving it. The charge of having sold out, or being co-opted, dogged intellectuals from the beginning. Julien Benda's (1969) *The Treason of the Intellectuals* claimed that 'clerks' who acted as 'checks on the realism of the people' and 'officiants of abstract justice and were sullied with no passion for a worldly object' soon 'began to play the game of political passion' by adopting political passions, bringing their passions into their actions as clerks, especially in their metaphysical reflections, and 'played the game of political passion by their doctrines'.[38] In entering the game of political passions, intellectuals succumbed to political commitment, national particularism and social partisanship that undermined their love of the spiritual and the universal. Fellow intellectuals had succumbed to the enticements of the politically powerful to change what they were saying or even become silent. That success may mean failure is tragic and affects even contemporary intellectuals, where the 'The intellectual', as Hofstadter puts it, 'is either shut out or sold out.'[39] Romantic or radical intellectuals may appear to avoid this tragic possibility, their questioning of the legitimacy of all contemporary institutions and denying the possibility of any solution to the problems they have diagnosed preserving them from the charge of collusion and complicity with corrupting politics. Yet their lives appear tragic in another guise – the more extreme their intellectual diagnosis, the more their intellectual cause appears pointless, so that in time they become modern Cassandras who speak the truth, but are never believed. Their sense of alienation and isolation from the public they seek to enlighten, combined with the evident impossibility of succeeding in their hopeless task, traps these intellectuals in a forlorn situation that is impossible to escape without sacrificing their insights or their integrity. Their selling out does not even have the cold comfort of a governmental sinecure as they are otherwise unemployable. They therefore risk becoming the poor lonely crank, at best amusing, certainly annoying, fundamentally tragic.

The heroic and tragic life of the intellectual as modern philosopher king suggests that it does not seem to ameliorate an important aspect of the paradox of the philosopher king – that ruling entails an unjust sacrifice for philosophers. How successfully does it resolve the other aspect of the paradox, whether the intellectual is salutary for politics?[40] The immediate and obvious answer was that the intellectual was essential for politics as its sole source of progress – without the intellectual, politics remained mired in superstition and tradition, darkness and backwardness. Accordingly, intellectuals were, as it were, the salt of the earth, essential for political health and material prosperity. History with its grim record of cruelty and injustice was proof of the necessity of intellectuals whose courageous actions and noble sacrifice transformed the world.

This persuasive claim was from the beginning met with objections, both from politics and philosophy. For those who took an active part in political life, the case was obvious and compelling. They charged intellectuals with incompetence and imprudence. Incompetence because they had never taken part in active political life and therefore were unaware of its onerous demands.[41] The daily requirements of office, the demands of limited budgets and resources, the conflicting policy mandates that were often irreconcilable all attested to the fact that politics was a 'strong and slow boring of hard boards', a world of compromise and second best rather than a forum for intransigent public indignation and declamation. The charge of imprudence was more serious as it questioned whether the intellectuals' judgement took into account the complex demands of contending stakeholders, and the delicate problem of acknowledging dignity and honour of all while making difficult choices. These were fine calculations that required judgement developed and refined over years of practice in lesser offices. Politics as the art of the possible seemed to elude the doctrinaire demands of intellectuals who insisted on change from an imperious and sanctimonious high ground. In short, philosophical abilities were qualitatively different from the political, and philosophers made bad politicians.[42]

The charge from philosophers was more serious, if only because it went to the heart of the intellectual project, questioning the notion of progress and the partiality of intellectuals. Whether abstract reason, geometric logic and theoretical speculations could be applied directly to politics was a question from the very beginning of philosophy. These concerns were subsequently raised by a variety of modern thinkers, including Hume, Rousseau, Burke and Tocqueville who in their own way feared the introduction of philosophy into politics by Enlightenment thinkers was comparable to the influence of theological contests that modernity had sought to temper if not eradicate. The Jacobinism of the French Revolution was thus diagnosed by Burke (1989) as a direct consequence of the 'political metaphysics' and 'mechanic philosophy' of 'speculatists' who deployed abstract principles instead of practical reasoning. Similar arguments were made in contemporary politics, with intellectuals indicted of being the unaccountable political advocates or ardent apologists for the worst excesses of the twentieth century.[43] Thus Popper was critical of Nazi intellectuals, Hayek disparaged socialist intellectuals as 'professional second hand dealers of ideas' and Aron saw Communism as the 'opiate' of intellectuals.[44] More recent critics charge intellectuals of supporting totalitarian regimes, with Lilla's (2001) *The Reckless Mind* indicating the tone and tenor of the accusation made against intellectuals. To what extent were Martin Heidegger, Paul De Man and Konrad Lorenz responsible for Nazism, and György Lukács, Jean-Paul Sartre and

John Desmond Bernal for Stalinism?[45] The problem is not only the question of 'dirty hands' and 'doctrine of double effect' regarding well-intentioned acts that have unintended consequences, but also 'negative responsibility' or responsibility for what one does not do.[46]

A specific charge has been the moral myopia of intellectuals due to their commitment to trans-political causes, entrenching a hatred of one's own and a willingness to turn a blind eye to failures of causes espoused. Rimon calls this the problem of 'lucrimax', a term she borrows from Russian literary critic and historian Alexander Etkind to signify a

> zealous striving on the part of the cultural elite for all things real, genuine, and original, and their rejection of their own culture as phony and conjured ... the acceptance of the authenticity of the 'Other' and the rejection of one's own culture as inauthentic.

Examples for Rimon include Chomsky's views of the Khmer Rouge and Foucault's perspective on the Iranian revolutions. As she puts it, 'Terror is the intellectual's temptation. Does this not make it doubtful that intellectuals are capable of performing the duty of the custodians of values? *Quis custodiet ipsos custodes?* Who will guard the guards?'[47]

Decline of the Intellectual

The discussion above has revealed the potential tensions for both the intellectual and politics in this modern version of the philosopher king. Even if we are prepared to dismiss these concerns, we nevertheless need to consider the feasibility of the intellectual as a modern philosopher king. Does it represent a viable modern alternative or is it merely a contingent historical curiosity, a consequence of a peculiar coincidence of different political and cultural trajectories that are not capable of replication? In exploring this question, we need to acknowledge that the reception and specific role of intellectuals will be influenced by the institutional, cultural and political settings of each nation.[48] The 'British exceptionalism' thesis, for example, even claims that Britain has never had intellectuals.[49] But the more substantial challenge to the viability of the intellectual is captured in the debate concerning the 'decline' of the modern intellectual. Whether the intellectual is in decline or even no longer possible is an important question, not only for contemporary politics, but for our understanding of the intellectual as it seems to suggest that it can only be, or ever was, a temporary or limited expression of a modern philosopher king.

As we have seen, the vulnerability of intellectuals to be tempted by personal advantages and therefore succumbing to corruption was a charge that accompanied intellectuals from the start. It is a persistent theme for those who prosecute the decline of intellectual thesis so that for contemporary critics the modern 'treason' has been to accept positions in universities and educational institutions, resulting in professionalisation and specialisation and the insular 'institutionalised intellectuals' who write for each other and for tenure.[50] Alternatively it has produced 'insipid anchormen', 'publicity hounds' and single-issue publicists, or television celebrities who emphasise the personal and sensational.[51] The decline thesis is not accepted by everyone. Some claim at issue is the very definition of the intellectual, with different constructed identities of the intellectual tending to favour an imagined past state of illusory autonomy.[52] Others argue that rather than a decline there has been a transformation in institutional contexts and the publics themselves, with a broader range of engagement strategies that now allow a more open and fluid conception of the intellectual.[53]

These varied and complex claims, I suggest, can be comprehended under two aspects – philosophical and political – that have important implications for viability of the intellectual as a modern philosopher king. Philosophically the intellectual has been defined and constituted by modernity and its tendency towards self-critique.[54] Therefore the dominant view of the intellectual as an Enlightenment agent of progress has been challenged variously by Romantic and anti-bourgeoise intellectuals informed by Rousseau, Hegel and Marx, as well as contemporary intellectuals favouring Nietzschean nihilism and perspectivism as well as Heideggerian radical historicism that advocates *Destruktion*. What the contemporary intellectual's 'accusation' is and who is being accused has therefore become unclear and questionable. Such lack of clarity, especially evident in widespread doubts about the notion of progress and claims about 'end of ideology' suggests the end of the intellectual.[55] If we accept this proposition, then the intellectual was not a fundamental or foundational modern expression of the philosopher king, but a specific answer in response to a philosophical experiment, so that its future was always mortgaged to the ambitions and success of the Enlightenment. Even if we accept this proposition, it does leave open the possibility of new intellectuals, those who were instrumental to the demise of the Enlightenment.

They may no longer resemble the traditional intellectuals because in emphasising the limits to human rationality their calls for revolutionary change bereft of programmatic reforms seem equivocal in their curious admixture of ruthless cruelty and hopeful naïveté. Yet one cannot deny they remain intellectuals, albeit shadows of their former selves.[56] They therefore appear as melancholic 'unquiet' spirits, reminding us of the heroic promise – and failure – of the 'traditional' intellectual.

The other, political argument concerns the recent economic, cultural and technological changes that have taken place, transforming the concept of the intellectual and of public space.[57] A distinctive feature of these changes has been the increasing importance of universities and think tanks as places of refuge for intellectuals.[58] Moreover, the advance of science has made the technocratic expert rather than the intellectual dominant.[59] On matters that reach beyond such instrumental concerns, the authority of the intellectual has been fundamentally transformed by changes in how we engage with each other. The ubiquity of new social media has not only changed the way we communicate, it has also transformed the way citizens consult and deliberate with each other and engage with the state.[60] The decline of 'mass media' and the rise of new virtual fora that blur boundaries between public, private and commercial has made us rethink the meaning of the 'marketplace of ideas'. It certainly has democratised access to the public: we all now have the potential to have our voices heard. These developments have in effect redefined the constituent elements of the intellectual. Individuals and groups and their relationships have become more contingent and amorphous, fragile, indeterminate and in flux. Like the concept of the 'expert', moral authority is now under challenge so that the moral superiority of any one individual is now in question. Similarly, the notion of a 'detached' intellectual has become even more ambiguous because what constitutes the boundaries of 'state' are increasingly uncertain and the threat of the state has become ubiquitous, diffused and invisible. The intellectual therefore appears to have been democratised yet this process has been at the price of effacing those elements – attachment to a cause and detachment from politics – that defined the intellectual. Everyone can speak, but it is now harder to be heard.[61] Consequently, the 'thinkers', 'influencers' and 'thought leaders' that have replaced intellectuals in modern liberal democracies have, in attempting to be heard, tended to displace public critique, dissent and deliberation with entertainment, amusement and consumption. The irony may be that the success of the modern project has meant the end of intellectuals, with their last vestiges in authoritarian regimes recalling an anachronistic legacy.[62] Taken together, these philosophical and political developments suggest the intellectual was an ambitious attempt that in its heroic and tragic aspects reveals the paradox and promise of the modern philosopher king.

Notes

1. Cited in Karabel (1996). See also Havel (1991: 167).
2. Said (1994: 23).
3. Said (2002: 39).
4. Chomsky (1967: 1).
5. Foucault and Deleuze (1977: 207).
6. Edward Said, who in delivering the prestigious Reith Lectures for the BBC in 1993, repeatedly emphasised that the task of the contemporary intellectual is 'to speak the truth to power'. The phrase 'speaking truth to power' is generally traced to the 1955 book opposing the Cold War, *Speak Truth to Power: A Quaker Search for an Alternative to Violence*, published by the American Friends Service Committee. On the tension between the intellectual and 'tradition' see Eisenstadt (1972).
7. See the thoughtful and thorough overview by Kurzman and Owens (2002); Gagnon (1987); Leonard (1996); and Shils (1968).
8. See, for example, Ignatieff (1997) on American intellectuals; Petras (1989) on Latin American; Pusey (2010) on Australian; Stapleton (2000) on British; Tănăsoiu (2008) on Romanian; Ross (1990) on French; Pasquinelli (1995) on Italian.
9. 'Any attempt to define intellectuals', according to Bauman (1992: 81), 'is an attempt at self-definition'.
10. See Danowski and Park (2009); Jacoby (1987); Gourgouris (2007).
11. For origin of the term, especially its English usage, distinguishing between the cultural expert, the university educated person and devotees of culture see Allen (1986: 349–50).
12. On the different types of Russian *intelligentsia* see Confino (1972).
13. Allen (1986: 348).
14. On the Dreyfus case and Zola's prominent role in organising *les intellectuels* see Coser (1997).
15. See Mannheim (1993); Todorov et al. (1997).
16. On the intellectual as 'child of the Enlightenment' see Jennings (2000); Rahe (2003); Melzer (2003). Compare with Schumpeter (1942: 147): 'But if the monastery gave birth to the intellectual of the medieval world, it was capitalism that let him loose and presented him with the printing press.'

17. See Bauman (1992: 83) who argues that the modern state is the birthplace of intellectuals, giving rise to three social groups: 'the elite, serving as a self-appointed model of *l'honnête homme, l'homayee civilisé*, or *l'homme des lumières*; the *masses* ("The Other" of the elite), accordingly raw, uncivilized and unenlightened; and the *trainers* meant to refine, civilize and enlighten the masses'.

18. See in this context Descartes, who begins with radical scepticism, Galileo, who claimed 'Mathematics is the alphabet with which God has written the universe' and Hobbes, who claimed to have discovered a new science of politics (Rahe 2003).

19. See Foucault and Deleuze (1977: 207) on how contemporary intellectuals are agents in systems of power.

20. For Todorov et al. (1997: 1121) an intellectual is 'engaged in an activity of the mind resulting in the production of a work', such as literature, science and philosophy, and is also concerned about the state of society and participates in public debate. He denies that politicians, preachers and propagandists are intellectuals for they do not produce a work. He also distinguishes between intellectuals and 'artists' such as painters, musicians and actors (though curiously making an exception for filmmakers) and those who work in isolation, such as poets in garrets and scientists in labs.

21. As Rimon (2013: 534) notes, 'Sartre, in his lectures in Japan (1966), declared that the "technicians of practical Knowledge" (doctors, lawyers, social scientists) will not be intellectuals, until they become aware of the contradiction between the particularity of their practice and the universality of their vocation for knowledge'.

22. Sowell (2009) argues that intellectuals, defined as people whose occupations are concerned primarily with ideas (writers, historians, academics), usually consider themselves as anointed, or endowed with superior intellect or insight enabling them to guide power brokers and the masses. This makes intellectuals different from other highly educated cerebral workers in the applied professions such as engineering, medicine or military service. Sowell claims that modern society needs to foster an attitude of healthy scepticism towards intellectuals.

23. Mannheim (1955: 154–5; 1993).

24. Parsons (1969: 11, 23).

25. Shils (1972: 26–8).

26. Shils (1968). But this had the unintended consequence of creating a sense of alienation in intellectuals. Similarly, Znaniecki (1968) saw them as explorers who did the unexpected, or in terms of Dahrendorf (1969) they appeared as court jesters or fools and were frequently rebellious.

27. See Collins (1998). This perspective allowed others to develop typologies – Shils (1972: 21–2), for example, distinguished between

the 'productive', 'reproductive' and 'consumer', while Sadri and Vidich (1992) identified four ideal types of intellectuals, distinguishing between other-worldly and this-worldly, paradigm-founders and paradigm-followers.

28. See Leonard (1996) who notes the tension between intellectual as critic and as expert.

29. Unlike elite theorists such as Michel, Mosca and Pareto, Gouldner (1975) proposes a 'new class', distinguishing between technical intelligentsia and intellectuals to argue that intellectuals are important for revolutions. Bourdieu (1989), who views the intellectual as constituted as such by intervening in the public sphere in the name of autonomy, asserts that intellectuals – in order to set up themselves as an autonomous collective force – need to draw on their intellectual capital.

30. Boggs (1979: 7), who provides a subtle analysis of these puzzles.

31. On Gramsci's theory see Olsaretti (2014) who argues that Gramsci took class into account by transcending it, and generally Showstack (1981) and Karabel (1976).

32. With Foucault this approach became a more complicated account of intellectuals as both objects and instruments of power, cogs in the machine that may expose and disable it. See also Foucault and Deleuze (1977: 208) where Deleuze states a theory is like a 'box of tools', and an 'instrument of combat'. Thus, recent scholarship has concentrated on the conditions that allow intellectuals to be 'organic': see Karabel (1996).

33. For a thoughtful discussion of the modernity of the intellectual see Melzer (2003); Rahe (2003).

34. Put in terms of 'culture', see Bourdieu's (1989: 99, 101) description of intellectuals as '*bi-dimensional* beings', between 'pure culture and engagement' and even an 'unstable synthesis'.

35. Bauman (1992: 91).

36. As Melzer (2003) notes, this approach is comparable to the Christian view that saw the otherwise weak clerisy gain authority by preaching the wisdom of a book to shape public opinion.

37. See, for example, the careers of Jamal al-Din al Afghani and Liang Qichao in Mishra (2012).

38. Benda (1969: 220, 218, 221, 225).

39. Hofstadter (1974: 417).

40. For an overview of the arguments and a defence for a special role for intellectuals because thought and action cannot be separated see Brecher (2004).

41. See, for example, Baert and Misztal (2012), and Galbraith (1972) who charges that intellectuals can only procure policy suggestions that are naïvely idealistic and lacking applicability.

42. See Collins (2011: 448), who argues that 'politics and intellectual

life are different spheres, played with different skills and subject to different pressures and criteria of success'. For an amusing reflection on the nature of the two worlds see Ignatieff (2013) who went from academic life to Canadian prime ministerial aspirant.

43. See in this context Maclean et al. (1990) and, more recently, Rickless (2012: 159) who argues that there is nothing about philosophy that should disable its practitioners from speaking publicly.

44. Popper (2012); Hayek (1949: 417); Aron (1957).

45. On the specific anti-democratic tendencies of intellectuals see Todorov et al. (1997: 1122), who argues that this situation came to an end in France around 1975 so that 'in the last quarter of the century, intellectuals seem to have reconciled with democracy, and when they criticize it, their criticism is founded on the ideal of democracy itself'.

46. See Fuller (2003) who also distinguishes between first and second-generation intellectual critics and his discussion of Kuhn and Geetz. The different but related problem is the nature of responsibility for philosophical ideas that are subsequently taken up and deployed politically by others for their own purposes: is Nietzsche responsible for Nazism? Marx for Marxism?

47. Rimon (2013: 546).

48. See Todorov et al. (1997), who suggest the history of the intellectual will be different in each country. For international case studies see Small (2002) and Jennings (2000). On American anti-intellectualism see Hofstadter (1974), and Lipset (1959) who explains why American intellectuals tend to the Left. Karabel (1996) attempts to theorise the conditions for intellectuals.

49. For an overview of the 'British decline thesis' see Collini (2002, 2006), who argues that how intellectuals have been defined explains the absence thesis, and more generally Stapleton (1999); Hickox (1986); Jennings and Kemp-Welch (1997).

50. Jacoby (1987) in the American context is the main proponent of the 'decline of intellectual' thesis, pointing to the rise of universities and politics of tenure as one of reasons for the decline. For Molnar (1961) they have become 'insipid anchorman', for Posner (2003) this has led to the absence of 'quality control', and for Jennings and Kemp-Welch (1997) it has limited their ability to cope with the challenges of the modern world. Bourdieu's (1989: 107) answer is the 'invention of forms of organizations which permit the creation of a voice for a larger collective of intellectuals, combining the talents of the ensemble of specific intellectuals'.

51. See generally Molnar (1961); Epstein (2006); Hudson (2003) in the context of French intellectuals.

52. Thus, the question is not of their decline but the problem of the intellectual as a 'character in search of a narrative' as Robbins (1990) argues.

53. See, for example, Cummings (2005); Drezner (2009); Baert and Shipman (2012); Michael (2000).
54. On the problem of modernity in a sense consuming itself see Smith (2016).
55. Consider Bell (1960: 439–40) who argues the 'exhaustion' of ideologies means they can no longer move the 'old radical intelligentsia' and the temptation of totalitarian economic reforms this presents to elites in Asia. See also Fuller (2004) who argues in a similar vein that the decline in the 'metaphysical ecology for such exotic creatures has virtually disappeared'.
56. See the discussion in Melzer (2003); Bauman (1992) thus calls them 'interpreters' rather than 'legislators'; McLennan and Osborne (2003) 'mediators' or 'critical insiders'.
57. See Misztal (2012) who refers to dramatic transformations, including the collapse of the Berlin Wall, the triumph of neoliberals around the world, the spread of new means of communication and the process of globalisation. For Eyerman (1994: 195), 'Professionalization, specialization and fragmentation rather than politization seem to be the fate of intellectual labour in late modern society.'
58. This problem was anticipated by Mills (1945). Also see Jacoby (2008) who claims that university appointment has deflected academics from becoming intellectuals; Elshtain (2001) who thinks the heroic dissenter is being replaced as academic expert; Misztal (2012) on 'think tanks'; Panton (2003) who claims modern universities cannot be a home for intellectualism; Epstein (2006) on 'public' intellectuals as publicity hounds; and Farganis (2003) who distinguishes between 'public' and 'dissenting' intellectuals.
59. The rise of the 'technician' was anticipated by Russell (1939).
60. See Dahlgren (2012) on 'mediated public spheres' and his view that a new historical phase for public intellectuals is taking place. See also Danowski and Park (2009) who examine living and dead intellectuals on the internet.
61. Intellectuals hardly 'are audible in the noise of the mass culture and politics' (Goldfarb 1998: 216). See also Davis (2009) and Baert and Booth (2012: 123) on 'the increased ability of intellectuals to cultivate their own publics through online platforms' so that the idea of a 'mega public intellectual' may be nearing its end.
62. See Kellner (1995) on how new technologies have given rise to the need for a 'new critical intellectual'.

Chapter 4

The Artist as Creator

In his celebrated *Las Meninas*, Diego Velázquez portrays himself with brush in hand at his easel, his brother Don José Nieto Velázquez in the distant doorway, Phillip IV of Spain and Queen Mariana reflected in a mirror and the central figure, the Infanta Margarita in the foreground, accompanied by attendants, the dwarfs Maribarbola and Nicolas Pertusato and a hound. *Las Meninas* shows Velázquez reflecting on his role in Court, and in doing so inviting us to confront the profound question of the relationship between the painter and the king, artist and politics. Are painters no more than the dwarfs and hounds, tolerated only for the amusement and entertainment they provide? Perhaps they're another useful resource at the disposal of power, celebrating, memorialising and thereby enhancing their patron's grandeur? Or are painters, indeed all artists, creative geniuses whose works disclose their uncanny abilities and profound insights, demonstrating their inherent parity if not superiority to kings and queens, so that they are philosopher kings?

Is the modern artist the most successful resolution of the paradox of the philosopher king? In our attempt to explore this possibility, we inevitably confront one of the most complex and contested threshold questions of 'what is art'. Art seems to comprehend an extraordinary range of things, from the familiar forms of painting, music, writing, dance and statues to modern forms ranging from extreme and confronting performance art displays that involve surgery and bodily mutilations, to Marcel Duchamp's 1917 readymade sculpture *La Fountaine* consisting of a porcelain urinal signed 'R. Mutt', Damien Hirst's 1991 *The Physical Impossibility of Death in the Mind of Someone Living* consisting of a preserved tiger shark submerged in formaldehyde in a glass-panel display case, Tracey Emin's 1998 *My Bed* consisting of her bed with bedroom objects in a dishevelled state, Maurizio Cattelan's 2019 *Comedian* created in an edition of three that appears as a fresh banana affixed to a wall with duct tape, and even silence in the form of John Cage's 1952 three-movement musical composition 4'33" where the score instructs performers not to play their instruments during the entire duration of the piece. And of course the meaning of art is inevitably complicated by the cultural, religious and historical contexts that sustain and give it substance.[1] Thus tattoos are religious and tribal symbols in the Pacific Islands, signs of Yakuza allegiance in Japan and artistic expressions of individual choice and authenticity in modern western societies.

In classical thought art traced its origins to the nine Muses, daughters of Zeus and Mnemosyne, goddesses of memory, poetry, history, music and dance who provided inspiration to artists. Such a divine view of the arts coexisted, however, with the influential approach that saw all art as *poesis* or 'making', a view that can be traced to the concept of 'art' as skill or craft, a refined form of artifice that consisted of *mimesis* or imitation of nature. Broadly speaking, these concepts were challenged in modernity with 'aesthetics', a scientific approach to judge the beautiful pioneered by German philosopher Alexander Gottlieb Baumgarten (1714–62) that subsequently informed the approach of major thinkers including Kant, Hume, Dewey and Tolstoy. 'Aesthetics' is therefore at the core of the contemporary attempts to define art. Consider for example, a recent definition: 'The arts, also called fine arts, are modes of expression that use skill or imagination in the creation of aesthetic objects, environments, or experiences that can be shared with others.'[2] It also gave rise to various theories of art, such as Emotionalism, Intuitionism, Formalism, Organicism, Voluntarism, Intellectualism, as well as powerful critiques that all theories that attempted to propose unity of art must fail.[3] Beyond these normative approaches, there have been attempts to classify, distinguishing, for example, between modern and tribal, and more comprehensively, literature, visual, plastic, decorative, performing, music and architecture. Though the question of 'what is art' inevitably solicits a diversity of answers, for our purposes it is sufficient to accept the broadest conception and formulation to see how its conceptualisation was shaped by influential contending views of the relationship between the artist and politics that are consequential for understanding whether the modern artist is a philosopher king.

L'art pour l'art or art for art's sake movement denied art had any moral, didactic or political purpose. Art was valuable as art, and artistic pursuits were their own justification. As Edgar Allan Poe (1850) put it in *The Poetic Principle*, this poem is 'written solely for the poem's sake'.[4] This conception of art was rejected by the influential modern view of the artist as an inspired creative genius who transforms the way we see, hear and think, radically altering the present or bringing into being new worlds. Seemingly divinely inspired, the artist transcends conventional moral and ethical strictures, reconstituting all and thereby transforming politics. As such, this creative artist appears as a compelling example of someone who has resolved the paradox of the philosopher king by combining creativity with political authority. This view of the creative artist as the modern philosopher king confronts and is challenged by competing alternatives which regard the artist as nothing more than a servant, panderer and flatterer of the wealthy and powerful or simply an entertainer or peddler of wares, constantly solicitous of what the customers find pleasing. To see if the artist is the successful modern resolution of the paradox and fulfilment of the promise of the philosopher king, we will therefore need to explore who artists are, what is the wisdom they possess, and importantly, how they negotiate the complex relationship between the arts and politics.[5]

In this chapter we start with the powerful and influential claim that seems to deny the possibility of the artist as philosopher king by arguing that the arts are never independent or authoritative, but rather are always children of politics, so that artistic endeavour is always within a political horizon and is ministerial to its demands. We examine this argument by exploring the claims of 'Marxist aesthetics', one of the most comprehensive and influential articulations of the view that relegates the artists to a subsidiary role in politics. We then turn to equally powerful alternative and contending Romantic and Heroic accounts of the artist as genius. In elevating the artist and the arts, these accounts seem to locate the artist somewhere removed from politics altogether or more ambitiously, altogether superior to politics and in some cases defining and constituting its substance as its founder and creator. If these approaches provide the theoretical foundations for the artist as philosopher king, we then must examine what constitutes the precise difference between the artist and the philosopher. To do so we will revisit what Socrates in Plato's *Republic* calls an 'old quarrel' between philosophy and poetry that reveals the nature of both and in doing so allows us to see the extent to which artists can be understood to be philosophers. As we will see, in recovering this debate we discern an older and until modern innovations the dominant view of the arts as *mimesis* or imitation, which allows us to locate Marxist, as well as Creative and Heroic approaches within a larger framework. In doing so we are able to distinguish a threefold relationship between politics and arts, where in the majority of cases the arts will entertain and please, and as servants of politics echo the dominant political regime, yet in rare cases the arts will also shape politics. It is in these exceptional works of artist philosophers, the poetical works of prophets and soothsayers, and in the creations of modern sophists in the form of 'ideology' that we may confirm the possibility of the artists as modern philosopher king.

The Worker–Artist

That art is defined, constituted and used by politics so that it is unavoidably entangled in contests for power presents a foundational challenge to the possibility of the artist as the modern philosopher king. The subservience of the arts to politics means the arts need to be primarily evaluated, promoted or censored for their political contribution or the extent to which they advance specific political goals. Consequently, this view of art presumes that the identity of the artist matters as much as the work of art itself.[6] To explore the strengths and limitations of such a claim, we will examine Marxist aesthetics as one of the most complex, sophisticated and influential approaches endorsing the view that the arts are subservient to politics.[7] Though both Marx and Engels were interested in and seemed to favour a special role for the arts, they never presented a comprehensive account of Marxist aesthetics, so that the theoretical development of the role of arts from a Marxist perspective was left to subsequent influential Marxist theorists and to the doctrinal advances in different socialist states.[8] Both of these sources drew upon and sought to reinterpret the core scientific insight of Marxist dialectical materialism that saw the economic organisation of society as its 'base', determining the political, legal and cultural organisation and consciousness of society in the 'superstructure'.[9] This theoretical starting point implied that art always reflected, justified and reproduced the social reality of the economic conditions of production that determines the general character of the social, political and spiritual processes of life. The dialectical evolutionary process that was a consequence of irreconcilable opposition between two social classes, those that own and control wealth, and those that are made to produce it, meant artists could never escape their social and historical circumstances. Art could never be disinterested; it was either decadent and reactionary defending the prevailing class, or dissident and revolutionary anticipating the next epoch.

'The ruling ideas of each age have ever been the ideas of its ruling class', according to Marx and Engels' *The Communist Manifesto* (2018). The capitalist system, which overturned feudal relations between slave and noble, intensified the alienation that existed in all epochs, separating the worker from what is produced, introducing competition for profits that alters the production process, exploiting and oppressing the worker for the profit of the owners of capital. Art thereby became for the first time a commodity, reducing all to its cash value so that the aesthetic potential of labour, with its potential for disinterested pleasure was debased and perverted by its subjugation to self-interest and hegemonic ideology of the era. Artists were like all workers alienated from their labour, and as petty bourgeois under the guise of free expression produced nothing more than entertainment and amusement as another product for consumption that gave false comfort to the suffering proletariat by celebrating the deceptive freedoms of bourgeois life. Capitalist art is therefore decadent, even if it contains vestiges from the earlier epochs.

Though this was the conclusive account of the role of art and artists in capitalist states, their role in socialist states was a more complex question. The question of what is art was addressed in the early years of the Soviet Union in the controversy over the meaning of revolutionary art. Should it draw on the best of the past as suggested by Lenin and Trotsky, or is it the work of only proletarians and should express solely the proletarian perspective as proposed by Bogdanov and his *Proletcult* group? In any case, both approaches concurred in repudiating the Formalists, avant-garde intellectuals who allied themselves to the revolution but rejected sociological interpretations in favour of artistic forms and techniques as the true source for the arts. These debates would soon be displaced by the adoption of Socialist Realism as the goal of Soviet art in 1934, where according to Gorky, Bukharin and Zhdanov, the Soviet writer was in Stalin's formulation 'engineer of the human soul' with an obligation to depict reality in its revolutionary development, so that truth and historical accuracy would be linked to ideological transformation, resulting in the education of the working people in the spirit of socialism.[10]

Similarly, Marxist theories of art in China were fundamentally shaped by Mao's views of the revolutionary potential of art and artists. After the 1949 victory of the Chinese Communist Party, Mao's (1942) *Talks at the Yan'an Conference on Literature and Art* determined China's cultural and artistic policy until the Great Leap Forward and the Cultural Revolution. In his *Yan'an Talks*, Mao argues that art and literature are a component part of the revolution, 'a powerful weapon in uniting and educating the people while attacking and annihilating the enemy'. Defending socialist realism, he states 'Revolutionary fiction, drama, film and so on can create all sorts of characters on the basis of real life and help the masses push history forward.'[11] The requirement to speak to the proletariat meant artists must, as much as possible, assume the class position of the proletariat, revolutionising themselves to destroy the petty bourgeois distinction between mental and manual labour to experience the feelings of the workers. Such an approach mandated an art that combines the 'poster and slogan' style of *agit-prop* with artistic principles that are not simply defined by politics. Important elements of Mao's *Yan'an Talks* could be seen in the subsequent Cultural Revolution where folk theatre was replaced with new forms of 'model opera' that combined traditional techniques with a new socialist 'positive hero' who would reveal an inherent communist spirit.[12]

This Marxist aesthetics was in continual tension with theoretical approaches that recognised the unique effects of art and therefore attempted to delineate a more autonomous and influential role for the artist and the work of art. We can see this tension in the early Marx (as well as Engels' writings after Marx's death), where he distinguishes between artists who transcended their class and ideology, which he called the 'triumph of realism', contrasting it with 'tendency' writing where doctrinal allegiance undermined the effect of art.[13] There was also Plekhanov's 'Art and Social Life' (2009) that attempted to accommodate both artistic and discursive forms in Marxist aesthetics, a view that was influential until the publication of Marx's early works.[14] Historical or cultural Marxists subsequently took up this approach, drawing on the ambiguities in Marx and Engels on the distinctive nature and autonomy of the arts from those of law and politics to charge the 'vulgar' view of causal link between base and superstructure as reductionist or mechanistic. This tension could be seen, for example, in the debates between Bertolt Brecht whose starting point was Marx's agonistic dialectic materialism and György Lukács who saw aesthetics as potentially distinct from politics, revealing the complexities in the contending positions within a developing Marxist aesthetics.[15]

Subsequent debates in Marxist aesthetics attempted to recover a distinctive role for art and artists. In the disputes between form and content, or quality and 'tendency', 'New Marxists', especially Walter Benjamin (1969), in his 'The Work of Art in the Age of Mechanical Reproduction', diagnosed the debasement of art in modernity through the elimination of its 'aura' and saw Communism's politicising of art as the means to counter the false consciousness of the masses. Comparable debates could be found in the writings of the Frankfurt School, where Adorno and Horkheimer (1972) in the *Dialectic of Enlightenment* criticised mass culture. Adorno thus favoured Schoenberg's atonal music over Stravinsky's regressive populism as the antithesis of the 'culture industry' in breaking through consciousness. In his *The Aesthetic Dimension*, Herbert Marcuse (1978) argued 'one dimensional' capitalism produced a harmonising pluralism where the most contradictory works and truths coexisted in indifference. Artists as the most alienated members of modern society therefore had a crucial role in a 'two dimensional' critique of this reactionary comfort and pleasure. This 'Great Refusal', as he called it, meant the artists had to reproduce or amplify alienation to negate reality. Art therefore should raise revolutionary consciousness and the artist is the foremost dissident or revolutionary at the forefront of revolutionary art. In his critique of Marxist aesthetics, Marcuse argues the 'political potential of art lies only in its own aesthetic dimension' so that the poetry of Baudelaire and Rimbaud is potentially more subversive than the didactic plays of Brecht.[16]

Marxist aesthetics, as our brief overview shows, makes a compelling case regarding the derivative or subsidiary nature of the arts and artists. The primacy of the political means that all aspects of art production or 'work' are political, especially the class of the artist and the intended effect of the work, which must serve revolutionary causes. Yet, as we have seen, Marxist aesthetics also appreciated that certain aspects of the artistic experience showed how art was not simply another form of work, and indeed, some forms of art could even be more revolutionary because of this distinctive, even unique nature of art. This recognition raised complex puzzles in Marxist aesthetics regarding the relationship between art and politics. It questioned the connection between the identity of the artist and the integrity of the work – could a petty bourgeois ever understand the plight of the proletariat? It also revealed the potential for different types of artists, distinguishing ones who merely reflect contemporary class structures from those who were agents of class change, celebrated as dissident, transgressive and revolutionary. Finally, it raised significant problems of aesthetics, where the primacy of the political over the form and quality of a work of art in effect redefined the meaning of the beautiful. In liberating itself from a powerful social realism, the engaged revolutionary artist seemed to favour the ugly, disruptive and alienating as subversive and revolutionary over the beautiful, whose pleasure and delight was now seen as reactionary. Pursued to its extreme such a sociological approach to art, where its true meaning and importance is found in its social function, rather than the work in itself, meant there was no inherent content to art, only those meanings discerned or recovered by Marxist critique.[17] In spite of these complexities, however, the overall insight of Marxism was that the artist was always at the service of politics, so that there could be no room for an independently powerful artist who could claim to be a modern philosopher king.

Artist as Genius and Creator

The worker–artist continues to shape modern aesthetics, with arguments developed from the concept of class now deployed with the more extensive vocabulary of 'identity'. Thus, race, gender and sexuality, like class, become the primary concepts for evaluating art and the artist, justifying the censorship of historical and contemporary works now considered 'incorrect' as well as stipulating the characteristics of good art.[18] Yet this view that made the artist and art subservient to the political was challenged by an equally influential approach that argued for the artist's superiority to politics and thereby provided the theoretical foundations for the artist as philosopher king. This approach that celebrates the artist as the rare creative genius who from Empyrean heights refashions the political can be traced to two distinct sources, the Romantic and the Heroic.[19] The idea of the genius anticipated the Romantics, with the poet and essayist Addison and others distinguishing between the 'natural' genius who was born, such as Homer, Pindar, the Old Testament poets and Shakespeare, and the genius who was made with the assistance of art or learning, like Plato, Virgil and Milton.[20] The natural genius was unique and seemed to partake in the divine, albeit in a mysterious or unfathomable and therefore naïve or even unconscious way. Moved by divine *enthousiasmos* or inspiration and therefore in a state of elation and rapture, the natural genius composed suddenly, effortlessly and even involuntarily and automatically. And on reviewing the completed work, even poets themselves were surprised to see their handiwork, which seemed as though written by someone else. The unique and transcendent nature of the genius therefore hinted at someone above or beyond ordinary morality and standards of justice.[21] The Romantic view, anticipated in Aristophanes' speech in Plato's *Symposium*, has its origins in Longinus's *On the Sublime* and its conception of the *hupsous* or sublime to be divined only by a 'natural genius', whose artistry was artless, ecstatic, and spontaneous, the 'echo of a great soul'.[22] Subsequently, such a notion of the sublime was taken up by Burke (1774) in his *A Philosophical Enquiry into the Origin of Our Ideas of the Sublime and Beautiful* and Kant (1774) in *Observations on the Feeling of the Beautiful and the Sublime*. Kant in his *Critique of Judgment* claims poets are geniuses, where 'Genius is the innate mental disposition (*ingenium*) through which nature gives the rule to art.'[23] Nature possesses the poet as an oracle, giving sensible expression to 'rational ideas of indivisible beings, the realm of the Blessed, the realm of hell, eternity, creation and so on'.[24] This idea of the sublime was influential in the Romantic Movement, adopted by its leading proponent the English poet Wordsworth, who in his autobiographical *Prelude* describes his night-time ascent of Snowdon in North Wales, where mind and nature are united in images 'awful and sublime'.[25] In his *Lyrical Ballads* we see a more ambitious conception of poetry and the poet that was widely adopted by his contemporaries such as the English poets Shelley and Coleridge, J. S. Mill and by the Europeans Schlegal, Schiller and Herder.[26] Poetry, according to Wordsworth, is 'spontaneous overflow of powerful feelings', or a process of imagination in which feelings play the crucial part and was therefore properly to be distinguished not from prose but from science.[27] It originated in primitive utterances of passions and used figures of speech and rhythm with the intention to foster and refine the sensibility, emotions and sympathies of the reader. The poet was a genius, endowed with more lively sensibility, enthusiasm and tenderness, someone who 'rejoiced in the spirit of life that is in him' and wrote poetry that was spontaneous and genuine. Such gifted and sensitive individuals were more blessed yet because they were susceptible to vice and misery also more cursed than others.[28] They were what would later to be called the *poète maudit*, the sensitive and suffering outcast of society who paid a high price for their more intense and refined sensibility. Yet poets, as Wordsworth indicated, were not simply outsiders, which meant that some Romantics had greater ambitions for poetry. Shelley in particular in his 'Defence of Poetry' (1840) presents poets as nightingales singing in the dark, transforming the world, as legislators and prophets who discover those laws according to which present things ought to be ordered.[29]

This overview of the Romantic genius shows the extent to which the natural geniuses and their art are not beholden to politics, with the artist impervious to political exigencies, and a poetry that seems to come from a mysterious or supernatural source, later termed 'supernatural afflatus'. The emphasis on enthusiasm and sensibility, with the intention to cultivate the affective elements of human nature suggested indifference rather than superiority to the political; lacking political sensibilities or ambitions, the romantic poet was at best unconcerned, at worst contemptuous of the world of politics. This disposition is confirmed by the Romantic celebration of lyrical poetry over the epic and dramatic that typically are concerned with political questions.[30] Other Romantics, however, anticipated a much more ambitious political role for poets and artists, seeing them as legislators and prophets.[31]

Like the Romantic artist, the artist as Hero was also not subject to the political, though moved by a powerful ambition to reshape politics by creating new worlds. Carlyle and Nietzsche are the seminal modern advocates of the heroic individual, subsequently influential for a diverse range of artists and philosophers, including Wagner, Shaw, Heidegger, Spengler, Stefan George and D. H. Lawrence. We will focus on Nietzsche's insights into the creative artist because of its significance for contemporary aesthetics and political philosophy.[32] Nietzsche was a great lover of music and poetry.[33] He admired the early Wagner and Bizet and the poetry of Goethe, Heine and Hölderlin (*Ecce Homo*). Yet he was also critical of artists, calling them vain (*Nietzsche Contra Wagner*), 'morally weak' and 'glorifiers of the religious and philosophical errors of mankind' or more enigmatically, claiming 'poets lie too much'.[34] What he proposed is an onerous burden on future creative poets who will have to be more than the romantic genius who is inspired or moved, even at the expense of truth. 'All great artists' according to Nietzsche, 'have been great workers, inexhaustible not only in invention but also in rejecting, sifting, transforming, ordering.'[35] Romantics such as Schopenhauer and Wagner strive for life not from superabundance but from poverty of life, so that they seek rest, peace and smooth seas.[36] In Nietzsche's (1988) *Birth of Tragedy*, his earliest and influential reflections on music and poetry, he distinguishes between the ecstatic Dionysian, and the rational Apollonian, showing how the creative tension between the two gave birth to Greek tragedy, and how the predominance of the Apollonian in the spirit of dialectic and progressive science denied the myths that ennoble humanity, issuing in contemporary nihilism. Nietzsche questions whether philosophy and science, to the extent that they too rely on metaphors and language, can ever claim to be 'true'.[37] The future poet will therefore have to be *Künstler-Philosoph* or artist philosopher who will necessarily combine the Dionysian and Apollonian to will both illusions and truth to create myths and values.[38] The creative artist philosopher will be overabundant, overfull, extravagantly generous – and malicious.[39] Consequently, the artist philosopher cannot be understood in terms of contemporary utilitarian calculus of comfort nor can it be comprehended by Christian and democratic morality that does not adequately acknowledge the need for cruelty and inequality for human physical and spiritual thriving. Beyond contemporary notions of good and evil, the character of such a creative artist can only be approximated by perplexing contradictions, such as 'music practicing Socrates' or 'a Roman Caesar with the soul of Christ'.[40]

We can gain an insight into Nietzsche's (1994) understanding of the nature of such poetry and philosophy in his greatest work, *Thus Spoke Zarathustra*, a dazzling combination of both. *Zarathustra* combines refined and subtle theoretical argumentations with poetic forms that draw on lyric poetry, satire and the gospels. It diagnoses the contemporary sources of nihilism and prepares the grounds for the future great artist philosopher, the *übermensch* or overman who will create new humanity and new nobility through the necessarily cruel transvaluation of values. And perhaps as an intimation of the nature of these values, *Zarathustra* announces a secular reinterpretation of Christian immortality and Hindu reincarnation that culminates in the Eternal Return of the Same. This new conception of ethical culpability and human excellence that demands we live each day as if it will be repeated forever is his celebration of *amor fati* or love of fate, the love (rather than endurance or concealment) of necessity.[41] What is incontestable with this conception of the artist philosopher is the almost divine creativity of the overman – all things, especially the political, but certainly the moral and the spiritual, are given meaning and substance by the extravagant and overabundant will to power or creativity of the individual; the political is therefore always epiphenomenal to the creativity of the artist.

The frequent contemporary references to artists as geniuses, and the characterisation of the artistic endeavour as 'creative' can therefore be traced to two related yet distinctive sources, the Romantic genius and Heroic creative artist philosopher. Unlike the dominant Marxist approaches, and resembling in some respects the various attempts at recovering a more ambitious role for the artist in Marxist aesthetics, both perspectives trace the origin of all art to the uncanny actions of unique individuals who stand above all conventional moral and legal standards. Their distinctive contribution lies in the practical ends of each, with the exquisite and refined sensibility of the Romantic genius seeking to heighten, refine and educate public sentiment, while the artist philosopher will necessarily transvalue all values and in such creative acts transform everything, 'legislating greatness'.[42]

Artist and Philosopher

The Romantic and Heroic perspectives with their more elevated conception of art and the artist provide the theoretical foundations for the artist as the philosopher king. In doing so, however, they make us wonder what is the precise difference, if any, between the artist and the philosopher? Is the artist king fundamentally different from the philosopher king? To examine this question, we will revisit the earliest and most influential discussion exploring the differences between the two, what Socrates in Plato's *Republic* called the 'old quarrel' between philosophy and poetry.[43] This discussion gave rise to the concept of art as *mimesis*, an approach that was dominant until challenged by modernity. It shaped Aristotle's famous and influential writings on *Rhetoric* and *Poetics*, and Boethius's *Consolation of Philosophy* where poets were seen as ministers to philosophy. It persisted when philosophy confronted revealed religion. Thus Augustine, influenced especially by Plato, regards poetry as essential but secondary to philosophy, which in turn was subject to divine revelation.[44] Aquinas too regarded poetry as a helpmate for philosophy, though he had to acknowledge and account for prophets, who were to be distinguished from both the philosopher and the poet in being inspired by and speaking for God and prophesying without necessarily understanding their prophecy.[45] It even continued in modernity, as we can see from Hegel's *Aesthetics: Lectures on Fine Art* where he distinguishes between the universalism and abstraction of philosophic judgement and syllogism and the particularity and unity of poetic imagination to argue that philosophy or speculative thought is higher than poetry because it is not limited to the particular and grasps abstract universals and therefore absolute knowledge.[46]

To understand the nature of the 'old quarrel', it is necessary to recall that the world was originally defined and constituted by the 'mythopoetic' rather than philosophic artists so that the arts have a much older provenance than philosophers and philosophy. Artists, and especially poets, were muses or speakers for the gods who through their works manifested divine orders, revealing the promise and manifestation of divine providence and thereby a legal and moral world suffused and made meaningful by the holy and sacred. These theological, cosmological and moral insights inevitably defined the models for human excellence, as well as the political ordering that fostered and sustained it. Consequently, artists through their works can be said to be the muses of the gods, founders of language, rituals, and the legislators of tribes and nations.[47] As we saw, these ancient accounts would in due course be challenged by natural philosophers who used poetic form to explicate the nature of the cosmos not in terms of gods but first principles and elements.[48] Subsequently, the Sophists drew on these insights to explore their political implications, questioning the divine provenance of rules and norms and suggesting they may indeed be *poiesis* or works of human artifice. It is in this context, and in his attempt to distinguish philosophy from the arts, that Socrates in Plato's *Republic* confronts what he calls 'an old quarrel between philosophy and poetry'.[49]

Why does Socrates present the relationship between poetry, understood to mean not only poems, but also other forms of *poiesis* such as music, painting and sculpture, and philosophy as a quarrel and what does this quarrel reveal about the nature and ranking of each? A useful starting point for understanding the nature of this debate is to reflect on its political and philosophical aspects as they are presented in the *Republic*. Politically, it is a contest over Glaucon, the talented and public-spirited young man who loves the poets yet is confused by their ambivalent celebration and denigration of the life of the self-sufficient tyrant. Philosophically, Socrates wants to differentiate the new discovery of philosophy from the ancient and enchanting poetry it resembles, distinguishing between dialectic as a means of overcoming ignorance from the ambitions of the few who exploit the ostensibly comprehensive insights revealed by the charming beauty of imitation and metaphor and the beguiling effects of meter, rhythm and diction.

In the course of discussing this quarrel, Socrates indicts poetry on two grounds, the first based on the nature of poetry itself, and the second on the specific aspects of Greek poetry. His theoretical critique of poetry and poets takes place predominantly in the final Book X, where he shows the limitations of poetry. Of the many forms of *poiein* or 'making', poetry is the exemplar. Poets, especially tragedians and comedians, and their helpers such as rhapsodes, actors and choral dancers, imitate, rather than narrate, so that this mimesis or imitation that pleases and charms us grants the poets their extraordinary authority.[50] But mimesis also reveals the weakness of poets since imitation is 'at the third generation from nature' or 'naturally third from king and the truth'[51] because 'painter, couch maker, god – these preside over three forms of couch', where the painter in imitating a couch is copying the work of a carpenter, which in turn attempts to approximate the idea of the couch.[52] Poets therefore imitate 'looks' rather than 'truth' because imitation can only be a small part of each thing, which is itself a phantom.[53] Consequently, when poets imitate, they lie and 'deceive children and foolish human beings' because they claim to know carpentry, and more generally, 'all arts and all things human that have to do with virtue and vice, and the divine things too'.[54] But is it not true that to imitate well one must know well what is being imitated?[55] Moreover, aren't poets superior to philosophers in using metaphors, similes and hyperbole to reveal the universal in each 'particular' dynamically, without distorting the particular? Socrates' response is that 'is' differs from 'looks like' and imitation is not knowing.[56] Imitation is therefore a kind of play, and not serious.[57] But perhaps the most telling critique of poetry is its inability to imitate and therefore intimate the good. Like fathers, and moneymakers, all poets love their works.[58] They also love the acclaim of the audience who takes pleasure in innovation and imitation.[59] The 'necessity of Diomede' thus means that poets produce what the many love, and thereby make the multitude their masters.[60] This will mean that poets will be predisposed to imitate certain aspects of the soul, such as reminiscences about pain or suffering, rather than deliberation that counters these passions because that 'prudent and quiet character, which is always nearly equal to itself, is neither easily imitated nor, when imitated, easily understood, especially by a festive assembly where all sorts of human beings are gathered in the theatre'.[61] The imitative poet who wants a 'good reputation among the many' will therefore be naturally directed to that part of the soul easily imitated and pleasing to the public so that poets are limited by their inability to imitate important aspects of the soul that will not readily appeal to or please the people.[62]

In addition to this theoretical critique, Socrates quarrels with influential Greek poets in the context of the musical education of the future guardians.[63] In classical thought music meant any activity performed under the guidance of the Muses, daughters of Zeus and Mnemosyne, especially lyric poetry sung to music.[64] That poetry pleases, and charms, may suggest it is merely for entertainment and, indeed, there is extensive discussion in the *Republic* of the achievements of the poets, especially Homer and Hesiod.[65] Yet in acknowledging that Homer 'educated Greece', Socrates confirms the political importance of the poets, evident in the frequent use of their authority and sayings in the *Republic* itself.[66] Poets matter because they provide an authoritative education concerning the gods, heroes and daemons, Hades and, importantly, about the goodness of justice.[67] It is this education that Socrates challenges and wants to replace with a new teaching. Socrates will therefore not oust the poets altogether, as they are unavoidable in the luxurious or feverish city; rather he proposes to censor incorrect teachings and in important cases use poetry himself, especially in telling *pharmakon* or noble lies.[68]

Socrates is particularly critical of the poets' false tales about the gods, implying that poets may be makers of gods.[69] Gods and heroes do not fight each other, they do not tell lies and they do not change or conceal themselves. Nor are there 'two jars' where Zeus dispenses good and evil or a terrible Hades. Simonides' definition of justice as helping friends and harming enemies shows justice as the art of stealing, and Pindar endorses the appearance of justice rather than justice itself. The poets show gods who punish, and gods who can be persuaded and therefore are corruptible. These teachings, however sweet, undermine individual courage, endorse ambitious tyranny and empower priests and mendicants to seek favours for 'initiations' to appease the gods and avoid terrible consequences.[70]

Concerning the human things, Socrates rejects the poets' teachings that 'many happy men are unjust, and many wretched ones just, and that doing injustice is profitable if one gets away with it, but justice is someone else's good and one's own loss'.[71] In place of these teachings, Socrates introduces a new 'theology' that will form the core of the new poetry. The gods are the cause of only the good, according to Socrates, so that bad has some other source. They are not the cause of evil to anyone.[72] As they are unchanging, they are not wizards, shifting shapes to deceive and bewitch people.[73] Socrates' new poetry will teach courage by showing that being dead is not a terrible thing.[74] It will instruct moderation in drink, sex and eating and not praise illiberality regarding money.[75] Socrates also demands a change in *lexis* or style of poetry, rejecting wailing and softness of Lydian and Ionian modes in favour of Dorian and Phrygian and preferring Apollo over Marsyas in rejecting lutes, harps and flutes.[76]

This critical view of the poets in the *Republic* seems to be countered, however, by the suggestion in other dialogues that poets are somehow divine. In the *Apology*, for example, Socrates claims that poets write tragedies and dithyrambs not through wisdom but some sort of inspiration, like the divines and those who deliver oracles and divine insights through a sort of *mania* or madness: 'So again, also concerning the poets, I soon recognized that they do not make what they make by wisdom, but by some sort of oracles. For they too say many noble things but they know nothing of what they speak.'[77] This mania may clarify why poets cannot explain, let alone teach others the source or implication of these insights. Similarly, in the *Phaedrus* Socrates claims that the 'god-inspired prophetic trances' of the prophetess at Delphi and priestess at Dodona resemble the mania of outstanding poets.[78] But what exactly is this mantic nature of poetry?

This is the question addressed in the *Ion*, a shorter Platonic dialogue between Socrates and Ion, the preeminent Homeric rhapsode. The dialogue reveals a deep tension in the heart of Ion regarding his abilities and how they are perceived by the public. That the poets are somehow divine suggests that like Korybants and Bacchantes they are 'light and winged and sacred things' who are given a divine dispensation, so that the gods use poets, just as they do soothsayers and seers.[79] Like a great magnet that draws a chain of rings, the gods inspire the poets, who in turn possess the rhapsodes and subsequently enchant the audience. Socrates' suggestion that Ion is an interpreter of the gods touches his soul, as it seems to capture an important aspect of what he does.[80] It is also, as he subsequently observes, flattering since it is noble to be called divine.[81] But Ion cannot endorse this view unreservedly since it presumes that the rhapsode in being 'magnetised' and 'possessed' no longer has his own mind.[82] He therefore rejects he is possessed or mad because it would imply that he personally did not deserve the prizes and awards he proudly claimed as his own. Indeed, as he indicates, though he is often moved to tears in presenting Homer, he is equally sensitive of the effect he is having on his audience, and in particular how it will affect his income.[83] Ion is unable to give Socrates a definitive account of his art, and forced to choose between a shape-shifting and dishonest Proteus or someone divine, he prefers the more noble view of someone possessed by the gods.[84] Socrates' conversation with Ion suggests that like soothsayers and seers, there is something uncanny in what the poets and their interpreters do. Yet this account does not completely capture and indeed seems to deny the craftsmanship of poets, leaving unanswered the initial puzzling question of what is the art of the poet and the rhapsode.

At the end the *Republic*, Socrates gives an 'apology' for having expelled the poets from the just or noble city he and his interlocutors have founded to examine the nature of justice. Yet as it becomes clear, Socrates' expulsion of the poets is not simply a repudiation of the poets, as his subsequent discussion reveals:

> If poetry directed to pleasure and imitation have any argument to give showing that they should be in a city with good laws, we should be delighted to receive them back from exile, since we are aware that we ourselves are charmed by them.[85]

Socrates wants to reconcile philosophy and poetry and does so by acknowledging the power of poetry to charm and entertain. Yet such a reconciliation is based on a new understanding of the relationship between philosophy and poetry. Poetry must concede the preeminence of philosophy due to the superiority of philosophical dialectic. At the same time, Socrates accepts that poetry with its ability to charm may be essential in politics. It is valuable for teaching and explication, as is evident from Socrates' use of metaphor and myth.[86] More generally, however, the power of poetry would appear to be essential for politics, which seems to require lies, even if noble. Socrates is willing to conciliate and cooperate with poets, but only if philosophy becomes their master and censor.[87]

Rethinking the Politics of Art

Socrates' examination of the quarrel between philosophy and poetry shows what is distinctive to each and why philosophy is superior to politics. What implications does this insight have for the possibility of the artist as the philosopher king? I suggest art as mimesis provides a comprehensive framework that can accommodate the conceptions of art as entertainment, as political tool, and creations of artists who can be said to be philosopher kings.

The pleasure of mimesis, and the 'necessity of Diomede' explains why the artist will always be, at some level, an entertainer. Marx's critique that artists in capitalist societies will be inauthentic 'producers' of content, participants in 'creative industries', with their 'product' to be consumed by the public who want to be amused and entertained therefore does capture an important aspect of art. Yet it cannot be denied that art has from its origins consisted of items that were produced to be exchanged. True, so-called 'tribal' art was not art in this sense, but use of decorative elements intrinsic to everyday and sacred items. But once one moved from these early and mythical orderings, we inevitably confronted art as variously pleasing and entertaining on its own and therefore something valuable to be bought, sold and traded, giving rise to artist–patron relationships evident in all cultures and throughout history. Thus patronage has always sustained artists, even if artists have sometimes parlayed them into grandeur, vaulting beyond their commissions to devise timeless works, as Bach's *Klavierwerke*, Michelangelo's *David* or Gaudí's *La Sagrada Familia* have outlived the memory of their patrons. Emile Zola anticipates and brings to life this view of art as primarily a marketable commodity in his novel *L'œuvre* or *The Masterpiece* (1886), where he tells of how Claude Lantier, a talented and innovative painter from the provinces who hopes to conquer Paris succumbs to disappointment and failure. Zola captures well the artist's single-minded ambition, and the high price of such an obsession for family and friends. Equally revealing, however, is the larger context, how new movements such as Impressionism challenged the Academies who can make careers, how art dealers, collectors and artists mutually exploit each other and how the world of models, art merchants and wealthy patrons decides who is the new 'genius' and what is, and is not art. To be sure, what Zola saw in the Parisian art world is now writ large, with an international network of Biennale, museums, art galleries, corporate sponsors, 'high net worth individuals' and art auction houses that bask in the reflected glow of refinement and exquisite taste, even as they extract both buyers' and sellers' commissions. This new market, combined with fashionable theories devised in art schools, contribute to innovations in the arts, including new types of art, (assemblage, kinetic, photography, animation, land and performance), use of new materials (collage, found objects, metals) and novel techniques (automatic drawing, action painting, 'Benday dots').

But art is not simply entertainment, and as Socrates shows, art as mimesis will also inevitably reflect the political and social world. So, consistent with Marxist aesthetics, the arts will tend to favour and support the prevailing regime and its view of justice. These influences are manifold, from the forms and substance of the art each regime endorses and occasionally enforces through laws and norms, to indirect channels, including commissions and sponsorships by preeminent individuals, curators of galleries both public and private, and corporations that favour the contemporary regime and the audiences' appetite for such mimesis as determined by their popularity. Pharaohs, Sons of Heaven, Sapa Inca, Maharaja and all monarchs and ruling families throughout history have employed the best architects, poets, painters and musicians to record their noble heritage, celebrate their rule, and declare and display their glorious power. Coins, mosaics, biographies, portraits and busts, minuets, symphonies and concertos, all gilt their benefactors' name and reputations while concealing and disguising the shameful or ugly. All art therefore took its coloration and substance from the character of the regime. Religion too imposed its strict rules on the arts, Protestantism decrying all previous Christian art, except for music, while Islam was Aniconistic, forbidding idolatry by rejecting figurative representation and thereby favouring calligraphy or geometric patterns.[88] Even modernity with its distinct ideologies made its demands. Leni Rienfenstahl's documentary *Triumph of the Will* celebrated National Socialism while Aleksandr Gerasimov surrendered Impressionism to document socialist realism, becoming President of the USSR Academy of Arts and four-time recipient of the Stalin Prize. Yet this mimesis is not a simple or crude endorsement of the prevailing political arrangements. To the extent that all regimes are in constant tension with vying alternative claimants to legitimacy, most art will also reproduce such tensions or struggles, even if it ultimately resolves them in favour of the powerful or dominant. Most artists are therefore unknowingly propagandists, even as they pride themselves to be revolutionary, because they are actually re-enacting a dramatic struggle over the regime that ultimately reinforces its authority. Contemporary democracies, for example, will celebrate either the 'little guy' or 'The People' by showing how a virtuous individual confronts and overcomes powerful and corrupt elites.[89] Ultimately, however, in addition to promoting and directing art that celebrates their ideals, principles and achievements, rulers and regimes will reserve the right to censor and even silence those who opposed them. Censorship, in its seemingly mild though potent form of social approbation or castigation, or more directed and brutish form of fines, imprisonment or death, was always the grim prospect faced by artists who had become too influential or troublesome. Andrei Zhdanov, the Soviet cultural ideologist criticised cosmopolitanism and 'formalism' or 'art for art's sake', resulting in attacks on the world's foremost composers such as Prokofiev, Shostakovich and Kachaturian for their 'hermetic' music. The Red Guards unleashed by Mao's Cultural Revolution destroyed priceless Chinese imperial art. More recently, the Taliban reduced to rubble the colossal sixth-century monumental statues of Vairocna and Gautama Buddha carved into cliffs in Bamiyan Valley of central Afghanistan. Even modern liberal democracies founded on freedom of speech and individual rights now confront demands that principles of equality or inclusiveness override artistic vision and creativity. Language, plot structure, directors and actors and the overall 'signal' or 'message' are required to comply with moral codes that specify who shall speak and what can be said, as adjudicated by self-appointed social media censors. In all these cases art is political, but only in the sense that like a Roman *signum* or standard it symbolises a regime that is being challenged. It becomes in effect a lightning rod for political contestation that is only incidentally about the work of art itself. Students did not campaign to remove the Cecil Rhodes sculpture at Oriel College Oxford because of its poor artistic quality, but because it seemed to endorse and celebrate British imperialist legacy.[90] Dutch and Catalan translators of Amanda Gorman's 'The Hill We Climb' poem read at Joe Biden's presidential inauguration stepped down in response to the charge that they were white authors translating the work of a black woman.[91] Similarly, Richard Wagner's operas have never been staged in Israel primarily because of his antisemitism.[92]

Yet even Marxist aesthetics acknowledged that there may be something unique about the poets that is not simply reducible to political exigencies of propaganda or the mandates of the 'creative industries'. The Romantic Genius and Nietzschean *Künstler-Philosoph* in important respects are the contemporary articulations of the Socratic insight into the divine madness of the poets in the guise of prophets, seers and soothsayers. That poets depict in striking and compelling colours and sounds the familiar and in doing so reveal profound insights that we have missed or only glimpsed in part distinguishes them as extraordinary, enthralling and beguiling. Their strange talents and ability seem both methodical and therefore *techne* or craft-like, so that they can be taught to others, yet mysterious, inspired and therefore unpredictable, resembling those who are moved by the gods to prophesy. The uncanniness of the artist and the artistic endeavour makes us to defer to their visions, even if they cannot account for them. It is for this reason that the more able and visionary the artist, the more authoritative they will become. This mysterious ability of artists can therefore make their works profoundly influential, even if they lack a specific political element. There is accordingly a sound basis for viewing a small number of artists as those who speak to the human condition, however understood, without seeing them as merchants and manufacturers, propagandists for their class or revolutionary advocates for political visions. The longstanding debates regarding the 'genius' of Shakespeare support this view.[93] This perspective helps to explain innovations within each artistic discipline – Beethoven's *Ninth Symphony* transforming the symphonic form; Picasso and Braque's Cubism repudiating expressionism; Cervantes' *Don Quixote de la Mancha* inaugurating the modern novel. And it is this ineffable nature of artistry that introduces a separation between the artist and the work, permitting a distinct moral and political calculus for each.

It is in this larger context that we are able to discern how art as mimesis and mania reveals the character and limitations of the artist as modern philosopher king, accommodating Nietzsche's hope for the 'creative artist' but on new terms. Socrates states that he did not meet poets who could give an account of themselves, yet left open the possibility that if they did, they would be called philosophers.[94] This statement yields three distinct possibilities of poets who transform politics with the potential of becoming philosopher kings. The first is perhaps the most subtle, the philosopher poets such as Heraclitus and even Plato himself who in revealing their thoughts to the world through writing are necessarily political yet, mindful of the civic potency of their insights, use cryptic and elusive poetical forms to mitigate their force. The second group consist of talented poets who use poetry to speak of ghosts, hell and heaven, and in doing so exploit the resemblance between the poet and oracle and seer, dissolving these distinctive aspects to inaugurate the poet as prophet so that poetry as the words of god has the potential to transform mundane politics. Though Socrates had in mind Homer and Hesiod, he anticipates future poets whose theology will make them indistinguishable from prophets precisely because of the uncanny power of poetry. From this perspective all great religions founded on writing or books are the handiworks of such artist kings as prophets. The third group was hinted at by Socrates in his discussion of sophists and rhetors such as Protagoras and Gorgias but has assumed prominence in contemporary thought. These are the new Homers, combining the talents of poet and sophist, who elevate glory and wealth above love of truth to bring into being new non-pious or philosophic poetry to transform the world. The ambition of all modern philosophers to become, as Machiavelli advised, partners to political leaders, or as Marx declared, to change the world, are early expression and anticipations of Nietzsche's hopes for the transformative overman.

Artist as Modern Philosopher King

For the great Romantic poet Percy Bysshe Shelley, poets are 'the unacknowledged legislators of the world',[95] yet according to the Irish poet William Butler Yeats who was influenced by Shelley, 'We have no gift to set a statesman right.'[96] This disparity of views presents a formidable challenge to the possibility of the artist as the modern philosopher king. Our recovery of the quarrel between philosophy and poetry has shown how, in important respects, both views are correct when reconceived within a larger architecture of mimesis, mania and philosophy to yield a more sophisticated tripartite understanding of the subtle links between the arts, philosophy and politics.

All art, to varying degrees, mimics and thereby entertains and gives pleasure. Most art is also fundamentally shaped by politics and therefore will display and reward the truths of each regime, either directly by beautiful depictions of what each regime elevates and venerates or in the course of dramatic portrayals of the victorious struggles of these principles in overcoming contending forces. In some rare cases, artist and politics will combine, resulting in the artist as philosopher kings. These cases elevate some artistic forms above others, so that writing tends to be politically more powerful than, for example, music, dance and painting. Thus philosophers may use poetry to declare and conceal their deepest thoughts; poets may sing into existence new gods; or sophists and demagogues will appeal to the fears and desires of their audience by promising them comprehensive and beautiful visions of just new worlds. But the rarity of such uncanny poetical skills will mean that there will be very few who will be able to succeed as philosopher kings. Even if they do rule, they will mostly do so in an attenuated or proximate sense, rarely exercising direct political authority. Their writings, even as they transcend time and space, will be buffeted by the cold winds of chance and the hot fires of censorship. Finally, and perhaps decisively, the artist confronts in modernity itself perhaps the greatest obstacle to achieving the promise of the modern philosopher king. Technical modernity, with its scientific austerity and complexity, flux and noise, seems indifferent to the Eros of poetry, promising barren ground to the rare and profound poet. The artist as the modern philosopher king therefore seems to be a child of the past, a forlorn hope and an unfulfilled promise.

Notes

1. See, for example, Segal (2016) for a comparative overview.
2. See <https://www.britannica.com/topic/the-arts> (last accessed 21 June 2022). Similarly, consider Beardsley (1983: 21): 'an artwork is something produced with the intention of giving it the capacity to satisfy aesthetic interest'. For a general overview or introduction see Freeland (2001).
3. For the influential critique and subsequent assessment see Weitz (1956); Kamber (1998); Volt (2002).
4. For an examination of the movement see Singer (1954).
5. For the diversity of approaches regarding the relationship between art and politics see, for example, Becker (1994); Bird (2019); Dasenbrock (2001); Edelman (1995).
6. On the role of arts as propaganda and their use by governments generally see, for example, Abbing (2002); Beech (2002); Chong (2010); Clark (1997); Hoock (2003); Lewis (2005).
7. For thoughtful discussions of the early debates see Laing (1978); Munro (1960). For more recent overviews see Graham (1997); Rasmussen (2006).
8. See the discussion in Baxandall and Morawski (1973: 4–8).
9. As elaborated by Marx (2010) in his preface to *A Contribution to the Critique of Political Economy*.
10. See generally Laing (1978: 39).

11. See Mao (1980: 50, 70).
12. For an early overview of Mao's influence on artists see Hsia (1963). For more recent reflections see, for example, Kraus (2004); Mittler (2008).
13. See Laing (1978: 8–14).
14. See generally Rubin (1956).
15. See, for example, the 'German Debates' in Laing (1978: 46–80).
16. Marcuse (1978: xii). As we have seen, similar attempts to recover a distinctive role for the artist can be seen in Gramsci's (1971) conception of ideology. Seeking to establish a proletarian hegemony of culture and consciousness over the ruling class he emphasised the universal and contradictory aspects of ideology and the importance of intellectuals in ideological struggles. He therefore suggested that in addition to the 'traditional' intellectuals who were functionaries of the prevailing class, 'organic' intellectuals of the working class could play a strategic role in ideological struggles.
17. See Rasmussen (2006) on the Marxist aesthetics of the ugly and monstrous. As Graham (1997: 114) puts it, 'if all the work is done by Marxist criticism, the object of that criticism may be anything whatever'.
18. See, for example, Caruso (2005).
19. For a history of the idea see Murray (1989).
20. Abrams (1953: 187).
21. See Bone (1989) regarding the contradictions inherent in the notion of a genius as an 'unfathomable exception'.
22. See Murray (1989: 73); Ferber (2010) and generally Steptoe (1998).
23. Kant (1987: 174).
24. Kant (1987: 183). It is for this reason that Kant rejects Baumgarten's scientific 'aesthetics'.
25. Wordsworth (1970: 74–9).
26. For an overview of the Romantics see Wu (2012). For a discussion of the varieties of Romantic theory focusing on Wordsworth and Coleridge see Abrams (1953: 100–24). Consider, for example, Tolstoy (2011), for whom art is a sort of 'infection' of spectators or auditors with the feelings felt by the author, a free and joyous activity that unites all to counter violence.
27. Wordsworth (2013: 111).
28. See Wordsworth's 'What is a Poet' cited in Wordsworth (2013: xliv) and his *The Prelude* in Wordsworth (1970).
29. See generally Dawson (1980); Scrivener (1982); Hoagwood (1988).
30. The Christian heroism and influence of Milton's *Paradise Lost* may also explain why the epic form was not subsequently adopted, though Pope's *Danciad* is a form of mock-epic and Wordsworth's *The Prelude* focuses on the growth of the poet's mind rather than a heroic epic.

31. Shelley was the most political, though his major works such as *Prometheus Unbound* were not read in his lifetime, while *Queen Mab* and some of his obviously political works influenced Chartists. Of the first generation of the famous English Romantic poets, Wordsworth and Coleridge were political in their youth but turned to nature after they were disappointed with the French Revolution. Wordsworth's *Lyrical Ballads* (2013), which included poems by Coleridge, ushered a new era of poetry and was considered radical and political. Byron, who belonged to the second generation of English Romantic poets and was friendly with Shelley, was radical and political all though his life. Keats was less political, and his later poems such as *La belle dames sans marci* and *Lamia* may be considered as early examples of 'art for art's sake', giving inspiration to the Pre-Raphaelite Brotherhood. I am grateful to Nahoko Miyamoto Alvey for these reflections, as well as Wu (2012).

32. See Bentley (1969) on the advocates of heroic individual. For an overview of Nietzsche's teaching on poets and poetry see Roberson (2012); Dennis (2011); Leib (1999).

33. On music see Liébert (2004); Davis (2019); for his collected poems see Nietzsche (2010).

34. Nietzsche (1996: 146, 220) and Nietzsche (1994: 39) respectively. On Nietzsche's views regarding poets as liars who enjoy lying, see generally Tuncel (2015) who distinguishes between poets who fabricate, making spectacles (more than a few) and those who make myths and thereby are value-creators (a few poets like Homer).

35. Nietzsche (1996: 155).

36. Nietzsche (1988: 370).

37. 'There is only a perspective seeing, only a perspective "knowing"' (Nietzsche 1989a: III, 12).

38. Nietzsche (1989b). Also see generally Conroy (1981).

39. Nietzsche (1988: Section 1).

40. See Nietzsche (1988: 15; 2017: 289).

41. See Nietzsche (1989a: 10; 1988: 276).

42. 'And so philosophy starts by legislating greatness' (see Nietzsche 2012: 43). There is a debate in the Nietzsche scholarship as to whether he is anti-political when he says this, meaning *self*-legislator (Thiele 1990) or to the contrary, whether this approach depreciates the political element in his thought (Ansell-Pearson 2015; Conway 1996).

43. *Republic* (607b).

44. For an examination of St Augustine's theory of art see, for example, O'Connell (1978).

45. See generally Steinberg (1941).

46. Hegel (1998: 1236).

47. On the importance of the passions as the true source of poetry, and

therefore verse predating prose in the thought of Plutarch, Vico and Herder see Abrams (1953: 78–84).

48. For an overview see Keyser and Irby-Massie (2008).
49. *Republic* (607b). See Lodge (1953) for Plato's theory of art. For scholarship on the quarrel see generally Bartscherer (2011); Burns (2015); Kannicht (1988); Nichols (2004); Levin (2001).
50. *Republic* (373b, 392c). Why does imitation please us? This question is not directly addressed. For alternative views, compare Hesiod's *Theogony*, where it is suggested that it makes us forget our unease and obligations, and Aristotle's *Poetics*, where he states imitation is pleasing because it approximates philosophical inquiry.
51. *Republic* (597e).
52. Ibid. 597b.
53. Ibid. 598b.
54. Ibid. 598c–e.
55. See the possibility of this with 'greatest imitator' (*Republic* 598b). Whether poets fabricate forms is the question not directly addressed (*Republic* 596d).
56. *Republic* 600a.
57. Ibid. 601b.
58. Ibid. 330c.
59. Ibid. 424b.
60. Ibid. 493d.
61. Ibid. 604e.
62. Ibid.
63. Ibid. Books II and III.
64. See Hesiod's *Theogony* on the origins of the Muses.
65. *Republic* (598e–600e).
66. Ibid. 606e. In the *Republic* see, for example, references to Hesiod (363a), Aeschylus (361b), Musaeus and Orpheus (363a), Pindar (365b) and Simonides (331d). Socrates also quotes favourably Hesiod (466c) and Homer (468d).
67. *Republic* 392a.
68. Ibid. 373b. See Rosen (1993) on the use of myths and poetry in *Republic*.
69. Thus, Socrates concedes the need for some lies that are noble or curative. He is ambiguous regarding the nature of poetic lies about the gods: even if the teaching is true, it should not be divulged to all and should be confined to the 'smallest number' (*Republic* 377d).
70. *Republic* 366b.
71. Ibid. 392b.
72. Ibid. 380a–c.
73. Ibid. 383a.
74. Ibid. 387d.
75. Ibid. 389e, 390d.

76. Ibid. 389c, 399d.
77. *Apology* (22b).
78. Ibid. 22c; *Phaedrus* (244b).
79. *Ion* 534c. Refences to *Ion* are to Plato (1991b).
80. Ibid. 535a.
81. Ibid. 542a.
82. Ibid 536b.
83. Ibid 535d, 536d.
84. Ibid. 541e–542a. The intriguing suggestion by Ion that his art concerns the relationships between master, slave and women, and that he is a general raises the question of an architectonic art that comprehends all others, both in times of peace and war (540b–541d).
85. *Republic* (607c).
86. Plato relies on poetry in the *Republic* with myths as *pharmakon* or good or noble lies. And poetic devices are used in the dialogues, for example the chariot in the *Phaedrus*, the spindle in *Statesman* and the potter in the *Timaeus*.
87. This suggests the need for a new form of poetry, that is both philosophic and poetic, one that is both dialectical and imitative. The Platonic dialogues in this context can be seen as the preeminent attempts to reconcile philosophy and poetry.
88. Music was permitted because it alleviated Luther's depression, authorising some of the world's greatest musical works by Bach and others.
89. See, for example, Tocqueville's *Democracy in America* (2000) for an early assessment of democracy's 'aptitude and taste for the sciences, literature and the arts' (Chapter 9), and his exploration of how democracy 'steers' the intellect in the sciences (Chapter 10); arts (Chapters 11, 12) and literature (Chapters 13–21). More generally see Melzer et al. (1999).
90. On Rhodes see Rawlinson (2016). Consider, more generally, the McCarthyism censorship in America (Doherty 2003) and the recent debates on the use of the 'N' word (Asim 2007).
91. Pineda (2021).
92. Hitron (2019).
93. See, for example, the debate between Kant and Herder regarding Shakespeare as a genius and how genius is related to philosophy: Cutrofello (2008).
94. *Phaedrus* (278d).
95. Shelley (1840).
96. Yeats (1919).

Chapter 5

The Hidden Philosopher King

The Capuchin monk François Leclerc du Tremblay, the close confident and counsellor of Cardinal de Richelieu, was referred to as the *éminence grise*. Since then, grey eminence has been the sobriquet for influential counsellors to political leaders, the hidden power behind the throne. History offers many instances of such a complex relationship between advisor and ruler. Joseph became counsellor to the Pharaoh, Seneca the Younger advised Nero, Averroes was physician and counsellor to Caliph Abu Yaqub Yusuf, Su Shi served Song Emperor Shenzong, Descartes was associated with Princess Elizabeth of Bohemia and Queen Christina of Sweden, Leibniz was employed in the House of Brunswick. But history also testifies to the dangers of such associations. Perhaps the most famous is Plato's failed attempts to instruct Dionysius I and II, tyrants of Syracuse. As we saw, though initially admired, Legalist philosopher Han Fei was later forced to drink poison by Emperor Qin, founder of Imperial China. Lord High Chancellor Sir Thomas More was beheaded by Henry VIII, King of England. Marxist theorist and revolutionary Nikolai Bukharin was executed by Stalin in the Great Purge.

That a philosopher may serve as counsellor or advisor to kings acknowledges the problems we have explored in the paradox of the philosopher king. It recognises the different character and virtues of philosophers and kings; that philosophers may be reluctant to rule and may not be skilled in ruling; and that rulers may seek wisdom to rule better but are jealous of their dignity and power. In doing so, however, such an advisory role also seems to offer the ideal solution to the paradox, overcoming these obstacles. By separating the philosopher king into its two constituent elements while link-ing them in the role of counsellor and ruler, it exploits the specific strengths of each while lightening the burdens they would otherwise bear, so that the philosopher need not sacrifice completely the life of the mind, while kings can defer to wisdom to enhance their rule without jeopardising their power and dignity. Does the philosopher as advisor to rulers therefore represent the conclusive union of the wisdom and power and the definitive answer to the paradox and promise of the philosopher king?

To explore this question, we first seek counsel and advice from a philosopher who is famous for advocating precisely such a political role for philosophers, turning to Machiavelli and especially his *The Prince* where he discusses the relationship between those who know and those who wield power. As we will see, and contrary to the general tenor of *The Prince*, Machiavelli is surprisingly not sanguine about the prospects of secretaries counselling princes, suggesting the effective truth of such a union will be a usurpation of power by the able advisor, resulting in the hidden philosopher king. We then examine implications of the hidden philosopher king for philosophy by turning to Confucius who favours what he considers the natural and necessary nexus between the sage and king. Our close examination of his teaching shows how the price of such union is a transformation in philosophy, with the dominance of political concerns directing its focus and thereby foreclosing important questions from philosophical investigation, such as the role of the individual, the place of the family and the importance of the gods in politics. In the concluding discussion we will see whether the institutionalisation of the advisor king relationship in the form of modern bureaucracy represents the successful modern resolution of the paradox of the philosopher king and its promise for just rule.

Hidden Philosopher Kings

A central theme of Plato's *Laws* is the best regime and how to secure it through laws. In the course of the conversation with the elder statesmen Megillus the Spartan and Klinias the Cretan who are considering the best constitution for the new Cretan colony of Magnesia, the Athenian Stranger proposes a provocative solution to the intransigence of politics to constitutional innovation. This 'oracular myth', or a 'prayer' proposes that a wise lawgiver should make use of a young tyrant with extraordinary natural qualities and youthful courage to effect the required changes.[1] Both Megillus and Klinias balk at this counsel as there seem to be insurmountable obstacles in finding such tyrants, how to direct their actions given their courage but lack of justice, grace or love of truth, and importantly how to assure their loyalty.[2] Confronted with these difficulties, the Stranger suggests an alternative, someone who has a 'divine eros for moderate and just practices' to counsel reigning authorities and thereby implement suitable reform, giving Nestor as the example of someone who will use persuasion rather than the violence of the tyrant to found the best regime.[3] Both solutions underline the enduring problem of how to combine wisdom and power to found the best regime, pointing to a solution in the form of philosophical advisors to kings.[4] Whatever its merits in cases of foundings, can this proposed solution be efficacious generally, even in established regimes? Plato's *Seventh Letter* chronicling his unsuccessful attempts to counsel the tyrants Dionysius I and II of Syracuse suggested otherwise, with his efforts exacerbating Syracuse's febrile politics and proving personally fruitless and perilous.[5] Yet the question has persisted and even taken a literary form, the genre of *Specula Principum* or *Mirror of Princes*, where philosophers seek to provide moral, ethical and legal counsel to rulers. Tracing their origins to Xenophon's *Cyropaedia*, these works encompass Islamic, Medieval and Renaissance writings. Consider, for example, St Augustine's *The City of God* (Book V); St Isidore of Seville's *Etymologies*; *On the Royal Office* by Jonas of Orléans; John of Salisbury's *Policraticus*; Godfrey of Viterbo's *Mirror of Kings*; Helinand of Froidmont's *On the Government of Princes*; and Gerald of Wales's *Book on the Education of a Prince*, all written between about 1180 and 1220. See also Gilbert of Tournai's *Education of Princes and Kings* and Vincent of Beauvais's *On the Moral Education of a Prince* (both *c*.1259). After the recovery of Aristotle's political writings, Giles of Rome's *On the Government of Princes* was the most widely copied mirror for princes of the Middle Ages, while Erasmus's *The Education of a Christian Prince* (1516) represented a renaissance version.[6] Machiavelli's *The Prince* appears to be within this tradition, but upon closer inspection reveals itself to be novel and innovative, with Machiavelli declaring 'I depart from the orders of others.'[7] *The Prince* warrants our closer attention because it is in this work that Machiavelli famously argues that philosophers should counsel rulers, and in doing so allows us to see clearly what this relationship entails both for the philosopher and the prince.[8]

Machiavelli writes *The Prince* soon after the fall of the Florentine Republic in 1512, when he is dismissed from office as First Secretary and banished by the new Medici regime to San Casciano in the countryside. As he makes clear from the first lines of the 'Dedicatory Letter' to *The Prince*, he is offering it as 'small gift' to 'acquire favour' from Magnificent Lorenzo de' Medici.[9] In doing so, he admits his neediness, due to 'a great and continuous malignity of fortune', and his hope that Lorenzo will raise him from his lowly place by employing him as advisor. This very personal introduction to *The Prince* reminds us that the question of advisors is an especially important one for Machiavelli. It is one that he addresses in a sense twice, first from the perspective of an ambitious and needy Machiavelli seeking patronage from Lorenzo, and second as a wise advisor counselling not just this prince, but all future readers and leaders. It is this double aspect of the book, of the specific relationship between Machiavelli and Lorenzo, and the more fundamental tension between all advisors and princes that determines the structure and rhetoric of *The Prince* as a whole. We can see this from the 'Dedicatory Letter' that immediately shows an inescapable fact about the disproportion in power between advisors and princes. Princes are 'high atop the mountains', while advisors are in 'low places'. Princes are self-sufficient, even great, while advisors are needy, hoping to please princes to acquire favour. The other notable difference is the disparity in interests of princes and advisors. Most princes tend to admire 'horses, arms, cloth of gold, precious stones and similar ornaments worthy of their greatness'.[10] It seems princes desire and value such objects not only for their intrinsic worth, but as an external sign or endorsement of their greatness. But advisors like Machiavelli value above all 'knowledge of the actions of great men' that can only be learned by 'long experience with modern things and continuous reading of ancient ones'.[11] One may infer from this that Machiavelli, in possessing such knowledge, is in an important respect superior to Lorenzo. Yet is it not clear that princes like Lorenzo believe they are deficient in this regard, or if they do whether they think such deficiency matters. The relationship between princes and advisors is therefore characterised by a disparity in power, interest and ability. These reflections on the nature of princes and advisors, from the perspective of a weak yet knowledgeable advisor, introduce and frame the subsequent discussion in *The Prince*. But the core of Machiavelli's insights regarding the role of advisors is found in two separate succinct chapters towards the end of *The Prince*. Chapter XXII, 'Of those Whom Princes Have as Secretaries', and Chapter XXIII, 'In What Mode Flatterers are to be Avoided', ostensibly address separate topics, but upon closer inspection appear to provide a comprehensive and self-sufficient essay on the relationship between the prince and advisors. It is only when they are read in this way that we see that Machiavelli contradicts his own counsel in the space of a few pages, initially extolling the merits of advisors, and subsequently questioning their usefulness and indeed indicating their possible dangerousness to the rule of the prince. To evaluate the cogency and force of these claims and the implication of such a contradiction for a comprehensive understanding of the nature of the relationship between rulers and philosophers, it is necessary to pay close attention to the subtle argumentation of each chapter.

Chapter XXII, 'Of those Whom Princes Have as Secretaries', starts provocatively: 'The choice of ministers is of no small importance to a prince; they are good or not according to the prudence of the prince.'[12] Provocatively, because it establishes prudence as an essential aspect of princely or political rule, and because it suggests that the goodness or otherwise of advisors is subject to this prudence rather than being innate to the character of the advisor. There is, it would seem, an ambiguity regarding the goodness of advisors, based not on their virtue, but on their usefulness and loyalty to the prince. Machiavelli follows this remark by appealing to the prince's vanity: 'the first conjecture that is to be made of the brain (*cervello*) of the lord is to see the men he has around him'. Distinguishing between *sufficienti* or 'capable' and *fedeli* or 'faithful' ministers, Machiavelli seems to exploit a prince's love of honour with his observation that a prince's reputation for wisdom is gauged by assessing the capacities of those he has around him, and especially by his ability to recognise competence and to keep advisors faithful. The prince's incapacity in this respect exposes him to 'unfavorable judgement', and importantly, 'the first error he makes, he makes in this choice'. Advisors seem like the 'ornaments' that Machiavelli in the 'Dedicatory Letter' said pleased princes and reflected their greatness, in this case for wisdom, but unlike these ornaments, their goodness depends on the nature of the prince. Princes, it seems, admire wisdom, but only to impress others, choosing the expedience of employing the wise rather than seeking wisdom themselves.

Machiavelli uses the example of Pandolfo Petrucci who is described as a prince of Siena and his minister Messer Antonio da Venafro to demonstrate the argument that it is the prince who determines the goodness of advisors. Pandolfo was judged a 'most worthy man' according to Machiavelli because of Venafro.[13] But this judgement is quickly challenged with Machiavelli's account of the 'three brains':

> And since there are three kinds of brains (*cervelli*): the one that understands by itself, another that discerns what others understand, the third that understands neither by itself nor through others; the first is most excellent, the second excellent, and the third useless – it follows, therefore, of necessity that, if Pandolfo was not in the first rank, he was in the second.[14]

Following Machiavelli's argument, we presumably know of 'prince' Pandolfo's excellence because of our judgement of Venafro his advisor. Yet this assessment also permits another possibility where Venafro could be a first brain, 'the one that understands by itself', while Pandolfo 'discerns what others understand'. Machiavelli's discussion of 'brains' therefore raises the possibility that ministers may be superior to princes in understanding.

Aware of this implication, Machiavelli now quickly seeks to comfort the potential 'second brain' princes. Even if such a prince does not have 'inventiveness by himself', as long as he has judgement to recognise the good or evil someone does and says, and extols the one while correcting the other, 'the minister cannot hope to deceive him and remains good himself'.[15] The problem of disparity of brains and the danger of deception can be overcome by the simple expedient of judging the goodness of deeds. These comments are intended to calm the fears of the second brain prince with a first brain minister, though in doing so the third brain prince is implicitly abandoned to the mercy of the first and second brain ministers, unless one can argue that a bad deed is evident even to those with the meanest capacities. But clearly Machiavelli thinks this may not be sufficient, because he immediately continues, 'But as to how a prince can know his minister, here is a mode that never fails.'[16] Yet as the tone of his discussion indicates, Machiavelli's helpful advice, which is in effect proposed as a permanent solution to the tensions in the prince–minister relationship, is directed to the second brains who may now see in ministers not a means to augment their reputation for wisdom, but rather a potential danger to their rule.

The problem concerns the faithfulness of ministers, who will be tempted to think more of themselves than the prince.[17] His proposed solution to making a minister always think of the prince, that is, 'to keep him good', is not to persuade or educate but rather bestow so much honour and wealth that the minister will not desire more of these, but in realising 'he cannot stand without the prince', he will fear changes. Goodness or faithfulness is to be achieved by concord of interest rather than an appeal to an idea or principle that transcends the interests of both prince and advisor. Machiavelli finishes this discussion (and the chapter) with the chilling observation, 'When, therefore, ministers and princes in relation to ministers are so constituted, they can trust one another; when it is otherwise, the end is always damaging for either one or the other.'[18] Trust, it seems, is not founded upon mutual respect and confidence, or a common commitment to some higher good, but on a subtle calculation of the advantages that outweigh the costs of mutually beneficial relationships.

The theme of secretaries, which was initiated as an important question for the prince and subject to his prudent management, and promised to burnish his reputation for wisdom, is now revealed to be an intractable problem of a struggle between princes and secretaries caused by differences in interest and the excellence of their 'brains'. This problem, according to Machiavelli, cannot reliably be resolved by a turn to a middle or common ground in wisdom, patriotism or religion to mediate and resolve the necessarily divergent ambitions of the princely and ministerial 'brains'. Rather, the only dependable means is the institutional use of rewards and punishments, the calculated dispensation of honour, wealth and fear by the prince to make the minister 'good'.

Chapter XXII seems to be Machiavelli's conclusive advice on how to manage secretaries. Yet the next chapter, Chapter XXIII, 'In What Mode Flatterers Are to Be Avoided', which is ostensibly about a different question, in effect reopens the discussion concerning advisors and in fact seems to offer completely different counsel. Machiavelli introduces Chapter XXIII almost as an afterthought, prompted by the discussion in the previous chapter: 'I do not want to leave out an important point and an error from which princes defend themselves with difficulty, unless they are very prudent or make good choices.'[19] All princes need to 'defend' themselves from the 'plague' of flattery and flatterers that crowd the courts. Yet the source of this problem lies not with the character of the flatterer, but in humanity itself. Because 'men take such pleasure in their own affairs' they deceive themselves so that powerful self-love makes princes seek the pleasure of praise, while blinding them to its truth. Consequently, they look needy and contemptible. Though he speaks of the 'plague' of flattery, Machiavelli's focus is not on the flatterer but on the deficiencies of character in princes that makes flattery possible. Such a diagnosis would suggest recourse to the conventional remedies for such a problem, such as an education in virtue to make princes impervious to such flattery. But Machiavelli does not take this opportunity to advocate a classical conception of magnanimity to moderate the prince's love of honour, nor does he remind the prince that pride is a sin and humility or meekness one of the foremost Christian virtues.[20] Instead he advises, 'For there is no other way to guard oneself from flattery unless men understand that they do not offend you in telling the truth', seeming to endorse the well-known solution of *parrhesia* or frankness, as the only means of countering flattery.[21] But the main difficulty with such truth-telling is that if everyone tells you the truth, 'they lack reverence for you'. The danger is that the prince will look contemptible in seeking honest advice. Honesty and truth-telling may overcome flattery, but seemingly at the expense of the dignity and therefore authority of the prince.

Having noted the significant obstacles associated with what Machiavelli stresses is the *only* solution to the problem of flattery, he proposes a 'third mode' ostensibly an attempt to retain truth-telling while remedying its potential threat to the dignity of the prince. Addressing the 'prudent' prince, this mode starts by dividing people into two groups, the 'wise men in his state' and the 'others'. Only the wise should be given freedom to speak the truth to the prince, but even in this case, not about everything – only about those matters that the prince has asked about and nothing else. Yet even this restriction on the wise is soon removed: 'But he should ask them about everything and listen to their opinions; then he should decide by himself, in his own mode; and with these councils and with each member of them he should behave in such a mode that everyone knows that the more freely he speaks, the more he will be accepted.'[22] As for the 'others', the advice is simple: 'he should not want to hear anyone', and once having decided he should be 'obstinate in his decisions'. Where this mode is not adopted, according to Machiavelli, the prince is exploited by flatterers or in changing views constantly is seen to be indecisive and therefore contemptible. With this advice we see that one major source of being contemptible is indecisiveness, due no doubt to the different advice a prince will receive. The price of frankness is contradictory advice, to be remedied by seeking advice only from the wise, and then by deliberating not in their company. How consistent is this 'third mode' with the advice he had given in the previous chapter on secretaries? In the emphasis on wisdom, this approach certainly reinforces what

Machiavelli had said about the necessity of prudence in politics, moving away from the other test, whether a minister is thinking of the prince or his own welfare. Indeed, it seems to go further in advocating a sort of deliberative council of the wise at the apex of political rule. But the solution he proposes seems to neglect altogether the problem of the 'three brains' and the tension between prince and advisor he identified, as well as the solution he proposed in terms of making advisors 'good' by a combination of reward and fear in the preceding chapter. Why should a 'first brain' prince be counselled, even by the 'wise'? Is there not a danger in the second, or even the third 'useless' brains in being advised, and therefore controlled by the wise? Who exactly are the 'wise' – after all, is there not an extraordinary range in human excellence, from the philosophically profound to the politically prudent? Finally, what about the problem of self-regard that distorts the prince's judgement and makes possible the plague of flattery? Will the prince's opinion of who is wise be inevitably distorted by this passion? If so, doesn't this third mode simply ignore the problem of flattery?

After the ambiguous example of Emperor Maximilian endorsing the 'third mode', Machiavelli seemingly summarises and restates it.[23] But the restatement is a reformulation since it abandons important aspects of the third mode. In his summary, Machiavelli states that the prince should always take counsel but only when he wants it, and 'he should discourage everyone from counselling him about anything unless he asks it of them'. Yet he should be a 'a very broad questioner' and a 'patient listener to the truth', going so far as to say, 'he should become angry when he learns that anyone has any hesitation in speaking to him'.[24] The distinction between the 'wise men' and others is now abandoned. The prince will now take counsel from everyone, the only limit being that he will initiate the discussion. It is as if Machiavelli wants to change the nature of the prince himself for, after all, isn't 'a very broad questioner' and a 'patient listener to the truth' a practical definition of a philosopher? Does this mean that the 'third mode' presupposes a 'first brain' or a 'philosopher-prince'? Perhaps it is not accidental that we have raised these questions. Machiavelli follows his summary or review with what appears to be a new theme, yet in doing so it soon becomes evident that this discussion goes to the core of the questions we have posed:

And since many esteem that any prince who establishes an opinion of himself as prudent is so considered not because of his nature but because of the good counsel he has around him, without doubt they are deceived. For this is a general rule that never fails: that a prince who is not wise by himself cannot be counselled well, unless indeed by chance he should submit himself to one person alone to govern him in everything, who is a very prudent man.[25]

Of course it was Machiavelli who had proposed at the very beginning of preceding Chapter XXII that 'the first conjecture that is to be made of the brain of the lord is to see the men he has around him'.[26] His initial discussion focuses on the various ways of managing the relationship between princes and secretaries, ranging from taking counsel as in the case of Pandolfo, to the mode that never fails in judging the counsellor ('is he thinking of himself more than you?'), to how to keep them 'good' (the judicious use of reward and punishment, and not appealing to the common good), and in the chapter on flattery, on the 'third mode', taking counsel from the wise, and finally, counsel from anyone as long as the prince does the asking. Now it seems that this entire discussion has ended in a complete repudiation of its starting point and its replacement with 'a new rule that never fails': 'a prince who is not wise by himself cannot be counselled well'. It is in particular the inability to overcome the problems with truth-telling, the only means of countering flattery, that seems to decide the issue. *Parrhesia* may solve the plague of flattery but at the price of undermining the authority of princes by elevating counsellors, by instituting a diversity of contradictory advice and by not overcoming the character of the prince (who may be prudent but too needy for the affection of others). The rule that never fails seems to question the usefulness of advisors altogether – why would a wise prince seek counsel at all, except in the most trivial sense of being provided with facts and detailed circumstances?

It is true that Machiavelli acknowledges an exception to this rule: 'unless indeed by chance he should submit himself to one person alone to govern him in everything, who is a very prudent man'. Yet this exception proves to be fatal for the prince: 'In this case he could well be [counselled well], but it would not last long because the governor would in a short time take away his state.'[27] With this observation, Machiavelli outlines how this situation cannot be remedied. A prince who is not wise, according to Machiavelli, cannot usefully take counsel from many, assuming that one can have many 'very prudent' counsellors because such a prince will 'never have united counsel, nor know by himself how to unite them'. Moreover, each counsellor will 'think of his own interest' and the prince will be unable to 'know how to correct them or understand them'. The reason for this is, 'men will always turn out bad for you unless they have been made good by necessity'. Thus Machiavelli denies the possibility of disinterested, 'scientific' or even public-spirited advice – all, and perhaps especially the 'very prudent', cannot help but seek rule and authority. Machiavelli concludes the chapter with a position that denies what he asserted in his chapter on secretaries that initiated his assessment of how princes should deal with advisors: 'So one concludes that good counsel, from wherever it comes, must arise from the prudence of the prince, and not the prudence of the prince from good counsel.'[28]

Machiavelli's reflections on princes and advisors are perplexing due to the contradiction in his account, where he seems to endorse advisors as attractive ornaments to rule, while in the very next chapter regards them as useless and even dangerous. He is too careful an author for us to assume that he simply makes a mistake. We therefore have to wonder what he means by such a blatant contradiction. I suggest that the contending teachings are an amusing practical demonstration of the power of flattery and the inability of truth-telling to counter it. That few if any readers of Machiavelli have seen the contradictory position he adopts in the space of a few pages is testimony to his view that either leaders are simply deficient 'third brains' or that their vanity or lack of ability will mean they will hear the advice that pleases them, rather than the advice they are offered. In the context of the specific chapters we have examined, leaders who will take the trouble to read these passages will always assume they are first brains, disregarding Machiavelli's view that at best they are 'second' brains who understand the first, but much more likely the 'infinite' others who are useless. They will therefore never take seriously or disregard the dangers advisors may present. Machiavelli thereby shows how *parrhesia* makes little difference if one can skilfully tell the offending truth in a way that vanity will interpret it as justified praise. But Machiavelli's contradictory discussion of flattery has a deeper lesson to offer. Having reviewed his advice on the dangers flattery poses to leaders, we cannot help but wonder if it is wise or even safe to be counselled by him. The reason for our wariness and reluctance is Machiavelli's clear-sighted assessment of the fundamental tension between power and wisdom in politics. Machiavelli shows that the relationship between leaders and advisors, especially at the highest level, is defined by a fundamental disjunction between wisdom and power, philosophy and politics – those who have power may not have the brains, and conversely, those who have brains may not have power. It is this discrepancy, according to Machiavelli, that is the reason for having advisors, and why they will be ineffective or, worse, dangerous. The philosopher as advisor or counsellor to kings appeared to be the ideal solution to the paradox of the philosopher king. Yet as Machiavelli reveals, the effective truth of this proposed remedy is that either advisors are treated as ornaments, to be disposed at the will of their political masters, or they become themselves the hidden philosopher kings, usurping the authority of their ostensible masters.

Confucian Literati and the Sage King

But perhaps we should be willing to tolerate the pretence if not duplicity of the hidden philosopher king as a small price for uniting wisdom and power to overcome the 'ills of the world'. If indeed the hidden philosopher king is salutary for politics, is it equally efficacious for philosophy? To see the possible price philosophy pays for becoming political in this way, we turn to the political philosophy of Confucius, who unlike Socrates sees no core ambiguity or tension between philosophy as a life devoted to inquiry and a life dedicated to politics, and indeed discerns an integral harmony so that philosophical excellence is essential for political prosperity. Our examination of Confucian political philosophy will therefore allow us to see if there are significant implications for philosophy, especially the questions it poses and the political practices it endorses, in favouring the hidden philosopher king.

There is an extraordinary similarity between Socrates and Confucius. Both Socrates and Confucius are elusive, so that even those who know them well attest to their mysterious character, requiring rare discernment and perseverance to see their seemingly concealed nature.[29] Both are famous for their love of learning, Socrates declaring during his trial that the 'unexamined life is not worth living', while Confucius, in responding to the question of who is Confucius posed by Duke of She advises his disciple Zilu to respond, 'Why didn't you just say to him: As a person, Confucius is driven by such eagerness to teach and learn that he forgets to eat, he enjoys himself so much that he forgets to worry, and does not even realize that old age is on its way.'[30] Socrates is famous for his ignorance and *zetetic* way of a life.[31] Confucius's pursuit of wisdom (*zhi*) appears fundamentally consistent with Socratic philosophising. He teaches his disciple Zilu, 'To know what you know and know what you do not know – this then is wisdom.'[32] Yet he denies he knows: 'Do I possess wisdom (*zhi*)? No, I do not. But if a simple peasant puts a question to me, and I come up empty, I attack the question from both ends until I have gotten to the bottom of it.'[33] Socrates frequently reminds us of his poverty and that, unlike the sophists and rhetoricians, he does not receive pay for teaching. Similarly, it is knowledge, rather than wealth or birth, that allows Confucius to understand and rank human beings, so that he is willing to teach all, rich or poor, or as he puts it, 'In instruction, there is no such thing as social classes.'[34]

That both Socrates and Confucius are moved by a powerful longing to know, and discern something profound about such a life of inquiry, reveals an extraordinary consensus at the heart of their philosophy. Yet it is also evident that there are fundamental differences regarding their teachings, which can be traced in part to their understanding of the paradox of the philosopher king.[35] Unlike Socrates, Confucius does not recognise a paradox in the possibility of the sage king. Indeed, as we will see, he considers it an aspiration and a duty. The reason for this can be traced to the Confucian rejection of the Sophistic argument that discerns in the discovery of *phusis* or nature the source of the tension between the individual and the city. The Confucian understanding of nature and the extent to which he considered it to be at tension with norms is a profound and complex question that has been approached from a range of perspectives, including his idea of human nature, his theology and, more comprehensively, whether Confucianism has a concept of 'natural law'.[36] The scholarly consensus is that Confucius sees a fundamental harmony and consonance between nature, individual excellence and political prosperity.[37] Confucius's view of nature, which can be inferred from his preference for Zengxi in the *Analects* who in late spring goes bathing in the River Yi, enjoys the breeze on the Rain Alter, after which goes home chanting poetry, over others who speak of how to administer the state, has been described as 'the most beautiful expression of the fusion between man and nature in Confucius's *Analects*'.[38] The cosmic order, from the overarching supervision of *tian* or heaven and sky to the rituals observed by individuals, reveals a natural ranking and hierarchy that favours human excellence and prosperity.[39] On human nature in particular, though it is true that Confucius, unlike his followers such as Mencius, remains ambiguous regarding its goodness, it is clear that he thinks we all share the same nature, which is capable of improvement: 'The Master said, "Human beings are similar in their natural tendencies, but vary greatly by virtue of their habits."'[40] The diversity in human ability and the importance of habits explain the central role of education based on nature that confirms the potential, and provides the model and the means for individual and political excellence and prosperity. Confucian education, which claims to be a recovery of an older teaching, therefore represents the correct articulation and development of nature's promise for humanity. Our natural openness to virtue and excellence is confirmed by Confucius's frequent references to how authoritative conduct and virtuous actions by individuals and leaders exercises a powerful influence on others, bringing out the best in them.[41] The substance of the education includes the virtues of benevolence (*ren*), righteousness (*yi*), ritual propriety (*li*), wisdom (*zhi*) and trustworthiness (*xin*). *Ren* or benevolence is especially notable for showing the nexus between nature and norms.[42]

The harmony of nature and norms is above all evident in the relationships he elevates and seeks to refine. The natural ordering that combines male and female, and develops it in the family, which in turn is mirrored in the state, all under *tian*, shows the harmonious place of humanity within the whole. It is within this hierarchy that Confucius singles out that most natural of human associations, the family, as the foundation for developing individual and communal virtues. The fivefold relations between husband–wife, father–son, brother–brother, friend–friend and ruler–ruled show the primacy of the family for the nurture and cultivation of the individual. Equally importantly, it shows the harmonious relationship between the family and politics, so that the family becomes the model for political organisations. Filial piety, for example, informs the nature of political loyalty, just as fraternal duty is seen to be a civic virtue. The family becomes the primary source of moral ordering and loyalty, prizing continuity, stability and peace as the foremost political (and by implication, intellectual and ethical) virtues. The ranking, hierarchy, obligations and responsibilities that defined familiar relations now become the models for political leaders and citizens. Confucian conceptions of virtue, merit and excellence are therefore founded upon the premise that there is no fundamental or inherent tension between nature and norms. Human instruction completes our natural potential, and therefore there is no inherent conflict between individual conceptions of happiness and the demands of either the family or politics.

Sage and Political Rule

The extent to which philosophy and politics are mutually accommodating is an important question for Confucius. But as we will see, rather than a paradox, he discerns an essential concord between the sage and the ruler, wisdom and power. Confucius is aware of the difference between the wise and the politically active. The wise seek the company of 'authoritative persons' (*ren*), according to Confucius, but differ from them: 'The wise (*zhi*) enjoy water; those authoritative in their conduct (*ren*) enjoy mountains. The wise are active; the authoritative still. The wise find enjoyment; the authoritative are long-enduring.'[43] He continues this distinction by noting that the person who is generous with the people and able to help the multitude is not only authoritative (*ren*), but also a sage (*sheng*).[44] Similarly, he distinguishes between a sage (*shengren*) and an 'exemplary' person (*junzi*). There is therefore some ambiguity between the different forms of human excellence explored in the *Analects*, ranging from the wise (*zhi*), the sage (*shengren*), the authoritative or authoritative conduct (*ren*), the exemplary (*junzi*) and the scholar apprentice (*shi*).[45] As each plant must be nurtured differently, the path to excellence will differ, though 'It is the sage (*shengren*) alone who walks this path every step from start to finish', suggesting a continuum of excellence, with the *junzi* occupying the middle.[46] This link or connection between the wise and the many, or between philosophy and politics, can be found in one of the most famous statements in the *Analects*, 'the excellence (*de*) of the exemplary person (*junzi*) is the wind, while that of the petty person is the grass. As the wind blows, the grass is sure to bend.'[47]

The political influence of the *junzi*, and by inference of the wise, lies not simply in the importance of excellence in subtly shaping politics. Confucius's own reflections reveal that he anticipates a much more powerful and engaged role for the sage in politics. Of course, there is some ambiguity regarding Confucius's views concerning himself. With suitable modesty he denies being a sage (*sheng*) or an authoritative person (*ren*): 'What can be said about me is simply that I continue my studies without respite and instruct others without growing weary.'[48] But this emphasis on teaching and instruction suggests that Confucius sees education as one of the most important roles of those who value learning. His rule for instruction is clear:

> To fail to speak with someone who can be engaged is to let that person go to waste; to speak with someone who cannot be engaged

is to waste your words. The wise (*zhi*) do not let people go to waste, but they do not waste their words either.[49]

Education of the promising young to become future sage or *junzi* is therefore an important aspect of what Confucius would regard as his public service or political duty. Yet Confucius does not limit his political ambitions solely to instruction and education. There are in the *Analects* frequent reflections by Confucius on contemporary politics, ranging from critique on the proper use of rituals, comments on the efficacy of barbarian tribes, commentary on advisors, including his own disciples, and critique of contemporary leaders for greed and cruelty. There are also numerous general remarks on how to rule. Perhaps the best known is the advice Confucius offers to Zilu should the Lord of Wey turn the administration of the state over to him. His counsel, which Zilu finds impractical, is to start with the proper use of names, because the proper use of names has implications for language, ritual propriety (*li*), playing of music (*yue*) and application of laws and punishments.[50]

In addition to the importance of the wise or the philosophic in being exemplary models for all, as well as in educating those who are keen to learn and in advising political leaders, Confucius's own ambitions suggest that he thinks the wise should seek political office for the common good. Public service, according to Confucius, is required where *dao* prevails – 'It is a disgrace to remain poor and without rank when the way prevails in the state; it is a disgrace to be wealthy and of noble rank when it does not.'[51] His counsel generally is to 'Make an earnest commitment to the love of learning (*haoxue*) and be steadfast to the death in the service to the efficacious way (*shandao*).'[52] But not excelling in love of learning does not deprive one of serving in office, as Confucius notes regarding Zilu, Zigong and Ranyou.[53] His model is the sage–king Yu, who was moderate in regard to his personal concerns yet was generous towards the gods and spirits of ancestors, was lavish in ceremonial expenses and generous in the construction of public works.[54] He thinks with truly efficacious people (*shanren*) in charge of government, violence could be overcome and killing could be dispensed with altogether, but they would have to govern for 100 years.[55] Confucius considers himself capable of such leadership.

> To serve the Duke and his ministers at court, and to serve my elders at home, in funerary matter not to presume to give less than my best efforts, and not to be overcome by drink – how could such things give me any trouble at all?[56]

Elsewhere he says, 'If someone were to make use of me in governing, in the course of a year I could make a difference, and in three
years I would really have something to show for it.'[57] Accordingly,
Yang Huo persuades Confucius to serve in office by arguing that
someone who has talent should help his country.[58]

It is clear, then, that for Confucius the sage king is not only
a possibility but is actually mandated by public duty. Yet there
seems to be more than a sense of duty evident in Confucius's ambition. We can see this especially in the way he confronts his lack
of success in fulfilling his ambitions. He encounters difficulties
in seeking office, as his experience in the states of Chen and Cai
suggests.[59] There is also a sense of frustration or desperation in
his search for office. When he is admonished by Zilu for want-
ing to join Gongshan Furao who was plotting a rebellion, seemingly because they had nowhere else to go, Confucius replies,
'How could this person who is summoning me be doing so for no
reason? If there were someone who would use me, I would give
him a "Zhou of the east".'[60] Similarly, when Bixi, who is plotting
rebellion with the Zhongmou stronghold, summons Confucius,
and Zilu again is critical of joining someone who behaves badly,
Confucius replies,

> 'You are right' said the Master. 'It is as you say. But is it not said,
> "With the hardest, grinding will not wear it thin". Is it not said,
> "With the whitest, dying will not turn it black". Am I just some
> kind of gourd? How can I allow myself to be strung up on the wall
> and not be eaten?'[61]

But his experience in office proves to be a failure, his advice seemingly ignored or disregarded.[62] His lack of success makes him
despair: 'No one appreciates me', and when asked by Zigong
why, he replies, 'I don't hold any ill will against *tian* nor blame
other people. I study what is near at hand and aspire to what
is lofty. It is only *tian* who appreciates me!'[63] Sensitive about
his lack of employment he explains how he can be employed
in governing by exercising filial piety.[64] But he comforts others
to not worry about having an official position or that no one
acknowledges them, consoling them by noting that it is because
he has never been appointed to an office that he learned many
arts.[65] What is unique to him, unlike others, is that he 'does not
have presuppositions as to what may and may not be done'.[66]
Confucius, criticised for flitting 'from perch to perch', never gets
the opportunity to exercise his prudence and judgement, ending

his days convinced of his failure: 'No intelligent monarch arises; there is not one in the land that will make me his master. My time has come to die.'[67] If we accept Confucius is a sage, despite his suitably modest protestations, we can see that he thought not only was the life of learning consistent with political rule, but that the two could not be separated. His love of learning was therefore of a piece with his ambitions to be an excellent model, a teacher and a political ruler who would reform politics for the welfare of all. He represented the beneficial union of wisdom and political ambition.

What implications does the Confucian endorsement of philosophers as advisors and even sage kings, have for philosophy? Our comparison of the Confucian and Socratic approaches to the paradox of the philosopher king, founded on their different conceptions of the relationship between nature and norms, reveals contending conceptions of the best life, for individuals and communities. Socrates poses a provocative challenge to those who aspire to political rule, questioning their motives, ambitions and longings. In doing so he points to the possibility of philosophy as the more comprehensive and satisfying life. Confucius in contrast regards political leadership by the sage as the apex of human endeavour, both for the individual and for communities. This ranking of lives has larger consequences for how they understand the relationship between wisdom and power, philosophy and politics. For Socrates the enduring tension between the life of thought and political power results in a depreciation of the political and therefore authorises philosophy to judge, evaluate and rank political regimes and the virtues and lives they endorse. For Confucius, the possibility and desirability of the sage king means there is a seamless unity and even a mutually enriching partnership between the two which tends to favour the primacy of political life above all others. It makes him depreciate the philosophical life that is not directly engaged with politics, and fashions political institutions on that basis. These differences have influentially shaped the problems they define, the solutions they propose and the questions they thereby neglect. The philosophical costs of the Confucian endorsement of the sage king, I suggest, is a foreclosing or limiting of important questions, as we can see in the Confucian depreciation of the 'individual', its elevation of the family as philosophical and political institution and finally the relative neglect of the gods.

Individual, Family and the Gods

The Sophists, in questioning the naturalness of the laws, revealed the potential tension between the happiness of the individual and of the city. Socrates acknowledged the importance of this tension but rejected the Sophistic answer that resolved the tension by defending the life of the tyrant. He instead raised the possibility that happiness for the individual may be found not in politics but the 'examined life', justifying a critical examination of the claims of politics.[68] How does this approach differ from Confucius's conception of individual happiness, the role of the family and the significance of myths and the gods? There is a continuing debate on the concept of the individual in Confucian thought.[69] Whatever this notion of the individual, Confucius, in so far as he seems to presume that political office is the aspiration, duty and hope of those who are wise, suggests the concurrence of individual and communal happiness, leading to a less clearly defined foothold for the idea of the 'individual'. Such an approach deprives the idea of the individual of the conceptual foothold we discerned in the Socratic view of the philosophic life, so that community and therefore politics and its hierarchies have a primacy for Confucius that remains questionable in Socratic thought. Indeed, unlike Socrates, he is prepared in crucial junctures to cease questioning or defer to the political.

Similarly, their different conceptions of the relationship between philosophy and politics explains their divergent views regarding the family.[70] Socrates, from his philosophical stance, is able to question the partial and limiting nature of family love, duty and affection. Consider, for example, his suggestion that the powerful familial bonds and affections present a formidable impediment to the requirements of justice (*Republic*), how love of one's own is an obstacle to philosophy (*Symposium*) and the way family poses a challenge to friendship (*Lysis*). His questioning of the family thus makes possible his examination of the nature of *politeia* or regimes as arrangements that superintend the family, revealing the potential foundations of republican rule and thus initiating the study of politics. Confucius too seeks to introduce and institute his new conception of the *junzi* as a new form of excellence that seems to challenge the powerful forces of family affection, loyalty and therefore partiality. Yet in a decisive respect, when the ideal of *junzi* confronts the demands of the family, Confucius defers to the family. The family becomes the primary source of moral ordering and loyalty, prizing continuity, stability and peace as the foremost political (and by implication, intellectual and ethical) virtues. It also becomes the model for the political regime so that the dynasty, which is a family writ large, is thereby institutionalised in Confucian thought.[71]

But perhaps the most striking consequence of the differences in the Socratic and Confucian approaches is evident in their distinctive response to the question of the gods.[72] It is true that Socrates is aware of the dangers of piety, as his own personal experience attests, and therefore seeks to moderate its force with a 'theology', speeches or reasoning about the gods that attempt a reinterpretation, even repudiation, of the Homeric and Hesiodic gods.[73] Yet his commitment to the examined life means that he persists in his quest to test the gods through reason, even seeking to disprove the Delphic oracle's claim that no one was wiser than Socrates.[74] Confucius too knows of *tian* or heaven, gods and spirits and thinks deeply about them.[75] Yet unlike Socrates he refuses to discuss this topic.[76] Confucius, it would seem, sought to discourage 'theology'.[77] The reason for this, in part, seems to be his concern for politics. When Fan Chi inquired about wisdom (*zhi*), 'The Master replied, "To devote yourself to what is appropriate (*yi*) for the people, and to show respect for the ghosts and spirits while keeping them at a distance can be called wisdom".'[78] Elsewhere Confucius observes, 'Not yet being able to serve the people, how would you be able to serve the spirits?' When Zilu asked about death, Confucius replied, 'Not yet understanding life, how could you understand death?'[79] Confucius seeks to moderate the influence of ghosts and spirits, at least for the general populace, by disregarding the origins and nature of *tian* and *dao* or the significance of the divine and the transcendent, in determining the nature of *yi*, *ren* and *li*. Socratic openness about the gods can be said to leave an important legacy in the form of 'theology' as well as cosmology, metaphysics and epistemology. By contrast, Confucius's reluctance to discuss *tian* and his prudent reticence regarding gods, spirits and ghosts has the great merit of removing the dangers of religious fanaticism and zealotry from politics, but at the expense of limiting 'metaphysical' conversations.[80]

We have turned to the thought of Confucius, an advocate of the union of wisdom and power, to see what implication such a combination has for philosophy. As we have seen, there is a remarkable consensus in the thought of Socrates and Confucius regarding the importance of love of learning or philosophy, what constitutes human excellence, and the educational and institutional means needed to secure such excellence. Yet there is also a divergence or dissensus concerning the nature and primacy of philosophy and politics that has far-reaching consequences for the character of philosophy. The Confucian sage king, in denying the philosopher king is a paradox and endorsing it as a means for securing virtue and justice, reveals there are significant implications for philosophy with such a union of wisdom and power, with our examination of individualism, the importance to be accorded to the family, and of the role of the gods showing how such an approach constrains or limits the range and scope of philosophical speculation.

Bureaucratising the Hidden Ruler

The philosopher who counsels kings appears to be a neat solution to the paradox of the philosopher king. Yet, as Machiavelli intimates, the practical effect of this solution is a new problem – the hidden philosopher king – which, even if successful, has the effect of transforming the core concerns and direction of philosophy, as we have seen from our examination of Confucian sage king. The Hindu *gurukula* system, the Buddhist *vihara* or monastery for renunciates, the Islamic *madrasas* for the mullahs and Quranic judges, and the Tokugawa *han* schools for Japanese samurai all represent attempts to structure the relationship between counsellor and ruler, philosopher and king.[81] Can these challenges to the philosopher as advisor to kings be addressed and resolved by institutionalising advisors? Is bureaucracy the modern answer to the paradox of the philosopher king? In Europe, universities, distinct from classical academies and lyceums and medieval monasteries, evolved through different historical and political contexts to continue as autonomous, permanent and corporate institutions of research and learning with an increasingly important instrumental role in modern states.[82] In Imperial China, merit-based Confucian examination of *literati* or scholar–officials and mandarins of the imperial bureaucracy were established in the Tang Dynasty (618–907) and consolidated in the Song Dynasty (960–1279), enduring until the end of the Qing Dynasty (1636–1912).[83] Though the Chinese models have been influential, the modern bureaucratic state can trace its origins to European cameralism, *étatism* and *Rechtsstaat* as well as English parliamentarianism and American constitutionalism, with each distinctive political and historical legacy challenging more recent attempts to globalise public management.[84] It is therefore difficult to evaluate in a comprehensive way whether the modern bureaucracy provides a definitive modern answer to the paradox of philosopher king. But a close examination of the contending views of the two influential theorists of modern bureaucracy, Hegel and Weber, will allow us to see whether and to what extent the tensions we have discerned above are resolved in the modern bureaucracy. As we will see, Weber's preference for a 'technical' bureaucrat who will not be 'political' contrasts with Hegel's bureaucrat who is more than a technical administrator and advisor and is someone who will exercise prudence and judgement in office. The existence and character of these theoretical contests, recalling important aspects of the debates we have explored above, suggest bureaucracy does not solve the paradox of the philosopher king but re-enacts it in different terms, locutions and forms.

Both Weber and Hegel agree on the nature of the modern state, founded on liberal rights. They also accept that modern bureaucracy is a new organisation, a consequence of the rise of the modern state that replaced feudal relations with institutionalised and impersonal structures. Accordingly, there is substantial consensus between them on important aspects of modern bureaucracies, such as their organisational structures that do not depend on the personal will of the ruler but are regulated by impersonal laws.[85] But there is also a fundamental difference between them regarding the nature of bureaucratic activity. Weber's conception of bureaucracy has been widely influential and continues to shape the way we think about bureaucracy and its legitimate role in the modern state.[86] He distinguishes between four types of human action: purposive-rational or instrumental-rational (*zweckrational*), value-rational (*wertrational*), affectual and traditional.[87] Purposive-rational action involves calculating and choosing the appropriate means to achieve a given end; it cannot determine the end of the action except by making pragmatic judgements as to whether a specific end is achievable.[88] This is based on Weber's distinction between facts and values, the 'ethic of responsibility' and the 'ethic of conviction'.[89] From this perspective, values are to be determined by politicians in the crucible of political struggle, while bureaucrats are to remain neutral, obliged to implement with disinterest, impartiality and precision those decisions that have emerged from these political struggles. This technical role of the bureaucrat, drawing on expertise in jurisprudence and administrative or business management, is to be contrasted with the more ambitious conception of their role by Hegel. Hegel is one of the most influential theorists of the modern state. In his *Philosophy of Right* (2002)

Hegel discusses bureaucracy in the context of his examination of the executive more generally, distinguishing between the power of the prince or monarch and that of the executive who mediates between the state and civil society. In executing and maintaining existing legal norms the executive makes the 'universal interest valid within these particular aims'.[90] This executive has the characteristics of modern bureaucracy, including functional divisions, hierarchic forms, formal offices requiring ability and talent as demonstrated through official examinations, fixed salaries and emphasis on speed and efficiency in handling state affairs.[91] But the most important consideration for our purposes is Hegel's claim that the bureaucrat, who is appointed due to knowledge and ability, should exercise authority according to the common good:

> What is really required by service to the state is that human beings shall sacrifice the selfish and capricious satisfaction of their subjective aims; by this very sacrifice, they acquire the right to find their satisfaction in, but only in, the dutiful discharge of their public functions.[92]

The reason for this emphasis on the common good can be found in Hegel's account of civil officials, which he designates as an 'universal class' because their end is to realise the universal interest as opposed to the particular interests of civil society. They are not appointed, like agents, 'to perform individual, contingent services; instead they invest in this relationship the chief interest of their worldly being, both spiritual and particular'.[93] They are therefore endowed with the highest political consciousness and knowledge about public affairs.[94] Such an ambitious role for the bureaucracy is reflected in its functions, which include the supervision of corporations in civil society and, more importantly, an advisory committee for the monarch regarding public matters that require his final decision.[95] Hegel's formal term for this is 'subsumption', which is activity that is based on knowledge, fitting forms to concrete situations so that right can be ascertained, mediating between universal legal norms and individual cases. Subsumption is therefore not simply mere application but use of practical judgement. As such, Hegel's bureaucrat has much greater discretion that is needed for exercising judgement.

As this brief overview suggests, there is a fundamental distinction between the duties of bureaucrats as they are understood by Weber and Hegel, founded on their conceptions of the state and ultimately their philosophical insights into the nature of politics. Weber wants bureaucrats to possess primarily technical skills, while Hegel expects them to exercise prudence and judgement. These contending conceptions of the nature and role of bureaucracy continue to inform debates in contemporary public administration, where the desire to assert democratic authority over powerfully unaccountable 'mandarins' in the form of New Public Management initiatives has met contrary proposals to ensure the bureaucracy remains the essential source for defending the public good.[96]

If these arguments seem familiar, it is because they represent the contemporary manifestation of the debates we have seen attempting to address the paradox of the philosopher king, starting from the proposal of the Athenian Stranger in Plato's *Laws*, Machiavelli's clear-sighted assessment of the benefits and dangers of counsellors, and the Confucian endorsement of the sage king. The persistence and salience of these contemporary debates suggests that modern bureaucracies have not definitively solved the paradox of the philosopher king by combining the wise advisor and the prince, as the continuing challenge of deciding who is to rule, the character of the counsel provided by philosophers to rulers and what to do with the problem of the hidden philosopher king shows us. If anything, they have obscured and complicated the tensions between wisdom and power with a novel lexicon and intricate and complex legal and administrative architecture.

Counsellors as Modern Philosopher Kings

The wise counsellor to the politically powerful seems to be the promising solution to the paradox of the philosopher king. By devising two separate offices for philosopher and ruler yet uniting them through the duties of counsellor, it promises a formidable unity and whole that combines wisdom and power, philosophy and politics, overcoming the limitations of the paradox of philosopher king. And history seems to agree, with numerous examples of close associations between philosophers and political leaders that have benefited both. Yet lingering doubts remain. As Machiavelli noted, the counsellor and the prince are such different beings that the union seems constitutionally fraught, with dangers to both. Princes see advisors as ornaments and on reflection fear the dangers of flattery, exploitation and usurpation that result in the hidden philosopher king. Philosophers may seek comfort in a new-found authority and dignity of the office of counsellor, but the price seems high for philosophy, its gaze now lowered, diverted from profound questions by the urgent and the necessary that characterise politics, as we saw in Confucian political thought. The institutional solution, refined in the form of the modern bureaucratic state, seemed to promise the conclusive solution to the problems of the hidden philosopher king. But, as we have seen, this answer does not resolve the core tensions, but rather reinstates them in the new vernacular of the modern bureaucratic state. The modern advisor to kings, whether as an individual or a bureaucracy, therefore remains a tantalising yet flawed answer to the paradox and promise of the philosopher king.

Notes

1. *Laws* (709c–e). References to the *Laws* are to Plato (1980). For a thoughtful commentary see Pangle (1980: 439–41).
2. *Laws* (711c).
3. But as we know from the *Iliad*, Nestor was not simply just, and his counsel was not always heeded.
4. *Laws* (712b).
5. For an overview of his experiences, and a detailed examination of the *Seventh Letter* see Lewis (2000); Levison et al. (1968); and the book length discussion by Edelstein (1966). More generally see Cimakasky (2017) and the concluding chapter of this book.
6. For an historical overview of the mirror for princes genre see Lambertini (2011). On the Jewish tradition see Melamed (2003).
7. *Prince* (15: 61). References to *The Prince* are to Machiavelli (1985) and are by chapter and page.
8. For an earlier discussion that explores these themes in the context of honour see Patapan (2021: 103–24).
9. *Prince*, Dedicatory Letter, 3.
10. Ibid.
11. Ibid.
12. *Prince* (22: 9).
13. Antonio Giordana da Venafro (1459–1530) was professor of law, Studio di Siena. In the *Discourses* (III: 6) Machiavelli calls Pandolfo 'tyrant of Siena' (cf *Prince* 20: 85), making us wonder if a good advisor may even efface the reputation of being a tyrant.
14. *Prince* (22: 92). Machiavelli alludes to Hesiod, *Works and Days* (lines 295ff.), but Hesiod, who is ostensibly counselling his brother Perses, refers to *noesis* rather than 'brains'.
15. *Prince* (22: 92).
16. Ibid. 22: 93.
17. Ibid.
18. Ibid.

19. Ibid.
20. On magnanimity see *Nicomachean Ethics* (1123b: 3–5). On Christian humility and the sin of *superbia* or pride see Aquinas (1920: II, II, Q. 132, art. 4).
21. *Prince* (23: 94). For an overview of flattery see Eylon and Heyd (2008). On *parrhesia* in Greek thought see Landauer (2012). On its effect in modern democracies see Foucault (2001).
22. *Prince* (23: 94).
23. The example of Maximilian reveals how his character, which seeks approbation, makes him susceptible to changing his mind, undermining his judgement.
24. *Prince* (23: 95).
25. Ibid.
26. Ibid. 22: 92.
27. Ibid. 23: 95.
28. Ibid.
29. See Plato's *Apology* (38a) as well as Alcibiades's account of Socrates in the *Symposium* (215 1-d). References to *Symposium* are to Plato (1993). All references to the *Analects* are to the Ames and Rosemount (1998) translation by section and page. When minister Shusun Wushu praises Confucius's disciple Zigong as being better than his master, Zigong replies that it is the high walls surrounding Confucius that deny entry to most and conceal the 'magnificence of the ancestral temple or the lavishness of the estate inside': *Analects* (19.23: 223–4).
30. *Apology* (38a); *Analects* (7.19: 115). See also *Analects* (2.4: 76, 7.2: 111, 7.3: 111).
31. *Apology* (29 b–c); *Meno* (79e–80b). References to *Meno* are to Plato (2004).
32. *Analects* (2.17: 79).
33. Ibid. 9.8: 128. Though he accepts that some are better in doing their utmost (*zhong*) and making good on their word (*xin*), he claims that in a town of 10,000 households 'there will be no one who can compare with me in the love of learning (*haoxue*)' (5.28: 102).
34. *Analects* (16.9: 199, 7.7: 112, 15.39: 192). He therefore distinguishes his students based on their excellence in their conduct, in eloquence, in statesmanship and in the study of culture (11.3: 142). On the diversity of disciples and the unpredictability of talent see (6.12: 106, 9.22: 131).
35. For a general overview of the differences between them see Yu (2005).
36. See, for example, Shih (2013) who traces a version of western natural law approach to, variously, the golden age, *t'en–chih* or the will of God, *dao* and the Canon of Confucian works, and finally reason or law. See also Greer and Lim (1998: 88) on the difference between Confucian and western theories of natural law.

37. Some such as Huang (2006: 324–9) argue that the virtues, especially *ren* or benevolence, provide the unity between 'man' and 'nature'. See in this context Hou (1997) on the harmony of nature and humanity and Bai (2020) who explores the nature and meaning of Confucian benevolence in a modern context.

38. *Analects* (11.26: 148–51); see Huang (2006: 318).

39. On the importance of *tian* in human affairs see, for example, *Analects* (7: 23, 12: 5, 17: 19, 20: 1).

40. *Analects* (17: 2, 203). See Dubs (1930) who argues Confucius never mentions the problem of human nature though there is the consensus that human nature is the endowment of Heaven. On equality, contrast the different views of Confucius (*Analects* 6.21, 17.2, 8.9) with those of Mencius regarding the human potential for 'merit' and also see Bai (2020: 44ff.).

41. *Analects* (12: 16, 157).

42. Generally interpreted as 'benevolence', its meaning ranges from the discipline of ritual action, filial piety and love of people to moral education of oneself. Thus, it can be seen in general acts such as caring for others (*Analects* 12: 22) or specific actions, including reticence in speaking (12: 3), avoiding clever speech (1: 3), and general respect and loyalty in dealing with others (13: 19). As these examples indicate, there is an intrinsic connection between personal development, the duties owed to family and the larger community, and more expansively to the natural order that encompasses all. See generally the discussion in Hou (1997) regarding *Tian Ren He Yi* or the harmony between humanity and nature.

43. *Analects* (4.1: 89, 6.23: 108–9).

44. Ibid. 6.30: 110.

45. Confucius appropriated and transformed terms that were traditionally used for social status. For example, *junzi* is literally 'ruler's son' but subsequently came to interpreted as 'gentleman', and *shi* originally referred to the lower nobility or 'knightly' class before becoming associated with 'scholar'. For a review of the key moral terms see Nivison (1999).

46. *Analects* (19.12: 221).

47. Ibid. 12.19: 158. Indeed, the 'common people' is an important theme in the advice he gives: see generally (2.19: 80, 2.20: 80, 14.41: 182).

48. Ibid. 7.34: 118–19. Confucius playfully suggests he may not have the ability of the *junzi*: *Analects* (14.28: 178; see also 9.6).

49. Ibid. 15.8: 186.

50. Ibid. 13.3: 162. There are a number of observations regarding the duties of officers (see 1.5: 72), how to employ ministers (3.19: 86), and primacy of good leadership over defence and food (12.7: 155; 20.2: 228).

51. Ibid. 8.13: 123.

52. Ibid.
53. Ibid. 6.8: 105.
54. Ibid. 8.21: 125.
55. Ibid. 13.11: 164–5.
56. Ibid 9.16: 130.
57. Ibid. 13.10: 164.
58. Ibid. 17.1: 202.
59. Ibid. 11.2: 142.
60. Ibid. 17.5: 204.
61. Ibid. 17.7: 205.
62. When in office, at a rank below high officials, his advice to send an army to punish Chen Chengzi who had assassinated his lord is referred by Duke Jian to the heads of the Three Families who refuse his petition (*Analects* 14.21: 177). When Duke Ling of Wey asks him about military formations, he replies he knows about use of ritual vessels but has never studied military matters, leaving the state the next day (15.1: 184). Duke Jing of Qi, hosting Confucius, ranks him between the Ji and Meng clans, but says he is unable to make use of him, whereupon Confucius takes his leave (18.3: 213).
63. *Analects* (14.35: 180).
64. Ibid. 2.21: 80.
65. Ibid. 4.14: 92; 9.7: 127.
66. Ibid. 18.8: 216.
67. Ibid. 14.32; Confucius (2013: II, Sect. I. ii. 20).
68. See Plato *Apology* (38a). The extent to which such a critical review is salutary for politics is a profound question for Socrates, theoretically and of course personally: see, for example, Leibowitz (2010).
69. Generally framed in Rousseauian and Kantian terms of 'selfhood', 'autonomy' and authenticity. On whether Confucianism makes room for 'individuals' compare, for example, Ames (1991); Ho (1995); Rosemont (1997) with those who see important elements of individualism: Tu (1972); Zhao (2009); and Brindley (2009).
70. There is an extensive scholarship on this divergence, most of which attempts to show the commonality between them: see generally Whitlock (1953).
71. On the debates regarding the role of the family in Confucian thought see Sarkissian (2010); Barbalet (2013); Liu (2007); Li (2012).
72. All the Socratic dialogues directly or implicitly engage with questions concerning the gods. On a direct confrontation with the question of the divine see the *Euthyphro* on whether the good is said to limit the gods; the gods are defended in the *Laws*; the *Statesman* examines the demiurge; *Parmenides* discusses the nature of being; and *Timaeus* explores the divine origins of the world. More generally, the question of justice in the *Republic* raises the problem of a providential god; the discussions concerning eros are unavoidably linked to a notion of

transcendent union with the divine (*Symposium*); death raises questions regarding the immortality of the soul (*Phaedo*).

73. *Republic* (377a ff.).

74. *Apology* (20c–24e).

75. See Confucius's autobiographical statement noted above (*Analects* 2.4: 76–7) and his numerous references to *tian*: (7.23: 116, 17.19: 208). For the importance of the divine in Chinese thought see generally Meir and Weller (1959); Lagerwey and Kalinowski (2009); Jaffe (2015).

76. As Zigong states, 'We can learn from the Master's cultural refinements, but do not hear him discourse on subjects such as our "natural disposition (xing)" and "the way of tian (tiandao)"' (*Analects* 5.13: 98). In the *Analects* we have the observation that 'The Master had nothing to say about strange happenings, the use of force, disorder, or the spirits' (7.21: 115).

77. The scholarship on Confucius and religion is broadly divided between those who question such theology or 'transcendence', see, for example, Hall and Ames (1987), and others who see a more significant religious aspect in Confucian thought, even if it is founded on ritual or *li* and not theistic or metaphysical principles: see, for example, Eno (1990); Kupperman (1971); Tucker (1998); Yong (2007); Sun (2013).

78. *Analects* (6.22: 108).

79. Ibid. 11.12: 144.

80. See, for example, Li and Perkins (2015).

81. See the discussion in Perkin (2007: 159).

82. See Perkins (2007) on the five stages of evolution of universities and compare with Scott (2006).

83. For an overview of the scholarship on the literati see Patapan and Wang Yi (2018). For a historical and cultural overview see Balazs (1964).

84. See Lynn (2005) who outlines the different origins of the modern bureaucracy and their developments as a result of Imperial French, Napoleonic, Prussian, English and American contexts.

85. On the affinity between Weber and Hegel see Avineri (1972); Jackson (1986).

86. On the influence of Weber see Rosser (2018); Fry and Nigro (1996).

87. See Shaw (1992: 383).

88. Ibid. 384.

89. Weber (1978: 24–6).

90. Hegel (2002: paras 287–97).

91. Ibid. paras 290–1.

92. Ibid. paras 291, 294.

93. Ibid.

94. Ibid. paras 205, 297.

95. Ibid. paras 283, 289.
96. On New Public Management (NPM) as well as use of key performance indicators, short-term contracts and golden handshakes in performance management of senior civil servants see generally Aucoin
(2012). On bureaucracy and the public good see Cooper's (2012)
'responsible administrator'; Moore's (1995) 'public value'; Rohr's
(1988) 'administrative discretion'; and Frederickson and Hart's
(1985) 'benevolence'. For a Weberian critique of such an approach
see Rhodes and Wanna (2007).

Chapter 6

The Scientist as Modern Benefactor

New Atlantis, Francis Bacon's 1626 incomplete and posthumous novel, depicts the ideal country of Bensalem administered by Salomon's House, the 'eye of the kingdom', a college of wise and philanthropic sages who will employ Bacon's new instruments and experiments to relieve man's estate.[1] *New Atlantis* anticipates how Bacon's discoveries would lay the foundations for a new society administered by scientists that would presage a life of health, wealth and peace. Though Bacon's unfinished novel seemed fanciful and far-fetched, in due course the claim that scientists should take a much more active role in politics assumed increasing prominence and support. Science was disinterested and its hard-won objective knowledge implicitly endorsed a notion of the common good. Politics, on the other hand, was subjective, partial and incoherent, leading to wasteful, inefficient and dangerous public policy. It therefore made a great deal of sense to have scientists take a greater role in politics, though the nature of this involvement and its implications for both science and politics remained less clear. For some, science could play a valuable advisory role, providing important insights for making better policy. For others who were more ambitious, there was the hope that scientific insights and methods would not only supplement but in due course supplant politics and politicians, leading to a new world of scientific rule. Here then we had a new manifestation of the paradox of the philosopher king and the ambition to resolve it on modern terms, where the philosopher is the scientist and rule is justified not on the basis of individual character and judgement, but on incontrovertible and demonstrated scientific truths. Does the rule by the modern scientist conclusively solve the paradox of the philosopher king? We begin to explore this question by examining the difference between the philosopher and the modern scientist and the increasing authority of science and scientists and their political role as advisors and rulers. We then evaluate the powerful contemporary headwinds against scientist advisors and kings, and in our concluding comments question whether ethical, democratic and philosophical challenges to science and scientists reassert in new terms the paradox of the philosopher king.

Philosopher as Scientist

The term scientist, an admixture of Latin and Greek, was coined by William Whewell in *The Quarterly Review* in 1834, in his attempt to reassert a unity to 'students of the knowledge of the material world' who tended to specialise into separate areas and subfields. Though initially resisted, it soon became the preferred term to describe what was formerly called the 'man of science' and the 'natural philosopher'.[2] The need to devise a new name and the reluctance by some to embrace it indicates that the term 'scientist' articulated deeper philosophical contests over the meaning of philosophy that had far-reaching epistemological, methodological and cosmological implications. *Scientificus* or scientific knowledge was the scholastic or Christian Aristotelian Latin term approximating Aristotle's concept of demonstrated knowledge that drew on *nous* and employed syllogism to demonstrate knowledge. Aristotle distinguished between theoretical sciences (such as physics or the study of *phusis* or nature, mathematics and theology), practical science that looked to knowledge of *praxis* or practical action, and *techne* or art of how to make things.[3] Following Aristotle, scholastics distinguished between branches of philosophy, such as grammar, logic, rhetoric, arithmetic, music, geometry and astronomy, and later between natural, moral and first or metaphysical philosophy.[4] The shift from philosophy to science took place after the publication of Francis Bacon's *Novum Organum* in 1620 where he promotes a new understanding of science as demonstrated knowledge, now requiring instruments, experiments and the work of many individuals over a long time to refine and clarify former partial truths. The goal of the sciences was therefore to endow human life 'with new discoveries and powers'.[5] This new goal transformed the meaning of science, from the contemplative life moved by curiosity in favour of pursing knowledge for the 'relief of man's estate'.[6] It was a transformation aided by the increasing success of the new sciences, so that in time philosophy was reserved to theology and metaphysics, while the more successful natural and physical philosophy became science, where any true knowledge could only be gained by examination of the material world. The increasing success and authority of the sciences led to distinctions between, for example, mathematics and chemistry, and within each even greater specialisation, prompting Whewell to propose the new term 'scientist' to comprehend this new diversity.

In addition to the Baconian method, the scientist was the child of theoretical and institutional innovations. These changes included a novel conception of cosmology, broadly captured by the idea of a scientific revolution that brought into being new disciplines of study and research, a new openness evident in the publications of latest findings and the foundation of new institutions such as the Royal Society of London for Improving Natural Knowledge (1662), and the Académie des Sciences of Paris (1666) where findings were made public and disseminated widely. The starting point for these changes was astronomy and especially Nicolaus Copernicus's (1473–1543) *De revolutionibus orbium coelestium libri VI* (*Six Books Concerning the Revolutions of the Heavenly Orbs*) published in 1543 and drawing on the observations of Tycho Brahe (1546–1601), which became a standard reference for advanced problems in astronomical research, particularly for its mathematical techniques. Subsequent findings by Kepler and Galileo transformed classical assumptions, such as the perfect circular motion of the planets, replacing Ptolemaic with heliocentric cosmology. These innovations in astronomy challenged Aristotelian mechanics with its notion of natural place, resulting in Galileo's idea of inertia and parabolic motion. They were aided by a new mechanistic conception of nature developed by René Descartes (1596–1650), founder of modern philosophy, which in turn led to the Dutch physicist Christiaan Huygens formulating the laws of conservation of momentum and of kinetic energy that contributed to Sir Isaac Newton's monumental *Philosophiae Naturalis Principia Mathematica* (1687; *Mathematical Principles of Natural Philosophy*), unifying celestial and terrestrial physics and developing the concept of force to synthesise mechanical philosophy and the mathematisation of nature. The importance of mathematics for modern science is especially evident in modern physics, from Galilean and Newtonian mechanics to the non-Euclidian geometry of curved space–time of Einstein's relativity theory, to the quantum physics of Planck, Bohr, Schrödinger and Heisenberg. Comparable advances in other disciplines such as chemistry, optics and biology and innovations in new disciplines such as genetics all confirm their debt to observational, mechanistic and mathematical elements of modern science.

The extraordinary success of the 'physical' sciences seemed to cast the achievements of the other non-scientific philosophies in poor light. Consequently, some suggested the successful methods of science should now be applied to these other approaches.[7] This approach had been anticipated by Hobbes' (1651) *Leviathan*, founded on materialism and positivism, Locke's (1689) *Essay Concerning Human Understanding* that rejected innate ideas, and Hume's (1739) *A Treatise of Human Nature*, defending empiricism and questioning causality and the Enlightenment *philosophes*, especially Condorcet. It was taken up in earnest in the nineteenth century by Auguste Comte (1842), who in his *The Course of Positive Philosophy* advocated 'sociology', a term he invented to encompass all the sciences on a new positivist foundation. Influenced by Comte, J. S. Mill (1845), who thought the 'moral sciences' were 'progressing towards the abstract and deductive character of classical physics', attempted to found a new positivistic social science, evident in his *A System of Logic* where he sought to reform and expand logic with a new 'inductive' approach.[8] Similar attempts at a science of society could be discerned in Spencer's *The Synthetic Philosophy* (1862–96). Even Weber, who along with Durkheim and others questioned such an approach, advocated 'value free' sociology.[9] But such initiatives in establishing a comprehensive social science did not succeed, and were replaced by a diversity of disciplines that sought to replicate the success of science.[10] Economics, for example, which had previously been *oikonomicus* or the art of household management, was for Adam Smith 'political economy' and by the time of Alfred Marshall's (1890) *Principles of Economics* had become neoclassical economics that relied on mathematics to combine the laws of supply and demand and the psychology of utility maximisation to develop a comprehensive scientific approach. It would change again with subsequent use of differential calculus, linear models and game theory.[11] Other disciplines, such as psychology, sociology, anthropology and politics would take similar approaches, inevitably deferring, either in 'methodology', research design or ambition, to scientific principles and methods, though with variable enthusiasm and limited success.[12]

Science as Philosophy and Politics

If the scientist is the modern philosopher king, we need to examine whether the modern scientist is identical to the philosopher and the related question of how the scientist engages with politics. Early modern scientific innovators were clearly also philosophers, as we can see from the writings of Bacon, Descartes and Newton.[13] The case for modern scientists is more complex.[14] Certainly to the extent that the Baconian scientific method succeeded in doing away with metaphysical speculations in favour of simple experimentation that was at least in principle within the province of everyone, a speculative or philosophical disposition in its broadest sense is not required for the average scientist in a laboratory. And the increasing dominance and complexity of modern mathematics in science suggests that it is now difficult for any one individual to contribute to both science and philosophy in a profound way – though Schrödinger and Heisenberg were familiar with Eastern philosophy, the specialisation and all too consuming nature of modern scientific research seems to leave little room for philosophical speculation.[15] Practically, this means philosophical innovations draw on scientific discoveries, rather than being their source, suggesting that major philosophical debates may now be taking place in physics rather than philosophy. Relativity theory and quantum theory, for example, have raised profound questions concerning the nature of space and time, causality and the origins and future of the universe.[16]

The scientist therefore was a new form of philosopher who used new methods and mathematics to discover general laws of nature that could be exploited to benefit the public. What, then, was the nature of the relationship between scientist and politics? The bounty of science, evident in the daily announcements of recent discoveries and innovations that would save and improve lives, increase efficiency and raise the standard of living, was persuasive proof of the public benefit of the scientific enterprise. It also presented scientists in an exceptionally favourable light, giving them unprecedented public respect and therefore political legitimacy and authority. Scientists now had the opportunity to influence politics in profound ways. For many scientists, reminiscent of the very origins of science as a natural philosophy, this was a temptation to be avoided because the fundamental disjunction between science and politics meant scientific research and discovery should avoid being tainted through political engagement. History provided ample evidence of the high price paid by science for its entanglement with politics, as the cases of ideologically informed but scientifically worthless Soviet or Nazi science demonstrated.[17] It was true that modern 'Big Science', such as the CERN accelerator, the Hubble Space Telescope and the Human Genome Project demanded substantial government support, but beyond seeking funding from government and private corporations, most scientists were happy to remain politically disengaged. For others, however, the new-found authority was the means to fulfil their ambition to pursue their political causes. Einstein, for example, would use his new-found fame and authority to defend democracy.[18] But more systematic initiatives to engage with politics took two divergent forms.[19] The first was the attempt to have more scientific politics, which entailed having scientists as an integral part of the governmental decisions on public policy, a very specific form of the philosopher as advisor to rulers we explored above. The second was more radical, seeking to reform politics to make it altogether scientific, transforming the scientist into a modern philosopher king. Whether direct or mediated, what was distinctive to both approaches was the fundamentally new foundation for political rule that did not rely on the well-trod paths to political power, exploiting wealth, family name or influential connections, or a record of achievement in public office to gain office. In contrast, the scientist's sole claim to political authority was scientific knowledge and discoveries that questioned ordinary or common sense, as we can see from the scientific truths that white light was made of many colours of the spectrum; that the natural state of any object was not rest; and that the sun did not revolve around the earth.[20] The new conception of philosophy therefore seemed to represent a successful union of science and politics, either as the scientist as advisor and potentially the hidden philosopher king, or more ambitiously the scientist king. We will examine each in turn to evaluate the extent to which each could justifiably claim to be a modern resolution of the paradox of the philosopher king.

Scientific Advisors

To what extent was the scientist as advisor to political leaders sufficiently distinctive to surmount the problems we discerned in the hidden philosopher king? In addition to the distinction between scientific knowledge and political judgement or prudence, the relationship between scientist and political leader was complicated by questions concerning the motives of both scientist and political leader. Did the scientist seek to counsel as a matter of duty or public service or were there other motives, such as bargaining for increased governmental funding to support research or, more directly, personal wealth and prestige? Equally, it was unclear whether rulers sought scientific advice for the obvious advantage of implementing evidence-based policy, or merely for trading on the legitimacy of scientists, having already decided on what was politically expedient. Clearly the answers to these questions would depend on each specific case, yet the very need to understand and explain these relationships suggests that the scientific advisor did not avoid the doubts about these relationships, that we noted in our discussion of philosophers as counsellors to rulers.[21]

Moreover, given the focus on scientific expertise as the basis and justification for the advisor role, larger foundational questions persisted. An enduring and distinctive concern was whether scientific knowledge could remain disinterested once it enters the political arena, or if it would inevitably be corrupted by political compromises. Initially this did not seem to present insuperable obstacles, as the American experience indicated. The decisive importance of science in the Second World War, and especially success of the Manhattan Project, the Second World War American initiative to build nuclear bombs, augured the prospect of salutary future scientific involvement in formulating public policy.[22] It was in this spirit that the office of science advisor to the president was created, systems analysis was deployed for making key decisions in the armed services on force requirements and weapon systems and scientists took an active role in nuclear policy.[23] The early optimism regarding the beneficial deployment of scientific advice in major policy initiatives soon gave way, however, to a more measured view of the promise of science, due in part to the complexity of policy making and the question concerning the politicisation of science. We therefore see the early optimism of Herbert Simon's *Administrative Behavior* (1947) now moderated by his acceptance of 'satisficing', an awkward neologism that combined 'satisfy' and 'suffice' as a replacement for 'maximising' or even 'optimising' alternatives.[24] Similarly, Charles E. Lindblom's criticism of rational models of decision making would find expression in his influential article 'The Science of "Muddling Through"' (1959), replacing the 'rational-comprehensive' approach with 'successive limited comparisons'.

As a consequence, there were increased attempts to understand the role of scientific advisor and the nature of the relationship between advisors and policy makers, evident in the various attempts to devise typologies of scientific advisors to understand who they were and the nature of advice they offered.[25] There was also increased focus on the institutional context and the extent to which it affected scientific advice.[26] For scientists who advocated taking part in the policy process, it was important to provide technical and scientific information as opposed to personal policy preferences.[27] Others who were critical of such an approach showed how scientific consensus may not exist or differ according to a specific discipline, while more radically, some argued that science was unavoidably normative and therefore the best way to proceed was to acknowledge this fact, raising the question of whether science and politics were in effect indistinguishable.[28] Whatever the substance of these debates, their complexity and range of concerns clearly showed that the scientist as advisor did not escape the problems of advisors more generally. Indeed, it seemed the new source of authority – scientific knowledge – generated a new set of questions concerning the ontology and epistemology of science in general, differences between disciplines within science, and most radically, the core challenge to the veracity of scientific knowledge itself. The scientific advisor was now doubly vulnerable as an advisor and as a scientist.

Scientific Kings

The challenges and complexities faced by scientists as political advisors suggest that the problems of the hidden philosopher king we examined reappear in the scientist as advisor to rulers but with a new complexity derived from the source of authority and the specific area of expertise. Less evident though present from the very foundations of modern science was a different conception of the relationship between scientists and politics. As we saw from Bacon's *New Atlantis*, this consisted of a much more ambitious role for the scientist, where science would in due course supplant politics so that scientists would rule. Such a solution promised a reasonable, efficient and prosperous world that displaced and relegated to history the partiality, corruption, inefficiency and instability that was the hallmark of all politics. In other words, the scientist as king was present as a potential solution to the human condition from the inception of modern science and has persisted as a possibility in various forms ever since. Consider, for example, Hobbes' *Leviathan* where he sought to transform politics into a form of administration to secure peace and thereby commerce and innovation. A more recent formulation of this ambition was Henri de Saint-Simon's vision in his *Essay on the Science of Man* (2014) of the rule by 'enlightened elites' of scientists and artists that would allow science to transcend politics. These views were endorsed, as we saw, variously by Hegel, who in *Philosophy of Right* (1814) envisaged rule by able bureaucrats, and similarly Comte, considered the originator of modern positivism and first modern philosopher of science who proposed in *Course on Positive Philosophy* (1830–42) a new scientific rule that would be favoured by the public since it was not founded on unreasoning belief.[29]

The hope of reconstituting all politics on a scientific foundation shows the enduring influence and fascination with the idea of the philosopher king. In its modern formulation it has been interpreted as a modified form of the scientist king or technocracy, rule by experts or technocrats.[30] The term 'technocracy' is attributed to the economist John Clark, though it was also used by William Henry Smyth, a Californian engineer, who used the word to describe 'the rule of the people made effective through the agency of their servants, the scientists and engineers'.[31] The technocracy movement was influential in America after the First World War, commencing with Frederick W. Taylor, who argued that industrial problems needed to be solved scientifically. The need to have scientific management of industry, and later society as a whole, was embraced by the Progressive reform movement which favoured a more rational form of government. Its early advocates included Thornstein Veblen who promoted engineering principles to address policy problems, and Howard Smyth who instituted a National Council of Scientists to control all national institutions. Veblen's *Engineers and the Price System* (1921) became a manifesto for the technocracy movement, with the radical engineer Howard Scott forming the Technical Alliance (1919) of scientists and engineers in New York, and after its disbandment in the mid-1920s, founding with Walter Rautenstrauch the Committee on Technocracy in 1932 with the intention of getting scientists and engineers to work together to overcome the effects of the Depression and lead to new abundance.[32] European attempts to transform politics in this way included the Manifesto of the Vienna Circle, launched in 1929 by the sociologist and economist Otto Neurath, the philosopher and logician Rudolf Carnap, and the mathematician Hans Hahn with the intention to realise an enlightened, rational and science-oriented society and culture.[33]

By the 1930s the need to restructure society along rational and scientific lines received wide support, though the lack of clarity concerning the political implications of these reforms meant the Committee disbanded in 1933. Later movements, Harold Loeb's Committee on Technocracy and Scott's Technocracy, Inc., would be challenged by the New Deal reforms. Subsequent works showed the continuing salience of technocracy, as we can see from J. K Galbraith's (1972) *The New Industrial State* with its new conception of 'technostructure' as indicative of modern post-entrepreneurial capitalism, Daniel Bell's *The Coming of Post-Industrial Society* (1973) pointing to the new 'intellectual technology' and knowledge class where technological decision making opposed ideology, Alvin Gouldner's *The Future of the Intellectuals and the Rise of the New Class* (1979), with its 'technical intelligentsia' and finally Foucault's (1978) 'Birth of Biopolitics' lecture on 'biopower' that showed how technologies of discipline and the new social sciences manifested the increasing power of technological domination disguised by concepts of rationality and productivity.

The idea that government should be run by technical experts has continued to be influential in contemporary thought. The European Union endorsed it as a valuable means for deciding policy.[34] It has been advocated in modern democracies as a tempting alternative to the inefficiency and instability of democratic politics that is especially vulnerable to the dangers of populist leaders, as we can see from the recent examples of the Fischer (Czech Republic) 2009–2010; Papademos (Greece) 2011–12; and Monti (Italy) 2011–13 technocratic governments.[35] It seems to have been the preferred choice for authoritarian regimes, with 'scientific management' the counterpart to Party control.[36] Perhaps the most advanced manifestation of this approach can be found in Singapore, where the government ministers are employed (and paid) on the basis of their technical expertise.[37] Yet as all these examples also demonstrate, there has been no successful example of the scientist king who has ousted politics altogether. Rather there have been various attempts at combining science and politics in the form of technocratic institutions or regimes that at best conceal politics, as in the case of Singapore, or otherwise coexist with it in significant tension, as the politics in the European Union demonstrate.

Decline in Science

Bacon's *New Atlantis* was famously parodied in Jonathan Swift's (1726) *Gulliver's Travels*, which tells the story of the flying island of Laputa populated by experts in mathematics, music, astronomy and technology who keep their island airborne by means of magnetic levitation. Absorbed in listening to the music of the spheres and contemplating the stars, the Laputans seem less able to address their immediate practical needs – not only are they ill dressed and poorly housed (because they do not see the 'human' and therefore use compasses and quadrants instead of tape measures), but they are forced to exercise a form of tyrannical rule over the Balnirabi, the land over which the Laputa hovers. Swift's amusing account of Laputa, recalling Aristophanes' *The Clouds* where Socrates the natural scientist is suspended mid-air in a 'think tank', is a modern reminder of the tension, even contest, that has always existed between the intoxicating charms of philosophical contemplation and the immediate and practical demands of political life. Of course, there have always been lingering doubts and misgivings concerning the human aspiration to acquire knowledge. Adam and Eve were expelled from Paradise for eating of the fruit of the Tree of the Knowledge of Good and Evil.[38] Daedalus was dashed to the ground in his hubristic attempt to fly to the sun. The transformation of philosophy into science seemed to have overcome these concerns by showing the beneficence of science. And, as we have seen, by the twentieth century the role of science seemed so secure that there were increasing demands for scientists as advisors, and even the possibility of realising the new Atlantis in the form of technocratic regimes. Thus the rise of the scientist as a new form of philosopher, and the increasing political authority and legitimacy of both scientist and science, suggested the possibility of a new, more successful version of the modern philosopher king. As we have seen, however, the scientist as advisor was susceptible to the problems of the hidden philosopher king, while the scientist king did not succeed, in effect restating rather than resolving the paradox of the philosopher king. Moreover, even these contingent hopes for the scientist as counsellor or ruler were soon challenged by increasing reservations concerning the goodness and legitimacy of science. Surprisingly these doubts were raised at the height of science's historically unprecedented success in improving the health and prosperity of humanity. The seemingly unconditional support for science was challenged from diverse sources that together raised once more fundamental questions regarding the goodness of science and its technological innovations. We will focus on three distinct yet influential critiques – epistemological, ethical and political – to show how the recently unrivalled authority of science is increasingly questioned, posing fundamental impediments for the hopes of a scientist as modern philosopher king.

A critique of science that goes to the heart of the scientific enterprise questions whether science reveals or uncovers the truth. Bacon indicated nature had to be put on trial to reveal her truths.[39] Galileo (1957) in *The Assayer* claimed the book of nature and the universe was 'written in mathematical language, and the symbols are triangles, circles and other geometrical figures without whose help it is impossible to comprehend a single word of it; without which one wanders in vain through a dark labyrinth'. But what if such trials and mathematical inquisitions did not yield the truth? What if as Locke (1689) showed in his *Essay Concerning Human Understanding*, Hume (1748) in his *An Enquiry Concerning Human Understanding* and Kant (1781–90) in his three *Critiques* there were fundamental limits on human ability to understand nature? And more radically, what if all knowledge, as suggested by Protagoras and Leibniz but influentially developed in modern thought by Nietzsche in *Thus Spoke Zarathustra* and the *Gay Science*, was perspectival, a form of will to power shaped by the character of the viewer?[40] These ontological and epistemological challenges to science became increasingly influential, seemingly endorsed by advances in physics, such as Einstein's general and special relativity with its conception of multiple universes, and quantum mechanics that suggested the observer affects the observed reality. As a consequence, the view that science is merely another truth, a poetic creation or a 'discourse' assumed increasing authority as we can see, for example, in Kuhn's (1970) influential *The Structure of Scientific Revolutions*, where he argued that science does not progress by a linear accumulation of new knowledge but undergoes periodic revolutions through incommensurable 'paradigm shifts'. Similarly, Feyerabend's (1970) *Against Method* argued a historical universal scientific method does not exist and therefore science is like any other ideology and does not deserve its privileged status. Consequently, the view that science and politics were indistinguishable as 'discursive practices' became increasingly influential, discounting the authority of scientists.[41]

These doubts about the truth of scientific insights were compounded by fears concerning the goodness of scientific endeavour.

The moral ambiguity of science was in question from early modernity. Few have been as searing and influential in their critique as Rousseau who was originally a *philosophe* but subsequently impugned the entire Enlightenment project. In his *First Discourse* (1750), an essay that won the Dijon Academy prize, he argued that the arts and sciences corrupt human morality. In doing so he clearly demarcated the ethical from the scientific, depicting in bold terms a continuing and seemingly irreconcilable struggle between the two. He was especially concerned with the way modern society, based on commerce and technology, would lead to the divided and inauthentic bourgeois, an influential insight that became central to Marx's critiques of capitalist alienation. It was depicted most dramatically in Mary Shelley's *Frankenstein*, where the dedicated scientist Frankenstein creates life and in doing so brings into existence a powerful yet desperately lonely creature who lacks any moral scruples in punishing his creator. These fears of an unbridled and dangerous science became a mainstay in subsequent literary and poetical presentation of science, resulting in the new genre of 'science fiction' that continued to depict the dangers of science-initiated dystopias. Though the beneficence of science was evident everywhere, as science assumed increasing political authority its power for good and ill became more visible and questionable. Perhaps the most dramatic manifestation of this ambivalence was the Manhattan Project, which showed the impressive achievement and promise of science, and equally its potential destructiveness, evident in the deathly beauty of the atomic mushroom clouds that wreaked so much devastation on Hiroshima and Nagasaki. The subsequent threat of atomic warfare, 'Mutually Assured Destruction', and long-term dangers of nuclear contamination showed what was at stake with untrammelled science. The view that scientific innovation was not unambiguously good became increasingly influential, abetted by concerns about environmental destruction, especially climate change, genetic engineering and the use of technology by authoritarian states. The various attempts to make science ethically accountable could be seen in the proliferation of ethics codes, from the first, the 1948 Nuremburg Code on medical research involving human subjects, to more recent principles, such as those developed at the 1975 Asilomar Conference by genetic engineers on limits to recombinant DNA research. These initiatives were proof that science was no longer seen as simply benevolent and now had to be accountable for what and how it pursued its research.[42]

The third powerful impulse that draws on the perspectival and unethical implications of science is perhaps the most formidable because it is political.[43] Our discussion above has anticipated the democratic concerns with science.[44] Technocracy or 'epistocracy' indicate by their very terms they are not ruled by the 'demos' or the many. But unlike the historical challengers to democracy, such as the rule of the *aristoi* or best, or even *oligarchy* or rule by the few wealthy, this new minority or in modern terms 'elite' derives its political legitimacy from *episteme* or knowledge.[45] This new source of authority accounts for the core tension or paradox in modern democracies that as Tocqueville showed, favour scientific innovation yet fear that a reliance on an 'expert' undermines the democratic notion of popular sovereignty.[46] Scientists in democracies are therefore both celebrated and viewed as 'elite' and undemocratic.[47] Consequently, there has been extensive debate on whether scientific elites exist, the nature of their influence and power, and whether they pose a threat to modern democracies.[48] This debate has been complicated and recast by the increasing democratisation of science, resulting in the proliferation of experts and expertise and an expansion in the number and types of institutions and institutional bases for experts beyond universities to include think-tanks and consultancy firms. Perhaps this was the inevitable trajectory of the Enlightenment's replacement of the Bible with the *Encyclopédie* and now Wikipedia, celebrating democracy by recognising the 'wisdom of the crowds', anticipated by Aristotle and now advocated by epistemic democrats.[49] Just as the claims for science are being challenged, the primacy of scientists is now being questioned, as we can see in the increasing legitimacy of participatory or deliberative practices in technical decision making. Consequently, this dispersal of expertise has now made the important threshold question of who is an 'expert' more difficult to answer, resulting in new attempts to reconcile science with democracy.[50]

These three challenges to the ascendency of science have not of course rejected science altogether. Science and technology now play such an integral role in modernity that it seems impossible to abandon them without profound and far-reaching economic and political consequences. In any case, technological innovations are proceeding at such a pace and are so comprehensively and enthusiastically favoured and adopted that it is hard to resist their force. So the contemporary concerns with scientist as a philosopher king and the lingering doubts about the goodness of science itself, with its authoritarian impulses, coexist with a wholehearted and almost unthinking embrace of scientist as innovator and public benefactor.

Back to the Future

Unlike the classical natural philosophers who avoided political entanglements, the modern scientists made their peace with politics by agreeing to devote their research to the benefit of humanity. In doing so they seemed to combine wisdom and power, seemingly realising the promise of the philosopher kings. But the two manifestations of this ambition, in the form of scientific advisors to political leaders or, more ambitiously, scientists as kings, confronted significant obstacles. The scientific advisor appeared to reanimate the problems we discerned in the hidden philosopher king, while the scientist king confronted the challenge of modern democratic politics where sovereignty resided with the people. Both also faced epistemological, ethical and political challenges to the scientific enterprise, questioning altogether the promise of the scientist as the modern philosopher king. The nature and diversity of the forces arrayed against the scientific enterprise suggest that the exceptionally favourable circumstances for the scientist king have now faded, with no prospect of imminent return. We therefore now confront a curious case of a wholehearted commitment to the fruits of science, accompanied with increasing scepticism regarding its moral and theoretical standing. This situation may not be significant were it not for the nature of contemporary scientific innovations that seem to promise a transformation in our conception of what it means to be human, the nature of the family, and the structure of political organisations. Rather than the scientist king, we now have science that is not simply unlimited but rather managed and controlled in partial, unpredictable and unexpected ways. We therefore seem to be drifting to new worlds, without the promise of the scientist king to guide us.[51]

Notes

1. For an overview of the way Bacon turns to instruments and experiments to correct defects in human senses see Prior (1954).
2. See Ross (1991) who provides an extensive discussion of the origin of the word, its subsequent popularity and unsuccessful attempts to reject its use.
3. *Nicomachean Ethics* (1094a–95a 10).

4. See generally Marenbon (2012).
5. Bacon (1960: I, lxxxi). For an overview of the major developments see Heller (2011).
6. See Bacon (2019: 4, 30).
7. On the history of social sciences see Cravens (1985).
8. For a comparison of Mill and Comte see Lewisohn (1972).
9. See generally his *Economy and Society* (1978).
10. See generally Trompf (1977), and in particular the exception or middle position of historical studies.
11. For a history see Weintraub (2002).
12. Leaving in the 'fringe', as Trompf (1977: 137) puts it, 'those branches of social enquiry called humanities, not social sciences. They include classical studies, literary and art criticism, theology and religious studies, philosophy (including ethics and socio-political theory), and sometimes history'.
13. Newton, for example, was a well-known theologian.
14. Thus Hall (1988) suggests that Leibnitz was the last philosopher to make a significant contribution to both philosophy and science. On a thoughtful discussion of the relations between the two see Parrini (2012).
15. On the possible tension between the two see Cimatti's (2018) exploration of the thought of the oncologist Giorgio Prodi. Interdisciplinary research can be seen as one attempt to address these challenges: see de Melo-Martin (2009).
16. See Parrini (2012). For an overview of the philosophical implications of relativity theory see Heller (2011). For the philosophical implications of major scientific discoveries see Weinert (2005). As Bowler (2000: 100) argues in the case of Lyell, Darwin, Owen and Pearson, 'On the model of scientific creativity I am suggesting, rational argument often plays a surprisingly limited role in the decisions that shape the choice of world view or research strategy. If philosophy is called in, it is to defend the resulting positions after they have been constructed on the basis of what the scientists did by instinct or intuition.'
17. See Ulam (1973); Renneberg and Walker (1994).
18. On the *bildung* of Einstein and his philosophical commitment to democracy see Scheideler (2002).
19. Distinguished by Ezrahi (1980) as pragmatic and utopian rationalists.
20. For an overview of the nature of science see Williams (2000).
21. See in this context the discussion of the vocational role of scientists by Shapin (2008, 2010). For a specific example of these tensions in the context of statistical agencies see Howard (2021).
22. For an overview of the American experience see Kimball-Smith (1971) and Strickland (1968) on the 'atomic scientists' movement'.

For an overview of the role of scientists after the war see Wang (1999, 2002).

23. For an early overview of developments see Leiserson (1965). Pielke and Klein (2010) review Eisenhower's 1957 appointment of James Killian as Science Advisor to the President and the subsequent decline of that office. On systems theory and MacNamara's regrets regarding the Vietnam War see MacNamara (1995). On the scientific contribution to nuclear policy see, for example, Gilpin (1962) and Rubinson (2011).

24. See Simon (1947).

25. On the different roles of scientists see Gilbert and Mulkay (1984) and on notional typologies (e.g. of Pure Scientist, Science Arbiter, Issue Advocate and Honest Broker of Policy) see Pielke (2007).

26. As Ezrahi (1980) argues, the contested nature of scientific advice and the potential to politicise science or to make politics scientific could be traced to the specific policy area and the extent to which there is consensus on the facts, the science, the means and the objectives of the policy. See, for example, Hay (1982) for an overview of the National Academy of Sciences; Gluckman (2016) on 'science diplomacy'; Gluckman and Wilsdon (2016) on advice to governments; and Steele (2012) on scientists and 'value judgements'.

27. Thus Lackey (2007) distinguishes in ecology policy between policy neutral and policy inculcated scientific information, and Caplan and Marino (2007) note the problem of scientific answers to the question of when does human life begin, especially in the context of abortion or cell therapy.

28. See the discussion by von Schomberg (1993) in the context of epistemic debate about the ecological effects of the deliberate release of genetically engineered organisms. Machamer and Wolters (2004) argue that values determined the problems selected for examination and the way insights were applied. On the latter see Schweber (2013) on the moral responsibility of scientists concerning nuclear research. On whether science and politics were indistinguishable see, for example, Brown and Malone (2004).

29. On the importance of morality for Hegel's bureaucracy see Jackson (1986).

30. For an overview see Fischer (1990); Burris (1993).

31. Smyth used the term 'Technocracy' in his 1919 article '"Technocracy" – Ways and Means to Gain Industrial Democracy' in the journal *Industrial Management*.

32. See generally Nelson (1980); Akin (1977).

33. For an overview of these scientific movements in the 1920s and 1930s see Mormann (2017). The Vienna Circle contributed with American pragmatists to the International Encyclopedia of Unified Science, with the aim to make scientific knowledge accessible to a general

public thereby fostering a general 'scientific worldview' for society as a whole. As Mormann notes, 'By the 1950s at the latest the project of the Encyclopedia had faded away and the issue of global scientific promises and scientific worldviews gradually disappeared from the agenda of mainstream philosophy of science' (Mormann 2017: 191).

34. For technocracy and the European Union see Radaelli (1999).
35. McDonnell and Valbruzzi (2014) list the twenty-four technocrat-led governments that have existed in twenty-seven European Union democracies from the end of the Second World War until June 2013. For an overview in Europe see Pastorella (2016) and Turner (2013). On professionals in global policy making see Sending (2015).
36. On Chinese technocracy see, for example, the scholarship on meritocracy: Bell (2015); Bell and Li (2013).
37. On Singaporean technocracy see Barr (2006); Jayasuriya and Rodan (2007).
38. Gen. (2: 17).
39. See, however, Pesic (1999) who shows the limits to the conventional view that Bacon advocated the 'torture' of nature.
40. For Nietzsche's influence on the debate, see, for example Brooks (2010) on the nature of the scientist.
41. See, for example, Brown and Malone (2004: 118) who draw on Bourdieu to argue science and politics are 'discursive practices – though each conducted within a distinct institutional domain', allowing them to shift from epistemological to 'social norms'.
42. See, for example Patapan (2015); Frankel (1989) on professional codes; Judd (2009) for an overview.
43. See generally Greenberg (1999); Guston (2010).
44. Consider, for example, Ezrahi (1990); Mormann (2017); O'Brien (2013); Yankelovich (2003).
45. On 'epistocracy' see Estlund (2008b) and more generally Bertsou and Caramani (2020).
46. On Tocqueville's (2000) insights see *Democracy in America*, Book 2.
47. See Bijker et al. (2009) and Weingart (1999) on the paradox of scientific authority, and Thorpe (2002) on scientific authority in liberal democracy.
48. For an early account of 'elites' as a 'New Priesthood' see Lapp (1965). On more sceptical views see Greenberg (1965); Weingart (1982); on scientists as an 'Elite Reserve Labor Force' see generally Mukerji (1989).
49. See also Ezrahi (1990) on the 'privatisation of science'.
50. For an overview of the nature of the recent challenges as well as epistemic and institutional means to address them see Maasen and Weingart (2005).
51. See generally Patapan (2015).

Chapter 7

The Wise and Sovereign People

The philosopher king, both as a paradox and a promise, challenges all regimes by introducing wisdom as the new, preeminent qualification for rule. But this new source of authority is especially problematic for democracy, understood in its most general signification as the regime where the people are sovereign. The democratic principle of equality presumes parity in wisdom and judgement, justifying the sovereignty of all. Consequently, the democratic presumption that no one person is sufficiently wise to warrant sole rule makes the people wary and suspicious of any attempts to do so, regarding claims in the name of wisdom as in effect concealed oligarchic or tyrannical attempts at usurping democratic rule. Indeed, the modern democratic impulse, as we have seen, tends to disperse power to increase participation, rather than focusing and concentrating authority.[1] It would therefore seem that democracy is the regime most opposed to the philosopher king so that the increasing contemporary authority of democracy portends the end of the modern philosopher king as a practical, if not theoretical, possibility.[2]

Upon closer inspection, however, we see a more complicated picture of democracy's response to the philosopher king and, more generally, the relationship between philosophy and democracy, characterised by two divergent impulses that vie for authority.[3] The first, as we will see, is an attempt to accommodate philosophy within the regime of popular sovereignty by locating and securing it within specific institutions overseen by larger representative structures. This solution is to be contrasted with the more ambitious democratic alternative, which claims that appropriate deliberative settings will allow 'the people' to become philosophers and sovereign, conclusively resolving the potential tensions between wisdom and power. Both approaches suggest that democracy provides the conclusive solution to the problem of philosopher king, not by rejecting wisdom but by democratising it by dispersing philosopher kings, either by locating them within institutions or by regarding the people together as the philosopher king. The success of these measures and their implications for both philosophy and politics is the core theme of this chapter. We start with the formidable obstacle, the longstanding view that democracy is inherently anti-intellectual, first articulated in the classical discussions of the ambiguous place of wisdom in democracies, followed by modern elite theorists who reject democratic rule on normative and empirical grounds.[4] As we will see, Tocqueville, the foremost theorist of modern democracy, reveals a more complicated picture, with his examination of American democracy indicating that modern democracy is not anti-intellectual but selective in its preference for practical and utilitarian insights over the abstract or theoretical. Having shown the openness of democracy to wisdom, however contingent, selective or subtle, we then examine the first possibility of the people as philosopher kings, the attempts to combine and reconcile wisdom and power in specific democratic institutions. Our exploration of distinctly democratic institutions, such as parliament, representative democracy, cabinet and opposition and specific institutions such as the judiciary and the reserve bank shows how democracy attempts to accommodate and reconcile wisdom with democratic sovereignty. As our discussion shows, these dispersed and protected philosopher kings represent the liberal remedy to the challenge philosophy presents to democracy, increasingly assailed by claims that these institutions are undemocratic and no longer serve the demands of modern citizens.[5] We therefore turn to the second democratic solution to the philosopher king, the deliberative and epistemic democrats who in effect attempt to replace the king with the infallible people, and in doing so provide the modern union and reconciliation of wisdom and power. The feasibility of this definitive solution to the paradox, and fulfilment of the promise of the philosopher king forms the substance of our concluding reflections.

Democratic Anti-intellectualism

A perennial charge against democracy is that it is fundamentally opposed to the life of the mind. But the democratic record seems genuinely ambiguous on this point. Athens was much more open to ideas, discussion and innovation than any other regime as Pericles proudly boasted in his famous Funeral Oration, though it did take all his authority to save his teacher Anaxagoras from public persecution.[6] Of course Athens is especially notorious for having put Socrates to death, yet it is also true that it let Socrates philosophise his entire life.[7] Oligarchs have always accused the democrats of being 'nothing more than beasts', and the fear of the 'many', the 'plebs', the 'mob' as an uneducated and unthinking force has been a perennial charge against democrats, even as *Vox Populi* has been celebrated as *Vox Dei*.[8] This ambiguity is evident in the critiques of modern democracy. Though celebrated for its commitment to equality and therefore justice, it was also accused of the new menace of 'soft despotism', using its numerical superiority to silence alternative views essential for innovation and progress.[9] In contemporary debates the critique of democracy has focused on the claim that democracy is inherently hostile to political meritocracy, or rule by those who are superior in ability and virtue.[10] Using Confucian meritocracy as the ideal, this critique of democracy argues the principle of one person, one vote is an obstacle to fostering excellence.[11] In a similar vein, electoral democracy and therefore the democratic commitment to merit is considered vulnerable to various forms of tyranny endemic to modern democracies.[12] Thus the 'anti-intellectualism' of democracy, especially its inability to favour and sustain merit, is a formidable threshold question to be resolved before we can examine the way democracy confronts the paradox of the philosopher king.

But what exactly is anti-intellectualism? A useful starting point for a definition of anti-intellectualism can be found in Hofstadter's influential *Anti-Intellectualism in American Life* (1974), where he defines it as, 'resentment and suspicion of the life of the mind and those who are considered to represent it; and a disposition constantly to minimize the value of that life'.[13] To see whether democracy is anti-intellectual it is instructive to turn to one of the most profound theorists of modern democracy, Alexis de Tocqueville. In his most famous work, *Democracy in America*, Tocqueville states,

> I confess that in America I saw more than America; I sought there an image of democracy itself, of its penchants, its character, its prejudices, and passions; I wanted to become acquainted with it if only to know at least what we ought to hope or fear from it.[14]

As he later notes, 'it is because I was not an adversary of democracy that I wanted to be sincere with it'.[15] Favourably disposed to democracy, Tocqueville examines how the animating principle of democracy – equality – accounts for diverse aspects of American institutions, its politics and culture. He is therefore especially useful for us because he addresses the nature of intellect in American democracy, its prevailing philosophies as well as its support of the sciences, arts and letters, tracing them to a political origin, democracy. Though Tocqueville does not have a specific chapter dedicated to the discussion of anti-intellectualism, an important starting point for our investigation is Volume Two, Part One, 'Influence of Democracy on Intellectual Movement in the United States', consisting of twenty-one chapters that, taken together, provide a comprehensive account of his view of how democracies influence the life of the mind.

Tocqueville starts his discussion of the democratic influence on the life of the mind with a bold claim: 'I think there is no country in the civilized world where they are less occupied with philosophy than the United States.' In spite of this, he discerns a distinct philosophic method in America, so that 'America is therefore the one country in the world where the precepts of Descartes are least studied and best followed.'[16] This philosophic method is not derived from speculative studies, but in spite of them. The absence of classes in democracies means equality of individuals, where proximity does not reveal 'incontestable signs of greatness and superiority' in anyone else.[17] Questioning all authority and assuming that everything in the world is explicable and nothing exceeds the bounds of intelligence, the democrat therefore 'withdraws narrowly into himself and claims to judge the world from there'.[18] Thus, Americans do not acquire their philosophical method from books; 'they have found it in themselves'.[19] But this democratic reliance on individual effort does not necessarily favour independence of thought because limitations of time and ability in proving all truths means that some opinions must be accepted on trust. Confronted with this difficulty, democracies turn to the unassailable authority of public or common opinion, which may become 'a sort of religion whose prophet will be the majority'.[20] The reason is that though the principle of equality in democracies and the similarity of everyone disinclines individuals to rely on the opinion of any one person or a class, this same similarity 'gives them an almost unlimited trust in the judgement of the public; for it does not seem plausible to them that when all have the same enlightenment, truth is not found on the side of the greatest number'.[21] As a result, the public in democracies has an extraordinary power, furnishing ready-made opinions and theories on matters of philosophy, morality and politics that are adopted without examination.[22] Consequently, democratic equality has a twofold and contradictory influence on the intellect, leading individuals to new thoughts, while inducing them not to think.[23]

Tocqueville next addresses another feature of democracy that shapes the way citizens think, its tendency to favour 'general ideas' or its preference for theory. In democracies individuals see those around them as almost identical, so that 'All the truths applicable to himself appear to apply equally and in the same manner to each of his fellow citizens and to those like him.'[24] This habit of general ideas is carried over to all others, so that 'to explain a collection of facts by a single cause becomes an ardent and often blind passion of the human mind'.[25] Thus, the equality of condition that encourages each to seek the truth by himself 'will imperceptibly make the human mind tend towards general ideas'.[26] Such love of theorising is alloyed, however, with the circumstances that prevail in modern democracies that affect the mind in two ways: by encouraging a superficiality of thought; and confining theoretical reflections to matters that are not practical. Democracies encourage curiosity but provide little leisure for its satisfaction. A democrat's life is 'so practical, so complicated, so agitated, so active that little time remains for thinking.'[27] This means that in their ambition democrats 'want to obtain great success right away but want to exempt themselves from great efforts'. These contrary impulses mean that they reflect on objects not only to gain general ideas but as a means to save effort, so that 'they hasten to arrange them under the same formula in order to get past them'.[28]

The discussion above has shown how in democracies the idea of equality has given rise to the primacy of the individual as thinker and the democratic love of general ideas or theory. Tocqueville's subsequent discussion shows how equality modifies ideas that are already in existence, ranging from the idea of human perfectibility to the way equality shapes the 'aptitude and taste' for the sciences, literature and the arts. Aristocracies where citizens are classed according to rank, profession or birth possess a notion of self-perfection, according to Tocqueville, but deny it is indefinite and view it in terms of improvement and not change, confining progress 'within certain impassable limits'.[29] In democracies where equality prevails, with all its variability in usages, customs and laws and innovations in new facts and truths, the 'image of an ideal and always fugitive perfection is presented to the human mind'.[30] Continual changes endow the democrat with the idea of the indefinite faculty of perfecting himself.

Such a notion of perfectibility can also be discerned in the question of whether democracy favours the study of science, literature and the arts. Tocqueville's response is to address democracy's 'aptitude and taste for the sciences, literature and the arts', and how democracy 'steers' the intellect in the sciences, arts and literature.[31] The overall argument of his detailed discussion is that it is

> not true to say that men who live in democratic centuries are naturally indifferent to the sciences, letters, and arts; one must only recognize that they cultivate them in their own manner, and that they bring in this way the qualities and faults of their own.[32]

Democratic and free societies will always have 'infinitely more numerous' wealthy individuals than aristocracies, who will be able to rise towards 'the infinite, immaterial and beautiful' and in doing so inform the tastes of the larger populace.[33] Moreover, equality highlights the force of intelligence, so that 'all that serves to fortify, enlarge, and adorn intelligence immediately brings a high price'.[34] Consequently, all citizens 'rise or fall with singular rapidity', imitating and envying each other and discerning ideas, notions and desires that they would not have had in fixed societies. The 'restive ambition' that arises due to equality results in an immense number who cultivate the sciences, letters and arts, so that a 'prodigious activity is awakened in the world of intellect; each one seeks to pen a path to it and strives to bring the public eye in its wake'.[35] Enlightened democracy will therefore loosen the restraints that bind the mind to the earth, allowing the entire population to variously partake in the sciences, letters and arts, even if they do so in a way that is different in spirit and manner to aristocratic peoples.

The precise nature of this difference is the focus of Tocqueville's subsequent detailed examination of science, the arts and literature. Tocqueville's discussion of science shows the tendency of democracy to favour practice rather than theory. Democratic states and institutions do not 'stop the ascent of the mind' but rather 'steer it in one direction than another'. The democratic endorsement of a philosophical method that makes each individual judge of everything, its taste for the tangible and real, and its contempt for forms encourages science so that the sciences have 'a freer and surer but less lofty style' in democracies.[36] But in America there is much greater emphasis on the practical part of science, while the theoretical and abstract is neglected. Therefore, unlike aristocracies that 'conceive an inconsiderate scorn for practice', desire for material enjoyments and the ever-present hope of improving their circumstances means the search for the shortest path to wealth, machines that shorten work, instruments that diminish production costs and inventions that facilitate pleasures are the principal ways 'democratic peoples apply themselves to the sciences to understand them, and honor them'.[37]

Having examined the way democracy influences the sciences, Tocqueville next considers 'in what spirit the Americans cultivate the arts'.[38] The dominant aspects of democracy – mediocrity of fortunes, universal desire for wellbeing and the constant endeavour to procure it – results in the predominance of the useful, so that democrats 'will habitually prefer the useful to the beautiful and they will want the beautiful to be useful'.[39] Consequently, artisans confront those with diminished wealth who still want to satisfy their desires but now have limited means to do so, as well as the newly rich, whose desires grow faster than their fortune.[40] Both citizens have needs above their resources, and look for shorter paths to their enjoyments, and above all, 'would willingly consent to be incompletely satisfied rather than to renounce absolutely the object of their covetousness'.[41] As a result, artisans try to lower prices by inventing ways to work more quickly and with less cost, or by diminishing the quality without rendering it completely unfit. Tocqueville's conclusion is that 'democracy not only tends to direct the human mind toward the useful arts, it brings artisans to make many imperfect things very rapidly, and the consumer to content himself with these things'.[42]

How democracy engages with literature is Tocqueville's final focus in his examination of the life of the mind in the democracies. Literature of a nation, according to Tocqueville, is always subordinate to its social state and its political constitution.[43] Though people in America are least occupied with literature, 'one nevertheless meets a great quantity of individuals there who are interested in things of the mind and who make them if not the study of their whole lives, at least the charm of their leisure'.[44] In democracies where places, sentiments and fortunes are always changing, there are no classes and therefore no conventions, traditions or permanent rules.[45] Those occupied with literature in democracies turn to the pleasures of the mind furtively, 'as passing and necessary relaxation in the midst of the serious work of life'. Habituated to the practical,

> they like books that are procured without trouble, that are quickly read, and do not require learned research to be understood. They demand facile beauties that deliver themselves and that one can enjoy in an instant; above all the unexpected and new are necessary to them.[46]

Equality will therefore profoundly influence both the style and form of writings. Tocqueville does not deny the existence of authors of superior merit in democracies; but he thinks they will be rare, and their works will often return to the dominant democratic mode.[47] Democracy therefore 'introduces the industrial spirit into the heart of literature', and the public in democracies treat authors as courtiers, 'they enrich them and scorn them'.[48]

Tocqueville's reflections on the intellect in America reveal the complex effect of the principle of equality on the life of the mind. Equality, and the way it removes distinctions between individuals, gives rise to and favours a specific theoretical disposition. Democracy is therefore not anti-intellectual, but rather directs the intellect along distinct paths and trajectories. The absence of fixed classes inclines individuals to rely on their own judgement, giving rise to a Cartesian doubt, a love of general ideas, a belief in progress and the idea of indefinite perfectibility. In addition to this theoretical outlook, unique aspects of democracy determine the way science, arts and literature flourish in democracy. Democracy is characterised by a fluidity, love of movement and enterprise. These democratic virtues, a consequence of an equality that makes possible the prospect of changing and insecure fortunes, reveal the price to be paid for democratic energy and innovation – frantic activity that favours the practical over the theoretical, body over mind, earth over heavens.[49]

Instituting Philosophy in Democracy

Tocqueville makes a compelling case for the intellectual credentials of democracy. Democracy's general openness to the intellect and philosophy is confirmed by an examination of uniquely democratic institutions that preserve and enhance the rule of philosophy in politics. There is of course an extraordinary diversity in modern democracies, defined and shaped by their unique history, culture, traditions and institutions. Yet in their variety we find common or consistent themes that reveal a deference or more accurately the endorsement and institutional defence and enablement of wisdom and philosophy.[50] Modern democracies reject the use of sortition or the lot in electing officials, favouring discretion and judgement over chance in choosing representatives, thereby entrenching the principle of ability rather than mere citizenship in the election of political leaders.[51] Similarly, the foremost political offices, such as president, prime minister and the executive, are selected after public debate and contestation based on their future plans and ambitions for the country, making their vision and abilities an important element of their selection. Once in office, members typically form a smaller executive unit, a cabinet that, subject to various conventions, discusses and deliberates on policy, just as congress or parliament openly debate the best course of action and enact laws. Especially in parliamentary systems, this public, deliberative forum is distinctive in having a formal or 'loyal' opposition that will review legislative provisions and in question time challenge the executive, presenting alternative views and courses of action. The importance of debate and oversight can also be seen in the existence of different houses of parliament or congress, with legislation typically requiring the endorsement of the senate or upper houses for its enactment of laws. In this way, the scrutiny and oversight afforded by bicameralism further institutionalises the role of judgement in democratic politics. And this entire arrangement is supported by a modern civil or public service, appointed through merit selection, as opposed to the sinecures and preferments gained through nepotism and cronyism, to counsel and implement policy measures. In some democratic states these arrangements take place in federal systems, where states and federal governments demarcate powers while replicating representative democratic institutions. Thus federalism has been described as 'laboratories' for experimentation, enhancing debate, discussion and contestation of ideas, permitting 'novel social and economic experiments without risk to the rest of the country'.[52]

In addition to this representative, bicameral and federal system of accountable and responsible government, there are other politically powerful institutions where members are not directly appointed by the people and are protected from direct political interference through security of tenure. The best-known instance of such an institution is the modern judiciary, whose authority is usually assured and safeguarded by the constitution and is shielded from direct political influence by security of income and tenure, guaranteed by constitutional entrenchment. Within the judiciary, judges themselves display the importance of wisdom in providing their decisions in the form of reasoned arguments based on law and facts, basing their determinations on precedent and *stare decisis*. Such institutional acknowledgment and protection of expertise is not limited to the judiciary. Modern democracies have used these principles to establish numerous other bodies with distinctive expertise, protecting them from the vagaries of democratic politics. Central or reserve banks are the preeminent example of such institutions that manage the currency and monetary policy of a state and oversees its commercial banking system. Other examples that address the complex and diverse policy domains of modern democracies include electoral commissions, ombudsmen, public service commissions, freedom of information agencies, human rights commissions and the numerous other independent regulatory bodies (environmental, finance, trade and commerce, energy and nuclear) and related international bodies (such as the World Bank, International Monetary Fund, World Health Organization, United Nations) that form an essential part of the institutional architecture of modern democracies.[53]

Democracy from this perspective seems to have solved the problem of philosopher king through the complex and interlinked use of institutions. How efficacious is democracy's institutional accommodation of wisdom and philosophy?[54] One of the most famous theoretical justifications for such institutional solutions can be found in Aristotle's defence of democracy.[55] In *The Politics* Aristotle defends the commendable virtues of democracy by offering a series of arguments to support its excellence.[56] He suggests, for example, that though each may have one part of virtue and prudence, combined the many becomes 'like a human being' with superior abilities. The famous example he gives for this 'combination' argument is that of dinners contributed to by the many, which are better than those from a single source of expenditure. It is for this reason, he argues, that the many are good judges of music and poetry. In the context of political rule, the argument becomes more complex, with Aristotle suggesting that it is appropriate that the many take part in politics through deliberating and judging rather than sharing in the greatest of offices. He justifies this in similar terms to the combination argument noted above, though the terms of the debate seem to shift, starting with the acknowledgment that necessity requires the many to rule because 'when there exist many who are deprived of prerogatives and poor, that city is necessarily filled with enemies'.[57] The combination argument is also framed differently, with the suggestion that the many, mixed with those who are better, become superior and 'bring benefit to the cities'.[58] Aristotle therefore provides a democratic defence for the institutions of expertise and oversight we find in modern democracies. Yet this defence is subsequently questioned by noting the complexities involved in judging. To judge doctors may require medical knowledge, yet in the case of other arts, it would seem that the person who uses a house may be a better judge than the builder, just as 'a pilot judges rudders better than a carpenter, and the diner, not the cook, is the better judge of a banquet'.[59] It is, in other words, an acknowledgment of the limitations of democracy where the many participate through judging and deliberation.[60] Indeed, the Aristotelian account may be turned on its head, showing how at best democratic involvement provides a regular check on the merits of innovations initiated by the few wise, or more seriously is merely a burden imposed by the necessity to accommodate the many for the stability and legitimacy of the regime. This democratic defence of the institutional accommodation of wisdom therefore also raises profound questions regarding our view of the democracy as a regime that is open to philosophy.

These reservations become more serious when we turn to the alternate modern defence for these institutional arrangements that draw on Montesquieu, Locke and *The Federalist Papers* to show how liberty is best secured through the defraying of power. From this perspective, parliamentary, representative and federal structures become a means to ensure that the sovereign people cannot exercise intemperate power against the rich, while those who have been entrusted with considerable power and authority cannot concentrate in their own hands the ability to enact, judge and enforce their own determinations and will. This approach is especially concerned with the force of ambition and will rather than wisdom and judgement, seeking to moderate their inordinate impulses by countering power with power rather than assuming they can be moderated through an education in virtue.[61] But more significantly, it represents a liberal moderation or correction of democracy and as such is an indictment of its openness to wisdom. It suggests that the institutional entrenchment of the philosopher kings we have outlined is essentially an ensemble of liberal innovations aimed at modifying or correcting democracy, rather than inherently democratic in its spirit and intention.

Taken together, then, both in its Aristotelian and liberal justi-fications for the democratic entrenchment of philosophy, we find more or less serious reservations regarding the extent to which democracy can solve the paradox of philosopher king institution-ally. These reservations become more pressing when we examine the implications of such institutional solutions for philosophy itself. Democracy's institution of philosopher kings in specific offices means in practice the protection of select and partial exper-tise, whether it be judicial, economic or scientific. Such expertise is not only partial, but is also fragmented, interspersed throughout the regime, leaving few offices that have the authority for conclu-sive and comprehensive exercise of judgement. Instead there is the potential for these offices to vie for authority, resulting in political contests between these institutions and their incumbents, requir-ing constant vigilance of institutional jurisdiction and protection of authority. We can see this, for example, in the recent debates regarding 'juristocracy' and the undemocratic credentials of the highest courts in deciding the constitutional validity of decisions.[62] But above all, even if such contests could be resolved and a com-prehensive institution was feasible because it would necessarily and properly be concerned with policy formulation and application, it could leave little scope for genuine philosophical reflection. In sum, in instituting philosophy, modern democracies also tend to undermine the authority of philosopher kings they seek to protect by fragmenting expertise, dispersing authority and thereby initiat-ing unintended contests between these institutions, and emphasis-ing the immediate and practical above the abstract and theoretical. Both democracy and philosophy therefore pay a high price for the democratic institutional solution of dispersed philosopher kings.

The Wise and Sovereign People

The alternative to institutional embedding of philosophy in democ-racy is a radically democratic claim that in effect argues that even if people individually may not be wise, taken together or as a whole 'the people' are wiser than any one individual. Consequently, the possibility that the people are both wise and sovereign would seem to provide the conclusive solution to the paradox of the philos-opher king and become the definitive expression of the modern philosopher king. This notion of the people as philosopher kings is implicit or can be derived from two different though associated schools of thought – epistemic and deliberative democrats. We will examine each in turn to see how they can be interpreted as versions of the people as philosopher kings.

At the core of epistemic democracy is a 'wisdom of the crowds' claim that taken together the people make better decisions than any one individual.[63] Its contemporary origins can be traced to attempts to counter the claim that representative democracy was fundamentally deficient because ordinary voting procedures could not in principle express a stable collective will. This challenge derived from the American economist Kenneth Arrow's impossibility theorem, stating that when voters have three or more distinct alternatives, no ranked order voting system can convert the ordered preferences of individuals into a community-wide (complete and transitive) ranking while also meeting a number of criteria that are the basis for a democratic voting procedure.[64] Based largely on Arrow's theory, it was claimed that democratic voting was impossible, arbitrary and therefore meaningless. Epistemic democracy was an attempt to respond to this challenge by arguing that democracy can be defended not only in terms of fair procedures for decision making, but also in terms of the quality of outcomes.[65] Epistemic democrats therefore defend democracy for its ability to contribute to better decisions or 'truth track'.[66] The main theoretical authority and provenance of epistemic democracy is Rousseau's Social Contract (1978: IV. 2) where he argues that each individual in a popular assembly does not simply advance a private interest but rather deliberates on how the proposal is consistent with the 'General Will'.[67] As a consequence, a combination of this Rousseauian insight combined with Condorcet's theorem on the probabilities of groups of individuals coming to correct decisions has given rise to the Condorcet Jury Theorem, which in effect argues that where an average voter has a greater than 50 per cent probability of choosing correctly between a pair of alternatives, the probability of the majority vote being correct increases to 1 as the size of the group increases.[68] It has also given rise to the Diversity Trumps Ability Theorem that claims functionally diverse groups of non-experts can be and often are more effective than homogeneous groups of experts at solving difficult problems.[69] Epistemic democracy therefore goes beyond the claim that democratic procedures will enhance legitimacy. More ambitiously it is a defence of democracy on the grounds that the people as a collective will make better decisions than individual 'experts' – that the sovereign people are philosophers.

Deliberative democracy, similar to epistemic democracy in focusing on the people as a source of good judgement, was a response to the claimed limitations to the legitimacy and efficacy of representative institutions. The 'deliberative turn' in democratic theory examined the extent to which the 'force of better argument' and reason, rather than interest and power, could favour the common good. It therefore focused on how citizens could use collective deliberations to discover how their problems ought to be addressed.[70] At the heart of deliberative democracy is the core normative claim that collective decisions are legitimate only to the extent that they rely on reason and deliberation and have considered and reflected upon the views of those potentially affected.[71] Rather than thinking of political decisions as the aggregate of citizens' preferences, deliberative democracy claims that citizens should arrive at political decisions through reason and deliberation of competing arguments and viewpoints. Its theoretical provenance can be traced to liberal thought, especially Kant who is influential in the more recent Rawlsian concept of 'public reason' and Habermas's 'discourse ethics' that saw in the structure of discourse itself the grounds for rationality. Thus, deliberative democrats defend the normative merits of a democratic politics informed by rational consensus reached through discussion. More recent deliberative democrats have shifted from these normative claims to the view that deliberation can enhance the legitimacy of consensual solutions to the moral dilemmas which divide citizens. The immediate practical consequence of this approach has been to develop models of deliberation that prescribe the essential features of legitimate deliberation, which have in turn led to the development of 'forum based' or participatory institutional architecture for such deliberative practices, such as citizens' juries, participatory budgeting or collaborative forums, aimed at engaging citizens in political decision making.[72] More recently, there have been concerns regarding these deliberative 'micro publics' with increasing attempts to overcome the limitations of discrete deliberative institutions by focusing on deliberative systems.[73]

Both epistemic and deliberative democrats make strong claims regarding the wisdom of the people and in appropriate settings could be seen to be making a case for the people as sovereign kings. Yet both approaches share similar limitations. A core question concerns who are the 'people'. If by the people we mean the constitutive founders, then we confront the problem of how the people can, in the founding moments, constitute both itself and the regime.[74] If by the people we mean a smaller grouping or subset of the people, then we return to the difficulties we noted above in instituting philosopher kings within democracy.[75] A related concern is the how epistemic and deliberative communities confront, deliberate on and resolve political problems. In addition to the inherent complexity of policy questions that do not readily admit to clear alternatives, this raises the perennial procedural problems that confront the practice of all democracies – the way structures of organisation and governance, the role of leaders and rhetoric and the claims of minorities, both powerful and vulnerable, can influence the wisdom of the crowd.[76] And perhaps crucially there is the question of whether the nature of episteme or knowledge, and wisdom in deliberation is presumed by both epistemic and deliberative democrats. Are the sovereign people wise in mere instrumental calculation, in prudence and practical judgement, in ethical judgement or in theoretical speculation?[77] As these questions suggest, epistemic and deliberative democrats may have a strong case for showing the resources of judgement and deliberation that reside in the 'many'. But it is not clear whether the formidable obstacles we have noted permit the more ambitious claim that the people can be sovereign philosophers.

Democracy of the Wise

> *Houyhnhnms* are endowed by Nature with a general Disposition to all Virtues, and have no Conceptions or Ideas of what is evil in a rational Creature, so their grand Maxim is, to cultivate *Reason*, and to be wholly governed by it.

Friendship and benevolence are the principal virtues of the Houyhnhnms, and so perfect is their society that there is no word in their language to express lying or falsehood.[78] Houyhnhnms have no known ruler, with a representative council meeting in 'General Assembly' on the spring equinox every four years to deliberate and debate on matters concerning their country.[79] Though Houyhnhnms live on an island known as 'Houyhnhnm Land' located off the southern coast of Australia, they are in fact a fictional race of intelligent horses who exist only in Jonathan Swift's *Gulliver's Travels*. Yet as Gulliver's tale of 'A voyage to the Houyhnhnms' reveals, the Houyhnhnms also have to contend with the human-like Yahoos who are naked and hairy in appearance, as well as nasty, greedy and brutish in disposition.[80]

In Swift's account, Gulliver is suspended between these two possibilities, aspiring to the higher though often degenerating to the lower. In a similar vein, democracies with their energy, openness and freedom represent the best possibility for combining wisdom and power. Yet they are also most exposed to the alternative, a form that insists on the most common and popular and, in its fleeting formulations, may neglect to reflect on what is the highest in all. Suspended between both possibilities, they reveal the potential and the limits of the people as the conclusive answer to the paradox and promise of the philosopher king.

Notes

1. In the context of our discussion above, consider, for example, the way modern communication technologies have democratised access to the public sphere, so that it is now possible to hear from a variety of public intellectuals. Similarly, the adoption of the modern scientific method has democratised science, so that scientists now include not just the preeminent innovators and discoverers but many relatively unknown individuals who work in teams in laboratories. The 2015 article providing the most precise estimate yet of the mass of the Higgs boson, Aad et al. (2015), had 5,154 authors.
2. For 'waves' of democracy see Huntington (1993). For recent overview of democratic regression see Diamond (2021).
3. On the relationship between democracy and knowledge see generally Ober (2008; 2013).
4. For classical formulations see Plato's *Republic* and *Minos* and Aristotle's *Politics*. For modern elite theorists consider Machiavelli's concept of the few and the many, the influential elitism of Mosca, Pareto and Michels, and the subsequent economic elitism of Schumpeter and later developments in behaviouralism and rational-choice theories justifying rule by the few. For recent Confucian-based forms of elitism see Bai (2020).
5. On the problem of technocracy and 'epistocracy' see Brennan (2016); Mounk (2018).
6. On Pericles's oration see Thucydides (1982: 2.34–2.46). On Pericles and Anaxagoras see generally Stadter (1991).
7. See generally Socrates' account of his life in Plato's *Apology*, *Crito* and *Phaedo* and Monoson (2000).
8. Consider Aristotle's re-enactment of the debate between the democrats and oligarchs (*Politics*, Book III).
9. See especially Tocqueville's *Democracy in America*, which prompted J. S. Mill's *On Liberty*.
10. For an overview and thoughtful critique of the scholarship see Kim (2014: 15–17, 72–97, 179–202). On meritocracy more generally see Bell and Li (2013); Bell (2015); Bai (2020). The political origins of

meritocracy can be traced to the 1990s when Singapore's Lee Kuan Yew argued for 'Asian Values' and subsequently 'meritocracy' derived from Confucian principles, primarily to counter charges of 'soft authoritarianism': see Barr (2000); Wong (2013). More recently, the debate has moved to Confucian influenced countries in East Asia, but primarily China which has under Xi Jinping rehabilitated Confucius from its previous Communist neglect: see Bell (2015); Chan (2013).

11. See the discussion of the four problems of one person, one vote (the suspicion of leaders, effects on non-voters, undermining the interests of the silent, and lack of judgement of voters) in Bai (2020: 52–67).

12. These forms of tyranny include the tyranny of majority, of minority, of the voting community and of the competitive individualist, resulting in limits on selection of good leaders: see Bell (2015: 14–62).

13. Hofstadter (1974: 7).

14. *Democracy in America* (2000: 13). References throughout to *Democracy in America* are to Tocqueville (2000).

15. Ibid. 400.

16. Ibid. 403.

17. Ibid. 404.

18. Ibid. 404.

19. Ibid. 406.

20. Ibid. 410.

21. Ibid. 409.

22. Ibid.

23. Ibid. 410.

24. Ibid. 413.

25. Ibid.

26. Ibid. 413–4.

27. Ibid. 414.

28. Ibid.

29. Ibid. 427.

30. Ibid.

31. Ibid., Chapters 9, 10, 11 and 12, 13–21 respectively.

32. Ibid. 432–3.

33. Ibid. 431.

34. Ibid. 432.

35. Ibid.

36. Ibid. 433.

37. Ibid. 436–7.

38. Ibid. 439.

39. Ibid. 439.

40. Ibid. 440.

41. Ibid.

42. Ibid. 441.

43. Ibid. 449.

44. Ibid. 445.
45. Ibid. 448.
46. Ibid.
47. Ibid. 449.
48. Ibid. 450.
49. In his examination of the 'Influence of Democracy on Intellectual Movement in the United States' (Volume Two, Part One of *Democracy in America*), Tocqueville indicates two ways for correcting this democratic bias. The first and more substantial one consists of an extended discussion of religion in America to show how it may help to elevate the democratic mind away from its immediate and practical concerns, countering its Cartesian individualism and doubt (Chapters 5–7). Tocqueville's second proposal to remedy democracy's limitations concerns the study of Greek and Latin literature (Chapter 15).
50. On the importance of experts in democracy see Holsta and Molanderb (2019). On the claim of increasing influence of unelected experts in democracy see Vibert (2007); Viehoff (2016).
51. For a comprehensive overview see Manin (1997).
52. As per Judge Louis Brandeis dissenting, *State Ice Co. v. Liebmann*, 285 U.S. 262, 311 (1932). More generally consider Hollander and Patapan (2017).
53. For an overview see Lijphart (1999).
54. See generally Kane and Patapan (2012); Kane and Patapan (2014).
55. See, for example, Waldron (1995); Cammack (2013); Lane (2013) on Aristotle's account of the virtue of the multitude.
56. *Politics* (Book 3, Chapter 11, 1281 a39–1283 b13).
57. Ibid. 1281b28–30.
58. Ibid. 1281b25.
59. Ibid. 1282a24.
60. The diner may not appreciate the skill involved in making a dish and, moreover, what tastes good may not always be good for us as Socrates demonstrates in distinguishing between the medical and culinary arts (*Gorgias* and *Protagoras*).
61. See, however, the role of ambition in elevating the soul in Mansfield (1993).
62. Consider, for example, Hirschl (2004).
63. See Schwartzberg (2015) for an overview, and Surowiecki (2004). See also Estlund (2008a); Anderson (2006); Geenens and Tinnevelt (2009); Goodin (2003); Williams (2002).
64. For earlier critiques see above on elite theorists. On the limitations of the social choice approach see generally Rothstein (2019); Mackie (2014).
65. The main work was Riker's (1982). See also Cohen (1986), who coined the term 'epistemic democracy', and Coleman and Ferejohn (1986).

66. See Estlund (2008a); Landemore (2013); Landemore and Elster (2012).
67. As we have seen, there is also some support in Aristotle's *Politics* (Book 3, Chapter 11) where he argues that since the many bring a diverse range of skills and abilities, they are in combination better judges than any one individual. For additional but contingent support from J. S. Mill and modern pragmatism see Schwartzberg (2015).
68. List and Goodin (2001) extended the concept to plurality voting. Note, however, that when Condorcet tried to generalise the method to the case of three or more alternatives, he found that his method can easily lead to contradictions, later called the Condorcet Paradox.
69. Hong and Page (2004) defend this by showing that groups of randomly selected individuals often beat groups of the individually best-performing agents in finding the peaks of random landscapes. According to Singer (2019), this is due to diversity rather than randomness.
70. See, for example, Christiano (2004); Gutmann and Thompson (1996).
71. See, for example, Dryzek (2000, 2010).
72. See Kohn (2000). On various models compare, for example, Fishkin (2009); Cohen (1989); Guttman and Thompson (1996). On participatory institutions see Nino (1996); Fung and Wright (2003); Smith (2009); Nabatchi et al. (2012).
73. Dryzek (2016); Elstub et al. (2016).
74. For reflections on the nature of the 'people' and in particular the puzzle of their self-constitution in revolutionary foundings see Canovan (2005); Loughlin (2014).
75. See generally Riker (1982) and the social choice theory claims that popular will is incoherent.
76. See, for example, Anderson (2006); and more generally, the extent to which the deliberative democracy literature does not address sufficiently the problem of language (Kohn 2000) and the eloquence and flattery of individuals originally diagnosed as a serious flaw of democracy by Hobbes (see Patapan 2021).
77. See, for example, the critique of epistemic democrats by Erman and Möller (2016) and of the limits to deliberative democracy by Gunn (2019). For a comprehensive challenge to democracy on the basis of the limited knowledge of the public see Caplan (2007); Brennan (2016).
78. Swift (2005: 249, 219).
79. Swift (2005: 253, 289).
80. Swift (2005: 209–10; 243–6).

Conclusion:
Modern Philosopher Kings

In this book we have explored the manifold, distinct and complex expressions of the seemingly indomitable impulse and spirit to resolve the paradox of the philosopher king to secure its promise of justice. What each account has revealed is that rushing through diverse channels and carving new courses, the powerful ambition to unite wisdom and power to fulfil the promise of progress and perfectibility has nevertheless met with limited or elusive success. The hope and promise of the pious king has in practice meant the prophet was soon displaced by the pope and pious prince, both exercising contending and questionable authority. The public intellectual was revealed as a tragic figure whose authority would dissolve with success or whose voice was increasingly drowned in the cacophony of views and opinions amplified by advances in modern information and communication technologies. Artists as creative philosopher kings were revealed to be either entertainers or minions of the powerful, with the few wise limited in their reach and influence. The combination of wise counsellor and powerful ruler seemed to be the conclusive resolution of the paradox of the philosopher king, though in fact it has meant an unstable relationship where the wise are at the mercy of wary and proud rulers or alternatively threaten to become hidden leaders. Modern scientists as the new philosopher kings increasingly confronted challenges to their legitimacy by a public now wary and watchful of their technocratic ambitions, even as their innovations were eagerly sought and acclaimed as benefactions. Finally, attempts to secure wisdom in democracy through institutions or, more ambitiously, the temptation to see the people as the wise sovereign had to be tempered by the limits to public deliberation and judgement.

The reasons for the frustrated ambitions and faltering hopes of these various expressions of the modern philosopher king are necessarily and inevitably complex and diverse. From a synoptic perspective, however, three persistent aspects reveal themselves as major obstacles to the promise of the modern philosopher king. Few would deny the goodness of wisdom and, equally, most concede that the coincidence of celerity of thought, facility with memory and above all the need to have measured temperament and disposition to attain wisdom means there are formidable obstacles to our possession of this virtue. Politically, such diversity in ability makes it difficult to discern and agree on who is wise and, compounded by our natural inclination to favour or appreciate our own abilities at the expense of others, provides impediments to the recognition of the wise and deference to their rule. At the same time, it is not evident that the wise would seek to rule, and indeed, whether the ability to discern first principles is necessarily accompanied by sufficient knowledge of particulars essential for political judgement and action.[1] Politics therefore inevitably comprehends a variety of human beings moved by diverse talents, hopes and desires demanding a share in office and rule, with the ever-present threat of the use of force to gain advantages requiring moderation and even restraint by attempts to persuade, compromise and frequently compel a practicable consensus that does justice to most if not all claims. It is therefore inevitably a realm of concession and accommodation where the wise, assuming they will seek office and are capable rulers, will at best have to share authority, or at worst be ignored, derided or even censored. Compounding these challenges is the realisation that the influence of wisdom, already dissipated by the erosive influence of diversity in interests, abilities and claims, will always confront the unyielding limitations of our impermanence. We may not be mayflies who flourish only for a day, yet our greater allotment, however uncertain, will be consumed in becoming wise, and even when we have attained something of this fugitive excellence, the brevity of our tenure means we struggle against an irresistible mortality, confining our influence and good works to the brief span of our short lives. Finally, our best wrought plans, our hopes to exercise wisdom by asserting authority, seem to always elude our mastery and control. The world seems resistant to our will and chance circumscribes the indeterminate outer bounds to our wisdom and power. That most of us are not wise or are too proud to admit our limitations, that our lives are short and we are at the mercy of fortune combine to become redoubtable obstacles to our noble ambition to realise the coincidence of wisdom and power, philosophy and politics and therefore justice. Is the promise of the philosopher king therefore a futile hope always destined to fail? More perniciously, does it nurture a dangerous illusion of progress and perfectibility that undermines sound political judgement?

Socrates and Plato as Philosopher Kings

The modern philosopher kings we have examined compel us to ask whether the paradox of the philosopher king was ever capable of resolution and therefore returns us to its origin in Socrates' initial proposal. When we do, we confront a curious tension between Socrates' claims regarding the feasibility of the philosopher king, albeit hedged with appeals to chance or divine dispensation, and the life he himself pursued. As a citizen of Athens, Socrates fulfilled his civic duties. He served as hoplite in the Peloponnesian War at Potidaea (where he saved Alcibiades), the Battle of Delium and Amphipolis. He was also his tribe's delegate to the *prytaneis* or executive of the *boule* or council of 500 when the generals from the Battle of Arginusae were tried, and was one of five who was ordered by the oligarchy of the Thirty to apprehend Leon of Salamis.[2] Beyond these civic responsibilities, however, Socrates never aspired to high political office or influence. In the *Republic* he justifies this decision as an act of piety, obedience to his *daimonion* or divine sign that counselled him on what not to do, though without giving reasons.[3] Socrates provides a more detailed explanation of his decision in Plato's *Apology* where he defends the prudence of the *daimonion's* counsel: 'For know well, men of Athens, if I had long ago tried to be politically active, I would long ago have perished, and I would have benefited neither you nor myself.'[4] When towards the end of his life he is indicted for bringing in false gods and corrupting the young, he portrays himself at the trial as a private individual, a sort of moral gadfly who exhorts others to virtue, rather than a political leader ambitious for office and authority.[5] In addition to the question of his safety, perhaps the most revealing reason why he does not engage in politics is his claim that the 'unexamined life is not worth living'.[6] This seemingly innocuous explanation and justification of his life can be seen upon reflection as his true assessment of the primacy of philosophy and a comprehensive indictment and repudiation of the claims to preeminence of all other lives, especially the political and pious. It would seem, then, that even in the best case of Socrates and Athens, and contrary to Socrates' claim, the philosopher king or the union of wisdom and power was an unrealisable political goal.

Perhaps Plato provides us with greater confidence regarding the feasibility of the philosopher king? Yet even in this case we cannot escape the paradox of the philosopher king. Plato's own reflections on how to combine wisdom and power are chronicled in his *Letters*, especially his *Seventh Letter* where he explains and justifies why he chose not to participate in Athenian politics.[7] At the time Plato wanted to enter politics, Athens was subject to the lawless rule of 'the Thirty', which included his uncle Charmides and his cousin Critias among its leaders who invited him to take part in their rule. Plato states he decided against political involvement on seeing the injustice of their administration, and especially the way they attempted to use Socrates and tried to implicate him in their actions by forcing him to arrest Leon of Salamis. When the Thirty were overthrown, he was 'impelled with a desire to take part in public and political affairs'.[8] Though the exiled democrats who returned under Thasybulus and Thasyllus were moderate in their retributions, Meletus, Anytus and Lycon accused Socrates of impiety and on conviction had him executed.[9] Reflecting on this incident and the types of men, laws and customs of the subsequent administration, Plato states he decided not to enter politics because it was difficult to find friends and trusted companions, and the corruption in laws and customs could not be repaired without major renovation.

Both Socrates and Plato, by the lives they favoured and their resolutions to eschew politics, therefore suggest the infeasibility of the idea of the philosopher king. Their reservation is compounded by the ambiguous role of the philosopher king in the *Republic* and in Plato's dialogues more generally. There is an unresolved debate concerning the relationship of the philosopher king to the just city outlined in the *Republic*, and especially whether the entire discussion of the just city and the philosopher king is intended as a comprehensive template for political reform or is indeed a meditation on the political limits of justice.[10] It is remarkable that the philosopher king does not appear in any other Platonic dialogue.[11] It also seems to be repudiated by Plato's *Laws*, where the Athenian Stranger defends and favours the rule of law and constitutionalism.[12] So, perhaps we should confine the philosopher king to its specific dialogic context and purpose, seeing it as an enchanting rhetorical trope to comfort Glaucon and others like him by persuading them that philosophy is a necessary first step for satisfying their noble political ambitions, thereby diverting and moderating their desires away from the tyranny promised by the poets and Sophists.[13]

If so, what are we to make of Socrates' repeated claims regarding the feasibility of the philosopher king? As he says regarding philosophers becoming kings or rulers philosophical, 'I deny that there is any reason why either or both of these things is impossible. If that were the case we would justly be laughed at for uselessly saying things that are like prayers.'[14] Similarly, he later states, 'Do you agree that the things we have said about the city and the regime are not in every way prayers; they are hard but in a way possible.'[15] That the philosopher king is possible 'in a way' makes us wonder whether we can resolve the paradox of the philosopher king in a way that differs from the various attempts we have explored in this book.

Philosophic Rulers

Plato's *Seventh Letter* explicates his reasons for not pursuing political office in Athens. It also provides an account of the sole instance where Plato did take part in politics directly. Immediately after his explanation of why he declined to participate in Athenian politics, and just before his account of his first visit to Syracuse, Plato states,

> So in my praise of the right philosophy I was compelled to declare that by it one is enabled to discern all forms of justice, both political and individual. Wherefore the classes of mankind (I said) will have no cessation from evils until either the class of those who are right and true philosophers attains political supremacy, or else the class of those who hold power in the States becomes, by some dispensation of Heaven, really philosophic.[16]

Plato here appears to repeat and endorse in his own name Socrates' famous statement in the *Republic* concerning the philosopher king.[17] In doing so soon after his discussion of Athenian politics he shows the ever-present and formidable obstacles to the first possibility, rule of the philosopher king. But this statement reminds us of the second aspects of the philosopher king we have not explored in detail. Is the answer to the paradox of the philosopher king to be found not in philosophers assuming authority, but in rulers becoming philosophical? This possibility directs our attention to the question of how rulers become philosophical, and especially the feasibility of such a proposed solution given Plato's cautious reference to the 'dispensation of Heaven'. One obvious way rulers may become philosophical is by being personally instructed by philosophers. Let us therefore examine a famous example of such an instruction, Plato's attempts to teach the tyrants of Syracuse, Dionysius the Elder and his son Dionysius II, as detailed in his *Seventh Letter*, to evaluate the opportunities and limits of such an education.[18]

Plato made three trips to Syracuse, with his first a part of a larger voyage after Socrates' death, when he travelled extensively from Athens to Megara, Cyrene, Egypt, Southern Italy, Sicily and finally to the city of Syracuse where he met Dion (408–354 BCE), brother-in-law to Dionysius I, tyrant of Syracuse.[19] Dion, according to Plato, was quick witted and exceptionally keen to learn, determined to live his life as a philosopher rather than the Syracusan life of excess.[20] Though praising Dion, Plato is more reticent about his dealings with Dionysius I, with subsequent authors suggesting that Dionysius I was displeased by Plato's repudiation of the life of tyrant and, more contentiously, had him sold to slavery, requiring his ransom from a slave market in Aegina.[21] Plato's second trip to Syracuse took place at the invitation of Dion, after Plato had founded the Academy and written his famous dialogues. Dionysius II of Syracuse inherited supreme power on the death of his father Dionysius I in 367 BCE and began ruling under the supervision of his uncle Dion. Dion exhorted Plato to visit Syracuse in the hope that he would educate and moderate the young and dissolute Dionysius. It was during this trip that Dionysius, jealous of Plato's attention and taking counsel from Philistus and other opponents of Dion's reforms, conspired to banish Dion and took complete power in 366 BCE, lodging Plato in the citadel.[22] The impasse created by these actions were overcome when Dionysius agreed to let Plato return to Athens, provided he could help reconcile him to Dion and assist him to resume the study of philosophy. Plato's final trip to Syracuse was in response to the request of the philosopher Archytas who had been visiting Dionysius and claimed that Dionysius had made great progress in philosophy, and who hoped that Plato's visit would reconcile Dionysius with Dion. For the sake of his friendship with Dion and others and hopes that Dionysius may have attained love of the best life, Plato travelled once more to Syracuse, only to find that Dionysius, though he claimed to know many important doctrines, was not 'enflamed' by philosophy, and that he loved the reputation rather than the practice of philosophy.[23] Moreover, though promising much, Dionysius confiscated and sold the property that until then had been used to fund the exiled Dion, and deprived him of his wife and child, whom he gave to another man.[24] Outside the security of the citadel and at risk of mercenaries, Plato was fortunate to make his trip back to the safety of Athens. He declined to take part in Dion's subsequent venture to overthrow Dionysius, with the loss of his property forcing Dion and his friends to recapture Syracuse in 357 BCE, though he was soon assassinated by one of his soldiers, resulting in civil unrest in Syracuse until its defeat by the Corinthian General Timoleon in 344–3 BCE who restored it to democracy.

Plato's Syracusan experience shows how even in the most promising case of a ruler well disposed to philosophy, his character and upbringing, the allure of glory and the ever-present, corrosive fear of losing office can undermine the prospect of rulers becoming philosophic through instruction by the wise.[25] Dion, who was philosophically inclined, could not moderate Dionysius whose father had neglected to adequately educated him. Plato, who was enlisted to help Dion, did not succeed because Dionysius loved the appearance but not substance of philosophy. Plato's involvement seems to have exacerbated the relationship between Dionysius and Dion by making Dionysius envious and suspicious of Dion, so that ultimately he expelled Dion. Plato's attempt to reconcile Dion and Dionysius II aggravated the situation, resulting in Dionysius's extreme measures against Dion, prompting Dion's overthrow of Dionysius, leading to the subsequent assassination of Dion, and thereby plunging Syracuse into greater instability and warfare.

Writing as Ruling

Plato's lack of success in attempting to introduce the tyrants Dionysius I and II to philosophy suggests that even in this most promising of circumstances formidable obstacles, such as pride, desire for authority and fear of losing office, stand in the way of making rulers truly philosophical. Importantly, such a failure had significant political consequences, with his interventions resulting in greater instability and violence in Syracusan politics. If personal instruction is burdened with such limitations, are there other forms of education that may surmount the obstacles Plato confronted in Syracuse? Between his first and second trips to Syracuse, Plato founded the Academy and wrote his famous dialogues. If we put to one side Plato the political actor, to what extent is it possible to say that Plato the author overcomes these obstacles? Is it possible for writing to make rulers philosophical so that it becomes the conclusive answer to the paradox of the philosopher king?[26]

Now as we know the best rulers have an uncanny ability to make the right decisions and choose the best course of actions in the given circumstances. In other words, they possess *phronesis* or prudence, the defining virtue of a ruler. Prudence or judgement, to the extent that it is concerned with *praxis* or deliberative action regarding what is good, is distinguishable from both theoretical wisdom and technical skills of production. It therefore would appear to be an intellectual virtue that does not need philosophical instruction. Yet to the extent that prudence is distinguished from mere instrumental cleverness and draws on opinions of the good, it is necessarily informed and indebted to wisdom that reflects on and comprehends unchanging principles.[27] A persuasive case can therefore be made that rulers can become philosophical not only by personal instruction, but through the intermediary influence of reading and meditating on the written works philosophers. Moreover, and significantly, as we noted in our discussion of philosophers as counsellors, there is the question of whether such counsel may become so influential that philosophers become in effect hidden rulers. If all rulers are in this sense children of philosophers, then rulers who are philosophical are, in their political actions, expressions of the will and judgement of philosophers, who thereby can be said to rule indirectly through their writing. Accordingly, the philosopher as writer who shapes the thoughts and actions of philosophical rulers is the conclusive resolution of the paradox of the philosopher king. Solomon the Wise, Saladin the Great and Asoka the Great were famous for their wisdom, but their judgement was fundamentally shaped and influenced by the Torah, the Qur'an and the *buddhavacana*. Similarly, Marcus Aurelius, Cicero and Boethius are celebrated as philosophical rulers, but they were students of the Stoa and the Academy. Montesquieu, Locke and Aristotle influenced the authors of *The Federalist Papers*, just as Marx was the intellectual forebear of Lenin, Stalin and Mao. There is therefore a puzzling ambiguity concerning the nature of writing, which as mere marks on parchment and paper seem to be the refuge of the least powerful, yet as philosophical and prophetic writing can be the most powerful form of mediated rule. To explore the nature of this ambiguity and the implications it has for the philosopher king we need to examine the character of writing, its great potency as well as its dangers and deficiencies in limiting prudence and instituting a new politics of books.

The Limits to Writing

Socrates in Plato's *Phaedrus* recounts the story of the old Egyptian god Theuth, inventor of numbers, calculation, geometry and astronomy, draughts and games of dice and written letters, who explains the advantages of each of these innovations to the god of all Egypt, Thamos Ammon.[28] In commending written letters, Theuth claimed it will 'make Egyptians wiser and provide them with better memory'.[29] But Thamos disagreed, arguing letters were not a drug for memory but for reminding, since they ensure forgetfulness in the souls of those who have learned it, trusting in alien markings and not themselves, providing the opinion of wisdom but not truth.[30] Socrates, who never wrote, concurs, detailing a more specific set of reservations concerning writing. Writing is clever, according to Socrates, resembling painting in seemingly presenting living beings. But when in the hope of learning something you interrogate writing about the things said they indicate one thing only, and always the same.[31] What is more, once written, 'every speech rolls around everywhere, read alike by those who understand as in the same way by those for whom it is in no way fitting, and it does not know to whom it ought to speak and to whom not'. Finally, 'when it suffers offence and is reviled without justice it always needs its father's assistance. For by itself it cannot defend or assist itself.'[32] Socrates' critiques of writing are the obverse of the advantages of conversation and dialogue that he considers the only true form of philosophical engagement.[33] Plato seems to concur, noting the limitations of writing in his *Second Letter* and in particular in his *Seventh Letter* where he denies that philosophical insights can ever be captured in writing that is unalterable, contrasting it to conversations that like a blaze kindled by a spark, yield insights that are self-sustaining.[34] The implication is that arguments in the form of a series of logical propositions are not by themselves philosophical – that they need to come to life in an individual who cares to make them relevant and powerful.[35] 'This is the reason', according to Plato, 'why every serious man in dealing with really serious subjects carefully avoids writing.'[36] These reflections insinuate a great divide between philosophy and writing, suggesting writing can only be an image of a speech 'living and endowed with soul', so that at best it is a means for recording what we thought for play or remembering in old age.[37] Given the extent and force of this critique of writing, the obvious question has been, why did Plato write? Reflecting on this question and puzzle allows us to gain a better insight into the strengths as well as limitations of writing as a form of rule.[38]

One way to answer this question of why Plato wrote is to examine its philosophical and political aspects. The Socratic critique of writing takes its bearing from the high demands of philosophy, where the primacy of individual conversations as the kindling for philosophical insight will always make writing appear insufficient. But is it possible for writing to approximate the highest standard of conversation and exceed it in other respects? To assess this possibility we need to explore the extent to which writing is more or less philosophical by starting with the diversity of writing and how it replicates conversations ranging, for example, from law and legislation at one extreme, speaking to all and attempting to guide mainly through instruction, command and compulsion, to the other extreme where philosophical reflections and speculations, divine oracles and artistic works approximate the experience of individual conversation and elenchus. Seen in this light, depending on the knowledge and ability of the author, writing may come close to recreating the philosophical experience, while also surpassing it by overcoming the limitations of the rarity of the wise, the brevity of life and the unpredictability of chance that we noted were formidable obstacles to the union of wisdom and power.[39] What is needed, then, is a distinctive form of writing that addresses the concerns noted by Socrates – that it should recreate the conditions for the kindling of philosophical spark; it should be able to formulate and answer questions posed to it; and it should speak differently to different readers. Plato's innovation of the dialogue attempts to remedy all these deficiencies of writing.[40] As Socrates notes in the *Phaedrus*, in addition to a playful form of writing for remembering in old age, there is a serious play,

> when someone using dialectical art, taking hold of a fitting soul, plants and sows with knowledge speeches that are competent to assist themselves and him who planted and are not barren but have seed, whence other speeches, naturally growing in other characters, are competent to pass this on, ever deathless, and make him who has it experience as much happiness as is possible for a human being.[41]

Platonic dialogue combines the dramatic form of those other Greek inventions, the comedic and tragic plays, with the philosophical treatise to re-enact a confrontation with Socrates who claimed to know only his ignorance, yet in conversation appeared either as a stinging moral gadfly or the numbing torpedo fish.[42] This form of writing recreates a philosophical conversation, yet one where the author is absent and the interlocutors shape and direct the course of the conversation. It poses questions while not conclusively answering them, thereby providing a depth of engagement that, depending on one's ability, yields wisdom without succumbing to the neat formula, facile injunction or comprehensive 'doctrine' that will tempt some to think they know by mere memorisation.[43] Finally, in having interlocutors present and defending their views, the dialogues endeavour to answer questions put to them. The Platonic dialogue preserves and re-enacts for posterity the experience of having a conversation with a philosopher.

Politically, the dialogues can be said to have two distinctive roles – of *apologia* and of legislation. The significant political role of Platonic dialogues is that of forensic rhetoric in defence of the new discovery of philosophy. That philosophy is useless, queer or pernicious is the accusation it faced from its inception and is a perennial political prejudice and indictment of its public worth. Consequently, all the dialogues can be reordered as a biography of Socrates, from his early encounter with Parmenides to his trial and death, intended as an extended defence to the criminal charge of impiety and corruption of the young that confronts all philosophy. Socrates emerges from the dialogues as the pious and just citizen who was moderate concerning the desires of the body, cared little for wealth or power, was just and law-abiding in his civic life and courageous in defending the city, pursing virtue both for himself and for the Athenian youth and in doing so paying the highest price for his public service. In defending philosophy this writing therefore has the benefit of persuading the able and ambitious young to befriend philosophy, just as Glaucon and others declare in the *Republic*.

This defence of philosophy also reveals how philosophy perforce transforms politics, with Socrates as the new Achilles and philosophy as the standard for appraising all regimes.[44] Each dialogue therefore also demonstrates in its concerns and argumentation how philosophy transforms all aspects of political life, from its conception of justice to the meaning of virtues, the nature of law and of the gods. This defence will therefore unavoidably issue in specific proposals for reform, in both regimes and in *nomos* understood as laws and norms. Plato will use writing as legislation, enacting in his dialogues laws and constitutions for future benefit, as approximations of the prudent and wise who may not always be present. Socrates' founding of *kallipolis* can in this light be seen as a political act by the philosopher king and an influential paradigm or perfected model for all future regimes. In this sense it is a more substantial founding than any actual regime because it will remain untouched by circumstances and chance and impervious to the vagaries of having good leaders and well-disposed followers. Socrates as the philosopher king who founds *kallipolis* therefore reveals the only way, and perhaps the sole instance (if the *Republic* is not lost), where the philosopher rules as king.[45]

Kallipolis is not, however, the sole example of Plato's use of writing as both an opportunity for philosophical reflection and a form of political rule. Plato shows how the wise can rule through writing not only in turning individuals around to philosophy, but more ambitiously, through lawgiving that moderates politics by constitutionally protecting philosophers and tempering the insatiable human passion for justice that in its ambition too readily flies to the gods or descends to cruelty. Socrates' defence of the rule of law and constitutions therefore represents his engagement with future rulers open to philosophy, inviting them to meditate on the dangers of the philosopher king and counselling them on the advantages of the rule of law. In Plato's *Laws*, for example, the Athenian Stranger acknowledges the primacy of the rule by the wise and seeks to protect philosophers and the wise in the Nocturnal Council while also conceding that the rule of law and the mixed constitution is the 'second best regime'.[46] This view is in accord with Socrates' defence of the law (*Minos*) and of the obligations imposed by a form of 'social contract' (*Crito*). Related to this approach is a range of initiatives to reform and thereby moderate civic life. These measures favour more lenient criminal laws with changes to notions of responsibility and accountability (*Euthyphro, Apology, Gorgias*), the renovation of spirited patriotism with new noble myths of metals in the soul to repudiate a rigid caste system (*Republic*), refashioning of vindictive and unpredictable divinity with a new theology of beneficent gods who do not directly intervene in human affairs (*Republic, Euthyphro*), and even changes to international relations to limit its brutality and undermine slavery (*Republic*). All these initiatives are intended to moderate politics by encouraging it to be gentler, more reflective and generous, even if not philosophical.

This entire political approach, however novel and transformative, is complicated by the dialogic form that resists formulaic resolutions, while the persistence of Socrates' notorious ignorance and irony undermines doctrinaire dogmatism, making it hard to know exactly what Socrates stands for or advocates. Platonic dialogues through rare imitative skills in recreating philosophical engagement compensate their acknowledged limitation as only partial approximations to true philosophy by immortalising through writing Socrates and the discovery of political philosophy. Writing in this sense can overcome its limitations to become more influential than any particular philosopher king. In its celebratory discovery, articulation and defence of political philosophy, Socrates understands how some will imagine the seemingly endless opportunities and promises of this innovation. It is perhaps with these temptations in mind that he also sounds a sombre cautionary note on the seemingly intransigent limits to wisdom that will always tempt some to conquer chance or long for divine providence to rescue us from these fraught circumstances.

Dangers of Writing

If rulers become philosophical through books, then philosophers rule by writing. How efficacious is such a mediated rule by philosophers? This question presents a twofold challenge to writing as a solution to the paradox of the philosopher king. The first concerns the extent to which writing can be said to liberate or silence prudence and political judgement of individual rulers.[47] The second is whether writing as a form of rule introduces a new form of contention and political agonism. We will examine each in turn.

Prudence is the virtue that pursues the good in light of the necessary and exigent. It therefore demands the ability to accommodate and reconcile the unchanging to the fluid and unpredictable. As we saw, the laws as second-best solutions seemed to overcome the dangers of imprudent rulers. The clarity and fixity of laws were therefore a bulwark against the fickleness and partiality of individual judgement. But in resisting change, laws seem to deny flux and therefore the need to exercise prudence. Is the philosophical rule through writing inherently imprudent or does it enhance judgement? In Plato's *Laws*, the Athenian Stranger brings to Kleinias's attention 'an extreme in lawmaking and political art', Egyptian laws forbidding innovations in the works of the Muses that has meant that painting, sculpture and song have not altered for over

10,000 years.[48] As this example shows, the written word in the form of laws can be extremely powerful, resisting and even defying change. Such conservation, however, is at tension with the need to encourage progress and innovation, raising the question of whether the written word will inevitably be opposed to prudence or judgement.[49] Aristotle's *Politics* raises the problem of laws speaking to the universal and therefore not acknowledging specific circumstances when he notes that even in Egypt, notorious for its inflexible application of medical laws written by famous doctors, 'it is permissible for doctors to alter the treatment after the fourth day, though before then they may do so at their own risk'.[50] Egypt preserved and protected from innovation the integrity of its medical laws, even at the expense of the health of a patient.[51] When we recall that philosophy and medicine were discovered at the same time in Egypt, we can see that this approach to medical laws comprehended political and philosophical innovations, so that the more dogmatic such laws, the less scope they provide to the doctors of body and soul.[52] The tendency of laws to limit change and innovation and therefore resist their prudential interpretation may be alleviated by introducing a flexibility in philosophical reflection, as we find in the Platonic dialogues. But this new and unique form of philosophical speculation and instruction appears the exception, with the subsequent dominance of the treatise form attesting to the powerful impulse to rule by instruction and clarification rather than philosophical puzzlement as 'midwifery'. The problem is compounded in laws and constitutions, which by their nature have to be clear and precise. It is true that room for judgement may be included even here, as the Athenian Stranger indicates in his discussion of Preambles as the most important educative parts of laws that will clarify their intention and application.[53] Nevertheless, it is difficult to make room for the exercise of judgement and discretion in laws without undermining their rule, so that this form of asserting the authority of the philosopher king will tend to deprive future philosophers and statesmen of the necessary discretion to accommodate principles to the demands of practice. In its extreme doctrinaire form, it will have the perverse consequence of insisting on dogmatic application in the face of imprudent, even disastrous consequences, and indeed celebrating such intransigence as proof of loyalty, courage and doctrinal correctness. It leads to the rule of sectarians and zealots who would rather preserve their purity than pursue practical advantage.

The other aspect of rule by writing concerns its openness to contention and therefore its potential to become the basis for a new politics of writing and books that replicate and exacerbate political contestations. Writing as a physical object will be subject to the vagaries of chance, and as history attests, many profound works have been lost to posterity through uncompromising censorship, or the inexorable spoilation of time. Philosophers as authors, however ambitious they may seem in overcoming chance, will therefore always be subject to fortune's fickle will that decrees the fate of their written works. Beyond this immediate concern, however, is the reception and subsequent influence of these works. Irrespective of the ability of the author and the quality of the work, we have seen how writing cannot speak for itself and in having interpreters, some better than others, the most profound philosophic works will engender alternative readings, contending views and in time factions, groupings and sects that will emphasise one aspect of the work above the other and in doing so pursue clarity of a part at the price of fragmenting the whole. All great works, and especially those that seek to preserve the potential for fresh zetetic encounters, will therefore be subject to the eroding, if not corrosive, effect of subsequent readers and readings.[54]

Exacerbating this problem of writing as polyphonous, polysemous and therefore prone to indeterminacy and ambiguity is the inevitable confrontation of these forms of rule with a contending challenger, who may seek to modify, or more ambitiously challenge altogether the authority of the philosophic writings. And it is here that we see how aspects of the paradox of the philosopher king will exacerbate these struggles. That only the best can adjudicate these contests means that those who are enamoured of philosophy though not possessing sufficient ability will be tempted to enjoin and recruit the many in their struggles.[55] In the spirit of pleasing the many, they therefore will remove all ambiguity from their account and in doing so promise once and for all complete and immanent justice. Those who speak for the gods, auguring a future happiness, philosophers who discern in the great movements of world forces and subtle, submerged and therefore opaque workings of the human mind a promised justice will be especially successful in these battles for minds and souls. The philosopher as author therefore means that in time there will be a struggle between philosophers, complicated even more by the ambitious few who seek to rule by claiming to be philosophers. Instead of bringing clarity, peace and justice the philosopher as author reveals the new terms and terrain of the contest over ideas. But not solely ideas. The contest between philosophers, with their followers, interpreters and students, will inevitably manifest these struggles in princely courts, courts of law and fields of war. It seems contrary, counterintuitive and perhaps perverse but the battle of the books, which is in fact the contest between philosophers as authors, is arguably the source of those grim and brutal political struggles that seem far removed from the hushed tones and subtleties of philosophical contest and contention.[56]

Conclusion

Brutal power wielded with fervour or cold cruelty bears grim testimony to the distance and, more dishearteningly, the disjunction between wisdom and power. Our examination of the paradox and promise of the philosopher king, and the manifold attempts to fulfil the promise of uniting the two, reveals a more complex truth – that power and politics are always shaped and informed by larger philosophical concepts and ideas. This insight is a welcome reminder that wisdom is not helpless, and that reasoning and judgement exercise a potent force in politics. It is a realisation necessarily accompanied, however, with the recognition of the harsh truth that political contests are not only shaped by blind self-interest, partiality and force, but are also inevitably defined, directed and distorted by theoretical and philosophical contestation that will always animate, and frequently exacerbate, them. Indeed, the influence of wisdom and philosophy is such that political struggles are unavoidably contests over different conceptions of the good life, however conceived.

Our reflections on the paradox of the philosopher king have therefore revealed the power of wisdom manifest in the actions and thoughts of the wise ruler and in the writings of philosophers. Our exploration of the promise of the modern philosopher kings as the hope for progress and perfectibility has also shown the limits to such power, moderating our formidable longings to achieve justice by finding conclusive resolution to the paradox of the philosopher king. The realisation of such limits, however disheartening, helps us to avoid that hubris and overreach that fuel and aggravate our desire to solve political problems definitively. In doing so it arms us to resist the temptation to surrender either to the tragic view of life as a world of force and unreasoning will that encourages political quietism, or the pious denigration of this world in the hope of transcendent salvation. Modern philosopher kings as experiments, aspirations and hopes therefore reveal reason's place in politics, lighting an expanse and terrain for genuine human discretion, where prudence and judgement can counter the force of both pride and fear, the brevity of our lives and the fickleness of chance. It provides a sober and measured assessment of the true grounds and prospects for empowering wisdom and ennobling politics to secure justice.

Notes

1. See the discussion in Aristotle's *Metaphysics* (980a–982a), regarding first principles and how someone with experience seems superior to the wise, as well as Xenophon's assessment of the Socratic view that those who know are the true rulers in Pangle (2018: 112–63).
2. See Plato's *Apology* (32c–d) for Socrates' account where he states that unlike the others he went home instead of arresting Leon because he didn't want to be implicated in their injustice in the execution of Leon.
3. *Republic* (496c).
4. *Apology* (31d). On Socrates' *daimonion* see Ehli (2018).
5. *Apology* (30e).
6. Ibid. 37e–38a.
7. *Seventh Letter* (324c–326b). For references to letters see Plato (1989).
8. Ibid. 325b.
9. Ibid. 325c.
10. It is not clear, for example, whether the philosopher king forms part of the city or is intended to found it. As Steinberger (1989) argues, the philosopher king is not part of *kallipolis* but a means to implement it in practice. Moreover, as Strauss (1978) notes, the philosopher king seems to make the preceding discussion of *kallipolis* redundant.
11. Aristotle does not mention it in his critique of Plato in his *Politics*. Schofield (1999: 28 ff., Chapter 2) explores the absence of the philosopher king in subsequent dialogues including *Timaeus*, *Statesman* and *Laws*, suggesting that it is nevertheless an implicit theme in them.
12. See in this context Plato's *Laws* (713c–14a, 875a–d), which defend the superiority of writing and constitutionalism over the rule of the wise. On Plato's conception of law see, for example, Nightingale (1999); Pangle (1980); Cohen (1993).
13. See Lampert (2010) who argues that this new rhetorical form is arguably the introduction of a wholly new teaching that is only found in the *Republic*. Thus 'ideas' or 'Forms', easily accessible and defensible but philosophically complex and obscure, become the public 'Platonic' form of philosophy that is otherwise inaccessible in its erotic and zetetic form.
14. *Republic* (499c).
15. Ibid. 540c.

16. *Seventh Letter* (326a–b).
17. *Republic* (473d, 501e).
18. *Seventh Letter* (326b–352a).
19. For an overview see Evangeliou (2017).
20. *Seventh Letter* (327b).
21. On the conflicting evidence see Porter (1943).
22. *Seventh Letter* (326b–330c; 332c–d).
23. *Seventh Letter* (340b–341a, 344e).
24. *Seventh Letter* (337e–345a).
25. It thus reiterated the limits to the Athenian Stranger's counsel in Plato's *Laws* to rely on or take advantage of a tyrant for major political reform.
26. Writing, unlike thought and reflection, reaches out or seeks a reader, manifesting its intrinsically social and potentially political character. For a brief overview of the history of literacy, especially the 'literacy myth', see Gee (1988).
27. See the discussion of *phronesis* in *Nicomachean Ethics* (1140a ff.), as well as Kane and Patapan (2014).
28. On commentaries on *Phaedrus*, including its insights into writing see Griswold (1986); Ferrari (1987); Rowe's Introduction in Plato (2005).
29. *Phaedrus* (274e).
30. Ibid. 275a.
31. Ibid. 275d.
32. Ibid. 275e.
33. A view endorsed elsewhere, for example in Plato's *Protagoras* (329a) where books are criticised for being incapable of answering or putting a question of their own. On the problem of authority of writing in Plato's *Laws* see Fraistat (2015).
34. *Second Letter* (314c–d); *Seventh Letter* (341c–342, 344c–d).
35. See Hyland (1968: 43). To this extent Plato would question the modern analytical approaches of Frege, Russell, G. E. Moore and Wittgenstein. On the philosophical superiority of writing over oral or recitative approaches see Gee (1988: 199–200).
36. *Seventh Letter* (344c). See in this context Plato's *Second Letter* (314c) where he says to avoid divulging information improperly, it is best to avoid writing, and that he has never written anything on these philosophical doctrines, and that 'no treatise by Plato exists or will exist, but those which now bear his name belong to Socrates become fair and young'.
37. *Phaedrus* (276a, 275d, 256c).
38. For an overview of the political role of writing see, for example, Fisher (1966); Hyland (1968).
39. See in this respect the amusing presentation of Aristophanes in Plato's *Symposium* (185c–189b) who is unable to speak due to hiccups.

40. See the discussion in Hyland (1968).
41. *Phaedrus* (276e–277a).
42. See Plato's *Apology, Meno*.
43. See for example Hyland's (1968) examination of Plato's *Crito*.
44. On Socrates as the new Achilles see the introduction by Thomas G. West in Plato's (1984a) *Apology*.
45. When we examine more closely the drama of the *Republic*, we see how Socrates assumes comprehensive authority over the community that meets in Piraeus on that eventful day and night. 'I went down', the first words of the *Republic*, reminds us of how the philosopher will leave the blessed regions to return to the darkness of the cave. Socrates does not do so out of desire, but initially because he is compelled to moderate Glaucon's political ambitions for the sake of Plato's friendship and affection. Later he is 'arrested' by Polemarchus and his party to stay for dinner and the festival, and finally he is compelled by Glaucon, Adeimantus and others to take part in their conversation regarding the nature of justice. In Cephalus's house, Socrates orchestrates the removal of the aged and pious paterfamilias by reminding him with his insensitive questions about his imminent death how little he knows about justice and therefore his fate on the other side. He next takes on the other contending authority, the rhetor Thrasymachus who represents the Sophists. Socrates' spurious victory over Thrasymachus where he conflates what is with what appears, elevates him as the leading interlocutor and authority. His subsequent defence of justice persuades the ambitious young to favour the philosopher and philosophy over the poets, foremost statesman, sophists and the tyrannical life they advocate. In persuading the philosophically inclined young, he rewards them by being joint founders of the just or beautiful city. Taken together, the *Republic* represents the rule of the philosopher king, with the philosopher compelled to rule by the ambitious young who become his defenders, following his guidance in the founding of *kallipolis* or the just city.
46. On the rule of the wise see, for example, *Laws* (875b–c). For an overview of writing and law in Plato's *Laws* and the relationship between laws and the philosopher king see Fraistat (2015).
47. On the problems of codification see Scott (2009); on its implications for prudence see Rabbås (2010).
48. *Laws* (656d–657c).
49. For a well-known example of this tension see the debates regarding Abraham Lincoln's *Proclamation 104* suspending the writ of habeas corpus (Halbert 1958).
50. *Politics* (1286a: 12–14).
51. According to Diodorus of Sicily (1.82.3), cited in Jouanna (2012: 12), doctors who followed the written rules were absolved from

blame if unable to save the patient, but if proceeding contrary to legal prescription, they had to submit to trial with death as penalty.

52. On medicine and philosophy as parallel discoveries in Egypt see Jouanna (2012: 11), who notes the decline in the respect accorded to Egyptian medical knowledge from Homer to Galen.

53. On the importance of preamble in laws for Plato see Cohen (1993). For a contemporary overview see Orgad (2010).

54. See in this context Derrida (1997) who goes further by arguing texts have multiple meanings, some of which may not even be known to the author. For the 'death of the author' debate that claimed the intentions of the author or personal details were irrelevant for the interpretation of the text see generally Barthes (1977).

55. A problem anticipated by Socrates who insists that 'the many natures now making their way' to philosophy or rule 'are by necessity excluded' (*Republic* 473d–e).

56. For an overview of the role of writing in contemporary tyranny see the amusing and chilling account of what Kalder (2018) calls the 'infernal' library.

Bibliography

Aad, G. et al. (ATLAS Collaboration, CMS Collaboration). 2015. Combined Measurement of the Higgs Boson Mass in *pp* Collisions at √s=7 and 8 TeV with the ATLAS and CMS Experiments. *Physical Review Letters* 114: 191803.

Abbing, Hans. 2002. Art Serves the Government: How Symbiotic Is the Relationship between Art and the State? In *Why Are Artists Poor? The Exceptional Economy of the Arts*. Amsterdam: Amsterdam University Press, 232–58.

Abrams, Meyer Howard. 1953. *The Mirror and the Lamp*. Oxford: Oxford University Press.

Adorno, Theodor W. and Max Horkheimer. 1972. *Dialectic of Enlightenment*. London: Continuum.

Akin, William E. 1977. *Technocracy and the American Dream: The Technocrat Movement, 1900–1941*. Berkeley: University of California Press.

Allen, Peter. 1986. The Meanings of 'An Intellectual': Nineteenth and Twentieth-Century Usage. *University of Toronto Quarterly* 55(4): 342–58.

American Friends Service Committee. 1955. *Speak Truth to Power: A Quaker Search for an Alternative to Violence*. Philadelphia.

Ames, Roger. 1991. Reflections on the Confucian Self: A Response to Fingarette. In *Rules, Rituals, and Responsibility*, edited by Mary Bockover. La Salle, Illinois: Open Court, 103–14.

Ames, Roger T. and Henry Rosemount, Jr. 1998. *The Analects of Confucius: A Philosophical Translation*. New York: Random House.

Anderson, Elizabeth. 2006. The Epistemology of Democracy. *Episteme* 3(1–2): 8–22.

Annas, Julia. 1981. *An Introduction to Plato's Republic*. Oxford: Clarendon Press.

Ansell-Pearson, Keith, ed. 2015. *Nietzsche and Political Thought*. London: Bloomsbury.

Aquinas, St. Thomas. 1920. *Summa Theologiae of St. Thomas Aquinas*. Translated by Fathers of the English Dominican Province. <https://www.newadvent.org/summa/> (last accessed 1 July 2022).

Aristotle. 1979. *Metaphysics*. Translated by Hippocrates G. Apostle. Grinnell, Iowa: The Peripatetic Press.

Aristotle. 1984. *The Politics*. Translated by Carnes Lord. Chicago: University of Chicago Press.

Aristotle. 2012. *Nicomachean Ethics*. Translated by Robert Bartlett. Chicago: University of Chicago Press.

Aron, Raymond. 1957. *The Opium of the Intellectuals*. Translated by Terence Kilmartin. London: Secker & Warburg.

Ash Jr, James L. 1976. The Decline of Ecstatic Prophecy in the Early Church. *Theological Studies* 37(2): 227–52.

Asim, Jabari. 2007. *The N Word: Who Can Say It, Who Shouldn't, and Why*. New York: Houghton Mifflin Harcourt.

Aucoin, Peter. 2012. New Political Governance in Westminster Systems: Impartial Public Administration and Management Performance at Risk. *Governance* 25(2): 177–99.

Augustine (St). 1994. *The City of God*. Translated by Marcus Dods. New York: The Modern Library.

Aune, David E. 1983. The Character of Early Christian Prophecy. In *Prophecy in Early Christianity and the Ancient Mediterranean World*. Grand Rapids, Michigan: William B. Eerdman, 189–231.

Avineri, Shlomo. 1972. *Hegel's Theory of the Modern State*. Cambridge: Cambridge University Press.

Bacon, Francis. [1620] 1960. *The New Organon and Related Writings*. Indianapolis: The Bobbs-Merrill Company.

Bacon, Francis. [1893] 2019. *Advancement of Learning*. Frankfurt am Main: Outlook Verlag GmbH.

Baert, Patrick and Josh Booth. 2012. Tensions Within the Public Intellectual: Political Interventions from Dreyfus to the New Social Media. *International Journal of Politics, Culture, and Society* 25(4): 111–26.

Baert, Patrick and Barbara Misztal. 2012. Introduction: A Special Issue on Public Intellectuals. *International Journal of Politics, Culture, and Society* 25(4): 91–3.

Baert, Patrick and Alan Shipman. 2012. Transforming the Intellectual. In *The Politics of Knowledge*, edited by Fernando Domínguez Rubio and Patrick Baert. Abingdon: Routledge, 179–204.

Bai, Tongdong. 2020. *Against Political Equality: The Confucian Case*. Princeton: Princeton University Press.

Balazs, Etienne. 1964. *Chinese Civilization and Bureaucracy: Variations on a Theme*. New Haven: Yale University Press.

Barbalet, Jack. 2013. Greater Self, Lesser Self: Dimensions of Self-Interest in Chinese Filial Piety. *Journal for the Theory of Social Behaviour* 44(2): 186–205.

Barr, Michael D. 2000. Lee Kuan Yew and the 'Asian Values' Debate. *Asian Studies Review* 24(3): 309–34.

Barr, Michael D. 2006. Beyond Technocracy: The Culture of Elite Governance in Lee Hsien Loong's Singapore. *Asian Studies Review* 30(1): 1–17.

Barthes, Roland. 1977. Death of the Author. In *Image, Music, Text*. London: Fontana, 142–8.

Bartlett, Robert C. 2013. Sophistry as a Way of Life. In *Political Life Cross-Examined*, edited by Thomas L. Pangle and J. Harvey Lomax. New York: Palgrave Macmillan, 5–16.

Bartlett, Robert C. 2016. *Sophistry and Political Philosophy*. Chicago: University of Chicago Press.

Bartscherer, Thomas Luke. 2011. *The Ancient Quarrel Unsettled: Plato and the Erotics of Tragic Poetry*. Chicago: University of Chicago.

Bauman, Zygmunt. 1992. Love in Adversity: On the State the Intellectuals, and the State of the Intellectuals. *Thesis Eleven* 31(1): 81–104.

Baxandall, Lee and Sefan Morawski. 1973. *Karl Marx and Frederick Engels on Literature and Art*. New York: International General.

Beardsley, Monroe. 1983. An Aesthetic Definition of Art. In *What Is Art?*, edited by Hugh Curtler. New Haven: Yale University Press, 15–29.

Becker, Carol. 1994. Herbert Marcuse and the Subversive Potential of Art. In *The Subversive Imagination: Artists, Society, and Social Responsibility*. New York: Routledge, 113–29.

Beech, Dave. 2002. 'The Reign of the Workers and Peasants Will Never End': Politics and Politicisation, Art and the Politics of Political Art. *Third Text* 16(4): 387–98.

Bell, Daniel. 1960. The End of Ideology in the West. In *The Intellectuals: A Controversial Portrait*, edited with an introduction and overviews by George B. de Huszar. Glencoe: Free Press, 439–43.

Bell, Daniel. 1973. *The Coming of Post-Industrial Society: A Venture in Social Forecasting*. New York: Basic Books.

Bell, Daniel. 2015. *The China Model: Political Meritocracy and the Limits of Democracy*. Princeton: Princeton University Press.

Bell, Daniel and Chenyang Li. 2013. *The East Asian Challenge for Democracy: Political Meritocracy in Comparative Perspective*. Cambridge: Cambridge University Press.

Benda, Julien. [1928] 1969. *The Treason of the Intellectuals*. New York: W.W. Norton and Company.

Benjamin, Walter. [1936] 1969. The Work of Art in the Age of Mechanical Reproduction. In *Illuminations*, edited by Hannah Arendt and translated by Harry Zohn. New York: Schocken Books.

Bentley, Eric. 1969. *The Cult of the Superman*. Gloucester, MA: Peter Smith.

Bertsou, Eri and Daniele Caramani, eds. 2020. *The Technocratic Challenge to Democracy*. Abingdon: Routledge.

Bijker, Wiebe E., Roland Bal and Ruud Hendriks. 2009. *The Paradox of Scientific Authority: The Role of Scientific Advice in Democracies*. Cambridge: MIT Press.

Bird, Gemma. 2019. Rethinking the Role of the Arts in Politics: Lessons from the Négritude Movement. *International Journal of Cultural Policy* 25(4): 458–70.

Bloom, Allan. 1968. Interpretive Essay. In *The Republic of Plato*, translated by Allan Bloom. New York: Basic Books, 305–436.

Boggs, Carl. 1979. Marxism and the Role of Intellectuals. *New Political Science* 1(2–3): 7–23.

Bone, Drummond. 1989. The Emptiness of Genius: Aspects of Romanticism. In *Genius: The History of an Idea*, edited by Penelope Murray. Oxford: Basil Blackwell, 113–27.

Bourdieu, Pierre. 1989. The Corporatism of the Universal: The Role of Intellectuals in the Modern World. *Telos* 81: 99–110.

Bowler, Peter J. 2000. Philosophy, Instinct, Intuition: What Motivates the Scientist in Search of a Theory? *Biology and Philosophy* 15(1): 93–101.

Brecher, Bob. 2004. Do Intellectuals Have a Special Public Responsibility? In *Philosophy and its Public Role: Essays in Ethics, Politics, Society and Culture*, edited by William Aiken and John Haldane. Exeter: Imprint Academic, 25–38.

Brennan, Jason. 2016. *Against Democracy*. Princeton: Princeton University Press.

Brindley, Erica. 2009. *Individualism in Early China: Human Agency and the Self in Thought and Politics*. Honolulu: University of Hawai'i Press.

Brooks, Shilo. 2010. The Soul of the Scientist of Man. *The New Atlantis* 26: 98–107.

Brown, Richard Harvey and Elizabeth L. Malone. 2004. Reason, Politics, and the Politics of Truth: How Science Is Both Autonomous and Dependent. *Sociological Theory* 22(1): 106–22.

Burke, Edmund. 1989. *Reflections on Revolution*. London: Penguin.

Burnet, John. 1950. *Greek Philosophy: Thales to Plato*. London: Macmillan & Co.

Burns, Timothy W. 2015. Philosophy and Poetry: A New Look at an Old Quarrel. *American Political Science Review* 109(2): 326–38.

Burris, Beverly. 1993. *Technocracy at Work*. New York: SUNY Press.

Cammack, Daniela. 2013. Aristotle on the Virtue of the Multitude. *Political Theory* 41(2): 175–202.

Canovan, Margaret. 2005. *The People*. Cambridge: Polity Press.

Caplan, Arthur L. and Thomas A. Marino. 2007. The Role of Scientists in the Beginning-of-Life Debate: A 25-Year Retrospective. *Perspectives in Biology and Medicine* 50(4): 603–13.

Caplan, Bryan. 2007. *The Myth of the Rational Voter: Why Democracies Choose Bad Policies*. Princeton: Princeton University Press.

Caruso, Hwa Young Choi. 2005. Art as a Political Act: Expression of Cultural Identity, Self-Identity, and Gender by Suk Nam Yun and Yong Soon Min. *Journal of Aesthetic Education* 39(3): 71–87.

Chan, Joseph. 2013. Political Meritocracy and Meritorious Rule. In *The East Asian Challenge for Democracy: Political Meritocracy in Comparative Perspective*, edited by Daniel Bell and Chenyang Li. Cambridge: Cambridge University Press, 31–54.

Chomsky, Noam. 1967. A Special Supplement: The Responsibility of Intellectuals. *The New York Review of Books*, 23 February, 1–26.

Chong, Terence. 2010. The State and the New Society: The Role of the Arts in Singapore Nation-building. *Asian Studies Review* 34(2): 131–49.

Christiano, Thomas. 2004. The Authority of Democracy. *Journal of Political Philosophy* 12(3): 266–90.

Cimakasky, Joseph. 2017. *The Role of Exaíphnes in Early Greek Literature: Philosophical Transformation in Plato's Dialogues and Beyond*. Lanham: Lexington Books.

Cimatti, Felice. 2018. Scientist Because Philosopher, Philosopher Because Scientist. In *A Biosemiotic Ontology: The Philosophy of Giorgio Prodi*. Cham: Springer, 15–22.

Clark, Toby. 1997. Introduction. In *Art and Propaganda in the Twentieth Century*. New York: Abrams.

Close, Anthony J. 1969. Commonplace Theories of Art and Nature in Classical Antiquity and in the Renaissance. *Journal of History of Ideas* 30(4): 467–86.

Cohen, David. 1993. Autonomy, and Political Community in Plato's Laws. *Classical Philology* 88(4): 301–17.

Cohen, Joshua. 1986. An Epistemic Conception of Democracy. *Ethics* 97(1): 26–38.

Cohen, Joshua. 1989. Deliberation and Democratic Legitimacy. In *The Good Polity: Normative Analysis of the State*, edited by Alan Hamlin and Phillip Petit. New York: Blackwell, 17–34.

Coleman, Janet. 2000. *A History of Political Thought*. London: Blackwell.

Coleman, Jules and John Ferejohn. 1986. Democracy and Social Choice. *Ethics* 97(1): 6–25.

Collini, Stefan. 2002. Every Fruit-Juice Drinker, Nudist, Sandal-Wearer . . .: Intellectuals as Other People. In *The Public Intellectual*, edited by Helen Small. Oxford: Blackwell, 203–23.

Collini, Stefan. 2006. Introduction: The Question of Intellectuals. In

Absent Minds: Intellectuals in Britain. Oxford: Oxford University Press, 1–12.

Collins, Randall. 1998. The Sociological Eye and its Blinders. *Contemporary Sociology* 27(1): 2–7.

Collins, Randall. 2011. Who Has Been a Successful Public Intellectual? *European Journal of Social Theory* 14(4): 437–52.

Confino, Michael. 1972. On Intellectuals and Intellectual Traditions in Eighteenth- and Nineteenth-Century Russia. *Daedalus*, Intellectuals and Tradition, 101(2): 117–49.

Confucius. 2013. *Book of Rites*. Translated by James Legge. Boston: Intercultural Press.

Conroy, Mark. 1981. The Artist-Philosopher in Nietzsche's Jenseits von Gut und Böse. *MLN* 96(3): 615–28.

Conway, Daniel. 1996. *Nietzsche and the Political*. London: Routledge.

Cook, Daniel J. 2009. Leibniz on 'Prophets', Prophecy, and Revelation. *Religious Studies* 45(3): 269–87.

Cooper, John M. 1977. The Psychology of Justice in Plato. *American Philosophical Quarterly* 14(2): 151–7.

Cooper, Terry L. 2012. *The Responsible Administrator: An Approach to Ethics for the Administrative Role*. San Francisco: Jossey Bass.

Coser, Lewis A. [1965] 1997. *Men of Ideas: A Sociologist's View*. New York: Free Press (Simon & Schuster).

Cravens, Hamilton. 1985. History of the Social Sciences. *Osiris* 1: 183–207.

Cummings, Dolan, ed. 2005. *The Changing Role of the Public Intellectual*. London: Routledge.

Curd, Patricia. 2021. Presocratic Philosophy. In *Stanford Encyclopedia of Philosophy*, edited by Edward N. Zalta. Stanford: Stanford University Philosophy Department. <https://plato.stanford.edu/entries/presocratics/> (last accessed 1 July 2022).

Cutrofello, Andrew. 2008. Kant's Debate with Herder about the Philosophical Significance of the Genius of Shakespeare. *Philosophy Compass* 3(1): 66–82.

Dahlgren, Peter. 2012. Public Intellectuals, Online Media, and Public Spheres: Current Realignments. *International Journal of Politics, Culture, and Society* 25(4): 95–110.

Dahrendorf, Ralf. 1969. The Intellectual and Society: The Social Function of the 'Fool' in the Twentieth Century. In *On Intellectuals: Theoretical Studies, Case Studies*, edited by Philip Rieff. Garden City: Doubleday, 49–52.

Danowski, James A. and David W. Park. 2009. Networks of the Dead or Alive in Cyberspace: Public Intellectuals in the Mass and Internet Media. *New Media & Society* 11(3): 337–56.

Dasenbrock, Reed Way. 2001. *Truth and Consequences: Intentions,*

Conventions, and the New Thematics. University Park: Pennsylvania State University Press.

Davis, Howard. 2009. Conclusion: Revisiting the Concept of the Public Intellectual. In *Intellectuals and their Publics: Perspectives from the Social Sciences*, edited by Christian Fleck, Andreas Hess and E. Stina Lyon. Farnham: Ashgate, 261–70.

Davis, Michael. 2019. *The Music of Reason: Rousseau, Nietzsche, Plato.* Philadelphia: University of Pennsylvania Press.

Dawson, P. M. S. 1980. *The Unacknowledged Legislator: Shelley in Politics.* Oxford: Clarendon Press.

de Melo-Martin, Inmaculada. 2009. Creating Reflective Spaces: Interactions Between Philosophers and Biomedical Scientists. *Perspectives in Biology and Medicine* 52(1): 39–47.

de Mowbray, Malcom. 2004. Philosophy as Handmaid of Theology: Biblical Exegesis in the Service of Scholarship. *Traditio* 59: 1–37.

de Saint-Simon, Henri. [1813] 2014. *Selected Writings on Science, Industry and Social Organisation.* Translated and edited by Keith Taylor. London: Taylor & Francis Group.

Dennis, Amanda. 2011. Dithyrambs and Ploughshares: The Cycle of Creation and Criticism in Nietzsche's Aesthetics. *The European Legacy* 16(4) 469–85.

Derrida, Jacques. 1997. *Of Grammatology.* Baltimore: The Johns Hopkins University Press.

Diamond, Larry. 2021. Democratic Regression in Comparative Perspective: Scope, Methods, and Causes. *Democratization* 28(1): 22–42.

Doherty, Thomas. 2003. *Cold War, Cool Medium: Television, McCarthyism, and American Culture.* New York: Columbia University Press.

Drezner, Daniel W. 2009. Public Intellectuals 2.1. *Society* 46(1): 49–54.

Dryzek, John S. 2000. *Deliberative Democracy and Beyond: Liberals, Critics, Contestations.* Oxford: Oxford University Press.

Dryzek, John S. 2010. *Foundations and Frontiers of Deliberative Governance.* Oxford: Oxford University Press.

Dryzek, John S. 2016. Reflections on the Theory of Deliberative Systems. *Critical Policy Studies* 10(2): 209–15.

Dubs, Homer H. 1930. 'Nature' in the Teaching of Confucius. *Journal of the American Oriental Society* 50: 233–7.

Duncan, Christopher M. and Peter J. Steinberger. 1990. Plato's Paradox? Guardians and Philosopher-Kings. *American Political Science Review* 84(4): 1317–22.

Edelman, Murray. 1995. The Cardinal Political Role of Art. In *From Art to Politics: How Artistic Creations Shape Political Conceptions.* Chicago: University of Chicago Press, 1–14.

Edelstein, Ludwig. 1966. *Plato's Seventh Letter.* Leiden: Brill.

Ehli, Bridger. 2018. Rationalizing Socrates' *daimonion*. *British Journal for the History of Philosophy* 26(2): 225–40.

Eisenstadt, Shmuel Noah. 1972. Intellectuals and Tradition. *Daedalus* 101(2): 1–19.

Elshtain, Jean Bethke. 2001. Why Public Intellectuals? *The Wilson Quarterly (1976–).* 25(4): 43–50.

Elstub, Stephen, Selen Ercan and Ricardo F. Mendonca. 2016. The Fourth Generation of Deliberative Democracy. *Critical Policy Studies* 10(2): 139–51.

Eno, Robert. 1990. *The Confucian Creation of Heaven.* New York: SUNY Press.

Epstein, Joseph. 2006. Intellectuals-Public and Otherwise. In *Public Intellectuals: An Endangered Species?*, edited by Amitai Etzioni and Alyssa Bowditch. Lanham: Rowman & Littlefield, 185–94.

Erman, Eva and Niklas Möller. 2016. Why Democracy Cannot Be Grounded in Epistemic Principles. *Social Theory and Practice* 42(3): 449–73.

Estlund, David M. 2008a. *Democratic Authority: A Philosophical Framework.* Princeton: Princeton University Press.

Estlund, David M. 2008b. Democratic Authority: A Philosophical Framework. *Critica* 42(124): 118–25.

Evangeliou, Christos C. 2017. Plato and Sicilian Power Politics: Between Dion and Dionysus II. In *Politics and Performance in Western Greece: Essays on the Hellenic Heritage of Sicily and Southern Italy*, edited by Heather L. Reid, Davide Tanasi and Susi Kimbell. Fonte Aretusa: Parnassos Press, 289–301.

Eyerman, Ron. 1994. *Between Culture and Politics: Intellectuals in Modern Society.* Malden: Polity.

Eylon, Yuval and David Heyd. 2008. Flattery. *Philosophy and Phenomenological Research* 77(3): 685–704.

Ezrahi, Yaron. 1980. Utopian and Pragmatic Rationalism: The Political Context of Scientific Advice. *Minerva* 18(1): 111–31.

Ezrahi, Yaron. 1990. *The Descent of Icarus: Science and the Transformation of Contemporary Democracy.* Cambridge: Harvard University Press.

Farganis, Sondra. 2003. A Public or Dissenting Intellectual? *Critical Review of International Social and Political Philosophy* 6(4): 157–71.

Ferber, Michael. 2010. *Romanticism.* Oxford: Oxford University Press.

Ferrari, Giovanni R. F. 1987. *Listening to the Cicadas: A Study of Plato's Phaedrus.* Cambridge: Cambridge University Press.

Feyerabend, Paul K. 1970. *Against Method: Outline of an Anarchistic Theory of Knowledge.* Minneapolis: University of Minnesota Press

Fischer, Frank. 1990. *Technocracy and the Politics of Expertise.* Thousand Oaks: Sage Publications.

Fisher, John. 1966. Plato on Writing and Doing Philosophy. *Journal of the History of Ideas* 27(2): 163–72.

Fishkin, James S. 2009. *When the People Speak: Deliberative Democracy and Public Contestation*. Oxford: Oxford University Press.

Fortin, Ernest. 2002. *Dissent and Philosophy in the Middle Ages*. Lanham: Lexington Books.

Foucault, Michel. 1978. *The Birth of Biopolitics: Lectures at the Collège de France, 1978–1979*. Edited by Michel Senellart, François Ewald and Alessandro Fontana. London: Palgrave Macmillan.

Foucault, Michel. 2001. *Fearless Speech*. Boston: MIT Press.

Foucault, Michel and Gilles Deleuze. 1977. Intellectuals and Power. In *Language, Counter-Memory, Practice: Selected Essays and Interviews with Michel Foucault*, edited by Donald Bouchard. Ithaca: Cornell University Press, 205–17.

Fraistat, Shawn. 2015. The Authority of Writing in Plato's Laws. *Political Theory* 43(5): 657–77.

France, John. 2005. *The Crusades and the Expansion of Catholic Christendom, 1000–1714*. London: Routledge.

Frankel, Mark S. 1989. Professional Codes: Why, How, and with What Impact? *Journal of Business Ethics* 8(2–3): 109–15.

Frederickson, H. George and David K. Hart. 1985. The Public Service and the Patriotism of Benevolence. *Public Administration Review* 45(5): 547–53.

Freeland, Cynthia. 2001. *But Is It Art?: An Introduction to Art Theory*. Oxford: Oxford University Press.

Freeman, Kathleen. 1983. *Ancilla to the Pre-Socratic Philosophers: A Complete Translation of the Fragments in Diels, Fragmente der Vorsokratiker*. Cambridge, MA: Harvard University Press.

Fry, Brian R. and Lloyd G. Nigro. 1996. Max Weber and US Public Administration: The Administrator as Neutral Servant. *Journal of Management History* 2(1): 37–46.

Fuller, Steve. 2003. The Critique of Intellectuals in a Time of Pragmatist Captivity. *History of the Human Sciences* 16(4): 19–38.

Fuller, Steve. 2004. Intellectuals: An Endangered Species in the Twenty-First Century? *Economy and Society* 33(4): 463–83.

Fung, Archon and Erik O. Wright, eds. 2003. *Deepening Democracy: Institutional Innovation in Empowered Participatory Governance*. London: Verso.

Fustel de Coulanges, Numa. 1980. *The Ancient City*. Baltimore: The Johns Hopkins University Press.

Gagnon, Alain G., ed. 1987. The Role of Intellectuals in Liberal Democracies: Political Influences and Social Involvement. In *Intellectuals in Liberal Democracies*. New York: Praeger, 3–18.

Galbraith, John K. 1972. *The New Industrial State*. Harmondsworth: Penguin.

Galileo. 1957. *Discoveries and Opinions of Galileo*. Translated and edited by Stillman Drake. New York: Anchor Press, 229–80.

Gee, James Paul. 1988. Essay Reviews: The Legacies of Literacy. *Harvard Educational Review* 58(2): 195–212.

Geenens, Raf and Ronald Tinnevelt, eds. 2009. *Does Truth Matter? Democracy and Public Space*. New York: Springer.

Gilbert, G. Nigel and Michael Mulkay. 1984. *Opening Pandora's Box: A Sociological Analysis of Scientists' Discourse*. Cambridge: Cambridge University Press.

Gilpin, Robert George. 1962. *American Scientists and Nuclear Weapons Policy*. Princeton: Princeton University Press.

Gluckman, Peter. 2016. Science Advice to Governments: An Emerging Dimension of Science Diplomacy. *Science Diplomacy* 5(2): 9.

Gluckman, Peter and James Wilsdon. 2016. From Paradox to Principles: Where Next for Scientific Advice to Governments? *Palgrave Communications* 2(1): 1–4.

Goldfarb, Jeffrey C. 1998. *Civility and Subversion: The Intellectual in Democratic Society*. Cambridge: Cambridge University Press.

Goodin, Robert. 2003. *Reflective Democracy*. Oxford: Oxford University Press.

Gouldner, Alwin W. 1975. Prologue to a Theory of Revolutionary Intellectuals. *Telos* 26: 3–36.

Gouldner, Alvin W. 1979. *The Future of the Intellectuals and the Rise of the New Class*. New York: Continuum.

Gourgouris, Stathis. 2007. Public Intellectuals. In *International Encyclopedia of the Social Sciences*, vol. 4, 2nd ed., edited by William A. Darity Jr. Detroit: Macmillan.

Graham, Gordon 1997. The Marxist Theory of Art. *British Journal of Aesthetics* 37(2): 109–17.

Gramsci, Antonio. 1971. *Selections from the Prison Notebooks*. London: Lawrence & Wishart.

Greenberg, Daniel. 1965. The Myth of the Scientific Elite. *The Public Interest* 1: 51–62.

Greenberg, Daniel. 1999. *The Politics of Pure Science*, revised ed. Chicago: University of Chicago Press.

Greer, Steven and Tiong Piow Lim. 1998. Confucianism: Natural Law Chinese Style? *Ratio Juris* 11(1): 80–9.

Griswold, Charles L. 1986. *Self-Knowledge in Plato's Phaedrus*. New Haven: Yale University Press.

Gunn, Paul. 2019. Against Epistocracy. *Critical Review* 31(1): 26–82.

Guston, David H. 2010. Science, Politics, and Two Unicorns: An Academic Critique of Science Advice. In *Presidential Science Advisors*, edited by Roger Pielke Jr and Roberta A. Klein. Dordrecht: Springer, 7–15.

Guthrie, William K. C. 1969. *A History of Greek Philosophy*, vol. 3. Cambridge: Cambridge University Press.

Gutmann, Amy and Dennis Thompson. 1996. *Democracy and Disagreement: Why Moral Conflict Cannot Be Avoided in Politics, and What Should Be Done About it.* Cambridge, MA: Harvard University Press.

Halbert, Sherrill. 1958. The Suspension of the Writ of Habeas Corpus by President Lincoln. *The American Journal of Legal History* 2(2): 95–116.

Hall, A. Rupert. 1988. Scientists and Philosophers: Allies or Antagonists? *Interdisciplinary Science Reviews* 13(3): 204–7.

Hall, David and Roger Ames. 1987. *Thinking Through Confucius.* New York: SUNY Press.

Hankins, James. 1990. *Plato in the Italian Renaissance.* Leiden: Brill.

Harry, Chelsea C. and Justin Habash. 2020. *Brill's Companion to the Reception of Presocratic Natural Philosophy in Later Classical Thought.* Leiden: Brill.

Havel, Vaclav. 1991. *Disturbing the Peace: A Conversation with Karel Hvizdala.* New York: Vintage Books.

Hawkins, Denis J. B. 1947. *A Sketch of Mediaeval Philosophy.* New York: Sheed & Ward.

Hay, Cynthia. 1982. Advice from a Scientific Establishment: The National Academy of Sciences. In *Scientific Establishments Hierarchies*, edited by Norbert Elias, Herminio Martins and Richard Whitley. Sociology of the Sciences, Volume VI. Dordrecht: D. Reidel Publishing, 111–19.

Hayek, Friedrich A. 1949. The Intellectuals and Socialism. *University of Chicago Law Review* 16(3): 417–33.

Hegel, Georg W. F. 1998. *Aesthetics: Lectures on Fine Art.* Translated by Thomas M. Knox. Oxford: Oxford University Press.

Hegel, Georg W. F. 2002. *Philosophy of Right.* Translated by Alan White. Indianapolis: Focus Publishing.

Heidel, William Arthur. 1910. Περὶ Φύσεως. A Study of the Conception of Nature among the Pre-Socratics. *Proceedings of the American Academy of Arts and Sciences* 45(4): 79–133.

Heller, Michael. 2011. Science as Philosophy. In *Philosophy in Science: An Historical Introduction.* Heidelberg: Springer, 129–51.

Herodotus. 1988. *The History.* Translated by David Grene. Chicago: University of Chicago Press.

Herring, George. 2006. *An Introduction to the History of Christianity: From the Early Church to the Enlightenment.* London: Continuum.

Hickox, M. S. 1986. Has There Been a British Intelligentsia? *British Journal of Sociology* 37(2): 260–8.

Hirschl, Ran. 2004. *Towards Juristocracy.* Cambridge: Harvard University Press.

Hitchens, Christopher. 2008. How to Be a Public Intellectual. *Prospect Magazine*, May. <http://www.prospectmagazine.co.uk/2008/05/what-is-a-public-intellectual> (last accessed 1 July 2022).

Hitron, Hagai. 2019. The Tradition of Not Playing Wagner in Israel is Silly. *Haaretz*, 15 August. <https://www.haaretz.com/israel-news

/2019-08-15/ty-article/.premium/the-tradition-of-not-playing-wag ner-in-israel-is-silly/0000017f-f006-d497-a1ff-f286a0b80000> (last accessed 1 July 2022).

Ho, David Y. F. 1995. Selfhood and Identity in Confucianism, Taoism, Buddhism and Hinduism: Contrasts with the West. *Journal for the Theory of Social Behaviour* 25(2): 115–39.

Hoagwood, Terrence Allan. 1988. *Skepticism and Ideology: Shelley's Political Prose and its Philosophical Context from Bacon to Marx.* Iowa: University of Iowa Press.

Hoel, Nickolas O. 2020. Hues of Martyrdom: Monastic and Lay Asceticism in Two Homilies of Gregory the Great on the Gospels. *The Downside Review* 138(1): 3–18.

Hofstadter, Richard. [1963] 1974. *Anti-Intellectualism in American Life.* New York: Vintage.

Hollander, Robyn and Haig Patapan. 2017. Morality Policy and Federalism: Innovation, Diffusion and Limits. *Publius: The Journal of Federalism* 47(1): 1–26.

Holsta, Cathrine and Anders Molanderb. 2019. Epistemic Democracy and the Role of Experts. *Contemporary Political Theory* 18(4): 541–61.

Homer. 1991. *The Odyssey of Homer.* Translated by Richmond Lattimore. New York: Harper Collins.

Hong, Lu and Scott E. Page. 2004. Groups of Diverse Problem Solvers Can Outperform Groups of High-Ability Problem Solvers. *PNAS* 101(46): 16385–9.

Hoock, Holger. 2003. *The King's Artists: The Royal Academy of Arts and the Politics of British Culture 1760–1840.* Oxford: Clarendon Press.

Horrell, David. 1997. Leadership Patterns and the Development of Ideology in Early Christianity. *Sociology of Religion* 58(4): 323–41.

Hou, Wenhui. 1997. Reflections on Chinese Traditional Ideas of Nature. *Environmental History* 2(4): 482–93.

Howard, Cosmo. 2021. *Government Statistical Agencies and the Politics of Credibility.* Cambridge: Cambridge University Press.

Hsia, T. A. 1963. Twenty Years after the Yenan Forum. *The China Quarterly* 13: 226–53.

Huang, Chun-chieh. 2006. Man and Nature in the Confucian Tradition: Some Reflections in the Twenty-First Century. *TD: The Journal for Transdisciplinary Research in Southern Africa* 2(2): 311–30.

Hudson, Alan. 2003. Intellectuals for Our Times. *Critical Review of International Social and Political Philosophy* 6(4): 33–50.

Huggett, Nick. 2019. Zeno's Paradoxes. In *The Stanford Encyclopedia of Philosophy*, edited by Edward N. Zalta. Stanford: Stanford University Philosophy Department.

Huntington, Samuel P. 1993. *The Third Wave: Democratization in the Late Twentieth Century.* Norman, Oklahoma: University of Oklahoma Press.

Hyland, Drew A. 1968. Why Plato Wrote Dialogues. *Philosophy & Rhetoric* 1(1): 38–50.

Ignatieff, Michael. 1997. Decline and Fall of the Public Intellectual. *Queen's Quarterly* 104(3): 394–403.

Ignatieff, Michael. 2013. *Fire and Ashes: Success and Failure in Politics*. Cambridge: Harvard University Press.

Jackson, Michael W. 1986. Bureaucracy in Hegel's Political Theory. *Administration & Society* 18(2): 139–57.

Jacoby, Russell. 1987. Missing Intellectuals? In *The Last Intellectuals: American Culture in the Age of Academe*. New York: Basic Books, 3–26.

Jacoby, Russell. 2008. Big Brains, Small Impact. *Chronicle of Higher Education* 54(18): B5.

Jaffe, Yitzchak. 2015. Questioning Religious Essentialism: Ritual Change and Religious Instability in Ancient China. *Journal of Social Archaeology* 15(1): 3–23.

Jayasuriya, Kanishka and Garry Rodan. 2007. New Trajectories for Political Regimes in Southeast Asia. *Democratization* 14(5): 767–72.

Jennings, Jeremy. 2000. Intellectuals and Political Culture. *The European Legacy* 5(6): 781–95.

Jennings, Jeremy and Tony Kemp-Welch, eds. 1997. The Century of the Intellectual: From the Dreyfus Affair to Salman Rushdie. In *Intellectuals in Politics: From the Dreyfus Affair to Salman Rushdie*. London: Routledge, 1–24.

Jouanna, Jacques. 2012. Egyptian Medicine and Greek Medicine. In *Greek Medicine from Hippocrates to Galen: Selected Papers*, edited and with an introduction by Philip Van der Eijk, translated by Neil Allies. Leiden: Brill, 3–20.

Judd, Diana M. 2009. The Ethic and Practice of Natural Modern Science. In *Questioning Authority: Political Resistance and the Ethic of Natural Science*. New Brunswick: Transaction Publishers, 87–106.

Kalder, Daniel. 2018. *The Infernal Library: On Dictators, the Books They Wrote, and Other Catastrophes of Literacy*. New York: Henry Holt & Co.

Kamber, Richard. 1998. Weitz Reconsidered: A Clearer View of Why Theories of Art Fail. *The British Journal of Aesthetics* 38(1): 33–47.

Kane, John and Haig Patapan. 2012. *The Democratic Leader: How Democracy Defines, Empowers and Limits its Leaders*. Oxford: Oxford University Press.

Kane, John and Haig Patapan, eds. 2014. *Good Democratic Leadership: On Prudence and Judgment in Modern Democracies*. Oxford: Oxford University Press.

Kannicht, Richard. 1988. *The Ancient Quarrel Between Philosophy and Poetry: Aspects of the Greek Conception of Literature*. Christchurch: University of Canterbury Press.

Kant, Immanuel. 1987. *Critique of Judgment*. Translated and with an introduction by Werner S. Pluhar. Indianapolis: Hackett Publishing Company.

Kantorowicz, Ernst. 1957. *The King's Two Bodies*. Princeton: Princeton University Press.

Karabel, Jerome. 1976. Revolutionary Contradictions: Antonio Gramsci and the Problem of Intellectuals. *Politics and Sociology* 6(2): 123–72.

Karabel, Jerome. 1996. Towards a Theory of Intellectuals and Politics. *Theory and Society* 25(2): 205–33.

Kellner, Douglas. 1995. Intellectuals and New Technologies. *Media, Culture and Society* 17(3): 427–48.

Kerferd, G. B. 1981. *The Sophistic Movement*. Cambridge: Cambridge University Press.

Keyser, Paul T. and Georgia L. Irby-Massie, eds. 2008. *Encyclopedia of Ancient Natural Scientists: The Greek Tradition and its Many Heirs*. London: Routledge.

Kim, Sungmoon. 2014. *Confucian Democracy in East Asia: Theory and Practice*. Cambridge: Cambridge University Press.

Kimball-Smith, Alice. 1971. *A Peril and a Hope: The Scientists' Movement in America, 1945–47*, revised ed. Cambridge: MIT Press.

Kohn, Margaret. 2000. Language, Power, and Persuasion: Toward a Critique of Deliberative Democracy. *Constellations* 7(3): 408–29.

Kraus, Richard. 2004. The Chinese Censorship Game: New Rules for the Prevention of Art. In *The Party and the Art in China: The New Politics of Culture*. Lanham: Rowman & Littlefield, 107–42.

Kuhn, Thomas S. 1970. *The Structure of Scientific Revolutions*. Chicago: University of Chicago Press.

Kupperman, Joel. 1971. Confucius and the Nature of Religious Ethics. *Philosophy East and West* 21(2): 189–94.

Kurzman, Charles and Lynn Owens. 2002. The Sociology of Intellectuals. *Annual Review of Sociology* 28(1): 63–90.

Kyrtatas, Dimitris. 1988. Prophets and Priests in Early Christianity: Production and Transmission of Religious Knowledge from Jesus to John Chrysostom. *International Sociology* 3(4): 365–83.

Lackey, Robert T. 2007. Science, Scientists, and Policy Advocacy. *Conservation Biology* 21(1): 12–17.

Lagerwey, John and Marc Kalinowski, eds. 2009. *Early Chinese Religion*. Leiden: Brill.

Laing, Dave. 1978. *The Marxist Theory of Art*. Hassocks, Sussex: The Harvester Press.

Lambertini, Roberto. 2011. Mirrors for Princes. In *Encyclopedia of Medieval Philosophy*, edited by Henrik Lagerlund. Dordrecht: Springer. <https://doi.org/10.1007/978-1-4020-9729-4_338> (last accessed 1 July 2022).

Lampert, Laurence. 2010. *How Philosophy Became Socratic*. Chicago: University of Chicago Press.

Landauer, Matthew. 2012. Parrhesia and the Demos Tyrannos: Frank Speech, Flattery and Accountability in Democratic Athens. *History of Political Thought* 33(2): 185–208.

Landemore, Hélène. 2013. *Democratic Reason: Politics, Collective Intelligence, and the Rule of the Many*. Princeton: Princeton University Press.

Landemore, Hélène and Jon Elster. 2012. *Collective Wisdom: Principles and Mechanisms*. Cambridge: Cambridge University Press.

Lane, Melissa. 2013. Claims to Rule: The Case of the Multitude. In *Cambridge Companion to Aristotle's Politics*, edited by Marguerite Deslauriers and Pierre Destrée. Cambridge, MA: Cambridge University Press, 247–74.

Lapp, Ralph E. 1965. *The New Priesthood: The Scientific Elite and the Uses of Power*. New York: Harper & Row.

Leib, Ethan J. 1999. Nietzsche's Playground/Battlefield in Thus Spoke Zarathustra: The Quarrel between Philosophy and Poetry. *Yearbook of Comparative and General Literature* 47: 125–65.

Leibowitz, David M. 2010. *The Ironic Defense of Socrates Plato's Apology*. Cambridge: Cambridge University Press.

Leiserson, Avery. 1965. Scientists and the Policy Process. *The American Political Science Review* 59(2): 408–16.

Leonard, Stephen T. 1996. Introduction: A Genealogy of the Politicized Intellectual. In *Intellectuals and Public Life: Between Radicalism and Reform*, edited by Donald M. Reid, Stephen T. Leonard and Leon Fink. Cornell: Cornell University Press, 1–25.

Levin, Susan B. 2001. *The Ancient Quarrel Between Philosophy and Poetry Revisited: Plato and the Greek Literary Tradition*. Oxford: Oxford University Press.

Levison, Michael, Andrew Q. Morton and Alban D. Winspear. 1968. The Seventh Letter of Plato. *Mind* 77(307): 309–25.

Lewis, Victor Bradley. 2000. The Rhetoric of Philosophical Politics in Plato's Seventh Letter. *Philosophy & Rhetoric* 33(1): 23–38.

Lewis, William S. 2005. Art or Propaganda? Dewey and Adorno on the Relationship between Politics and Art. *The Journal of Speculative Philosophy* 19(1): 42–54.

Lewisohn, David. 1972. Mill and Comte on the Methods of Social Science. *Journal of the History of Ideas* 33(2): 315–24.

Li, Chenyang and Franklin Perkins, eds. 2015. *Chinese Metaphysics and its Problems*. Cambridge: Cambridge University Press.

Li, Yong. 2012. The Confucian Puzzle. *Asian Philosophy* 22(1): 37–50.

Liébert, Georges. 2004. *Nietzsche and Music*. Translated by David Pellauer and Graham Parkes. Chicago: University of Chicago Press.

Lijphart, Arend. 1999. *Patterns of Democracy: Government Forms and*

Performance in Thirty-Six Countries. New Haven: Yale University Press.

Lilla, Mark. 2001. *The Reckless Mind: Intellectuals in Politics*. New York: New York Review of Books.

Lindblom, Charles E. 1959. The Science of 'Muddling Through'. *Public Administration Review* 19(2): 79–88.

Lipset, Seymour Martin. 1959. American Intellectuals: Their Politics and Status. *Daedalus* 88(3): 460–86.

Lisi, Francisco L. 2013. Plato and the Rule of Law. *Méthexis* 26: 83–102.

List, Christian and Robert E. Goodin. 2001. Epistemic Democracy: Generalizing the Condorcet Jury Theorem. *Journal of Political Philosophy* 9(3): 277–306.

Liu, Qingping. 2007. Confucian Ethics and Social Morality: The Deep Paradox of Confucian Ethics. *Contemporary Chinese Thought* 39(1): 15–24.

Lodge, Rupert. 1953. *Plato's Theory of Art*. New York: Russell & Russell.

Loughlin, Martin. 2014. The Concept of Constituent Power. *European Journal of Political Theory* 13(2): 218–37.

Lull, Timothy, ed. 2012. *Martin Luther's Basic Theological Writings*. Minneapolis: Fortress Press.

Lynn Jr, Laurence E. 2005. Public Management: A Concise History of the Field. In *The Oxford Handbook of Public Management*, edited by Ewan Ferlie, Laurence E. Lynn Jr and Christopher Pollitt. Oxford: Oxford University Press, 27–50.

Maasen, Sabine and Peter Weingart. 2005. What's New in Scientific Advice to Politics? In *Democratization of Expertise? Exploring Novel Forms of Scientific Advice in Political Decision-Making*, edited by Sabine Maasen and Peter Weingart. Dordrecht: Springer, 1–20.

McCoy, Joe, ed. 2013. *Early Greek Philosophy: The Presocratics and the Emergence of Reason*. Washington, DC: Catholic University Press.

MacCulloch, Diarmaid. 2005. *The Reformation: A History*. London: Penguin.

MacCulloch, Diarmaid. 2010. *A History of Christianity: The First Three Thousand Years*. London: Penguin.

McDonnell, Duncan and Marco Valbruzzi. 2014. Defining and Classifying Technocrat-Led and Technocratic Governments. *European Journal of Political Research* 53(4): 654–71.

McFarland, Ian et al., eds. 2011. *The Cambridge Dictionary of Christian Theology*. Cambridge: Cambridge University Press.

McGrath, Alister E. 2017. *Christian Theology*. Hoboken: John Wiley & Sons.

Machamer, Peter and Gereon Wolters. 2004. Introduction: Science, Values, and Objectivity. In *Science, Values and Objectivity*, edited by Peter Machamer and Gereon Wolters. Pittsburgh: University of Pittsburgh Press, 1–13.

Machiavelli, Niccolò. 1985. *The Prince*. Translated by Harvey C. Mansfield Jr. Chicago: University of Chicago Press.

Machiavelli, Niccolò. 1996. *Discourses on Livy*. Translated by Harvey C. Mansfield Jr. and Nathan Tarcov. Chicago: University of Chicago Press.

Mackie, Gerry. 2014. The Reception of Social Choice Theory by Democratic Theory. In *Majority Decisions: Principles and Practice*, edited by Stéphanie Novak and Jon Elster. Cambridge: Cambridge University Press, 77–102.

Maclean, Ian, Alan Montefiore and Peter Winch, eds. 1990. *The Political Responsibility of Intellectuals*. New York: Cambridge University Press.

McLennan, Gregor and Thomas Osborne. 2003. Contemporary 'Vehicularity' and 'Romanticism': Debating the Status of Ideas and Intellectuals. *Critical Review of International Social and Political Philosophy* 6(4): 51–66.

MacNamara, Robert. 1995. *In Retrospect: The Tragedy and Lessons of Vietnam*, with Brian VanDeMark. New York: Times Books.

Mahoney, Timothy A. 1992. Do Plato's Philosopher-Rulers Sacrifice Self-Interest to Justice? *Phronesis* 37(3): 265–82.

Manin, Bernard. 1997. *The Principles of Representative Government*. Cambridge: Cambridge University Press.

Mannheim, Karl. [1932] 1993. The Sociology of Intellectuals. Translated by Dick Pels. *Theory, Culture and Society* 10(3): 69–80.

Mannheim, Karl. [1936] 1955. *Ideology and Utopia*. Boston: Mariner Books.

Mansfield, Harvey C. Jr. 1993. *America's Constitutional Soul*. Baltimore: The Johns Hopkins University Press.

Mao. [1943] 1980. *Mao Zedong's 'Talks at the Yan'an Conference on Literature and Art'*. A translation of the 1943 text with commentary by Bonnie S. McDougall. Ann Arbour: University of Michigan Center for Chinese Studies.

Marcuse, Herbert. 1978. *The Aesthetic Dimension: Toward a Critique of Marxist Aesthetics*. London: Macmillan.

Marenbon, John, ed. 2012. *The Oxford Handbook of Medieval Philosophy*. Oxford: Oxford University Press.

Marx, Karl. 1888. Thesis on Feuerbach. Supplement to *Ludwig Feuerbach and the End of Classical German Philosophy* by Friedrich Engels. Moscow: Marx-Engels-Lenin Institute of the Central Committee of the All-Union Communist Party.

Marx, Karl. 2010. A Contribution to the Critique of Political Economy. In *Marx Today*, edited by John Sitton. New York: Palgrave Macmillan, 91–4.

Marx, Karl and Friedrich Engels. [1848] 2018. *The Communist Manifesto*. New York: Vintage Classics.

Meir, Shahar and Robert Weller. 1959. *Unruly Gods: Divinity and Society in China*. Honolulu: University of Hawai'i Press.

Melamed, Abraham. 2003. *The Philosopher-King in Medieval and Renaissance Jewish Thought*. New York: SUNY Press.

Melzer, Arthur M. 2003. What is an Intellectual? In *The Public Intellectual: Between Philosophy and Politics*, edited by Arthur M. Melzer, Jerry Weinberger and M. Richard Zinman. Lanham: Rowman & Littlefield, 3–14.

Melzer, Arthur M., Jerry Weinberger and M. Richard Zinman. 1999. *Democracy and the Arts*. Ithaca: Cornell University Press.

Michael, John. 2000. Fundamental Confusion. In *Anxious Intellects: Academic Professionals, Public Intellectuals, and Enlightenment Values*. New York: Duke University Press, 1–22.

Mills, C. Wright. 1945. The Powerless People: The Social Role of the Intellectual. *Bulletin of the American Association of University Professors (1915–1955)* 31(2): 231–43.

Mishra, Pankaj. 2012. *From the Ruins of Empire*. New York: Picador.

Misztal, Barbara A. 2012. Public Intellectuals and Think Tanks: A Free Market in Ideas? *International Journal of Politics, Culture and Society* 25(4): 127–41.

Mittler, Barbara. 2008. Popular Propaganda? Art and Culture in Revolutionary China. *Proceedings of the American Philosophical Society* 152(4): 466–89.

Molnar, Thomas. 1961. The Emergence of the Intellectual. In *The Decline of the Intellectual*. Cleveland: World Publishing Company, 1–39.

Monoson, S. Sara. 2000. *Plato's Democratic Entanglements: Athenian Politics and the Practice of Philosophy*. Princeton: Princeton University Press.

Moore, Mark H. 1995. *Creating Public Value: Strategic Management in Government*. Cambridge: Harvard University Press.

Mormann, Thomas. 2017. Scientific Worldviews as Promises of Science and Problems of Philosophy of Science. *Centaurus* 59(3): 189–203.

Morrison, Donald S. 2007. The Utopian Character of Plato's Ideal City. In *Cambridge Companion to Plato's Republic*, edited by Giovanni R. F. Ferrari. Cambridge: Cambridge University Press, 232–55.

Mounk, Yascha. 2018. The Undemocratic Dilemma. *Journal of Democracy* 29(2): 98–112.

Mukerji, Chandra. 1989. Scientists as an Elite Reserve Labor Force. In *A Fragile Power: Scientists and the State*. Princeton: Princeton University Press, 3–21.

Munro, Thomas. 1960. The Marxist Theory of Art History. *The Journal of Aesthetics and Art Criticism* 18(4): 430–45.

Murray, Penelope, ed. 1989. *Genius: The History of an Idea*. Oxford: Basil Blackwell.

Mydans, Seth. 1998. Death of Pol Pot; Pol Pot, Brutal Dictator Who

Forced Cambodians to Killing Fields, Dies at 73. *New York Times*, 17 April. <https://www.nytimes.com/1998/04/17/world/death-pol-p ot-pol-pot-brutal-dictator-who-forced-cambodians-killing-fields-di es.html> (last accessed 1 July 2022).

Nabatchi, Tina, John Gastil, G. Michael Weiksner and Matt Leighninger, eds. 2012. *Democracy in Motion: Evaluating the Practice and Impact of Deliberative Civic Engagement*. Oxford: Oxford University Press.

Nelson, Daniel. 1980. *Frederick Taylor and the Rise of Scientific Management*. Madison: University of Wisconsin Press.

Nichols, Mary. 1984. The Republic's Two Alternatives: Philosopher-Kings and Socrates. *Political Theory* 12(2): 252–74.

Nichols, Mary. 2004. Socrates' Contest with the Poets in Plato's Symposium. *Political Theory* 32(2): 186–206.

Nietzsche, Friedrich W. [1882] 1988. *The Gay Science*. Translated by Walter Kaufman. New York: Alfred A. Knopf.

Nietzsche, Friedrich W. 1989a. *On the Genealogy of Morals and Ecce Homo*. Translated by Walter Kaufmann. New York: Vintage Books.

Nietzsche, Friedrich W. [1886] 1989b. *Beyond Good and Evil: Prelude to a Philosophy of the Future*. Translated and with commentary by Walter Kaufman. New York: Vintage Books.

Nietzsche, Friedrich W. 1994. Thus Spoke Zarathustra. In Walter Kaufmann, *Portable Nietzsche*. New York: Penguin.

Nietzsche, Friedrich W. [1878] 1996. *Human, All Too Human: A Book for Free Spirits*. Translated by R. J. Hollingdale. Cambridge: Cambridge University Press.

Nietzsche, Friedrich W. 2010. *The Peacock and the Buffalo: The Poetry of Nietzsche*. Translated by James Luchte. London: Continuum.

Nietzsche, Friedrich W. 2012. *Philosophy in the Tragic Age of the Greeks*. Translated by Marianne Cowan. Southlake: Gateway Editions.

Nietzsche, Friedrich W. 2017. *The Will to Power*. London: Penguin Classics

Nightingale, Andrea Wilson. 1999. Plato's Lawcode in Context: Rule by Written Law in Athens and Magnesia. *The Classical Quarterly* 49(1): 100–22.

Nino, Carlos Santiago. 1996. *The Constitution of Deliberative Democracy*. New Haven: Yale University Press.

Nivison, David S. 1999. The Classical Philosophical Writings. In *The Cambridge History of Ancient China: From the Origins of Civilization to 221 BC*, edited by Michael Loewe and Edward L. Shaughnessy. Cambridge: Cambridge University Press, 745–812.

Nussbaum, Martha C. 1997. *Cultivating Humanity: A Classical Defense of Reform in Liberal Education*. Cambridge, MA: Harvard University Press.

Ober, Josiah. 2008. *Democracy and Knowledge*. Princeton: Princeton University Press.

Ober, Josiah. 2013. Democracy's Wisdom: An Aristotelian Middle Way for Collective Judgment. *American Political Science Review* 107(1): 104–22.

O'Brien, Timothy. 2013. Scientific Authority in Policy Contexts: Public Attitudes about Environmental Scientists, Medical Researchers, and Economists. *Public Understanding of Science* 22(7): 799–816.

O'Connell, Robert J. 1978. *Art and the Christian Intelligence in St. Augustine.* Cambridge: Harvard University Press.

O'Connor, David. 2007. Rewriting the Poets in Plato's Characters. In *Cambridge Companion to Plato's Republic,* edited by Giovanni R. F. Ferrari. Cambridge: Cambridge University Press, 55–89.

Olsaretti, Alessandro. 2014. Beyond Class: The Many Facets of Gramsci's Theory of Intellectuals. *Journal of Classical Sociology* 14(4): 363–81.

Orgad, Liav. 2010. The Preamble in Constitutional Interpretation. *International Journal of Constitutional Law* 8(4): 714–38.

Orwin, Clifford. 1997. *The Humanity of Thucydides.* Princeton: Princeton University Press.

Pangle, Thomas L. 1980. Interpretive Essay. In *The Laws of Plato.* Chicago: University of Chicago Press, 375–510.

Pangle, Thomas L. 2018. *The Socratic Way of Life: Xenophon's 'Memorabilia'.* Chicago: University of Chicago Press.

Panton, James. 2003. What are Universities For? Universities, Knowledge and Intellectuals. *Critical Review of International Social and Political Philosophy* 6(4): 139–56.

Pappas, Nickolas. 1995. *Plato and the Republic.* London: Routledge.

Parrini, Paolo. 2012. Science and Philosophy. *Diogenes* 57(4): 89–101.

Parsons, Talcott. 1969. *Politics and Social Structure.* New York: Free Press.

Pasquinelli, Carla. 1995. From Organic to Neo-Corporatist Intellectuals: The Changing Relations Between Italian Intellectuals and Political Power. *Media, Culture & Society* 17(2): 413–25.

Pastorella, Giulia. 2016. Technocratic Governments in Europe: Getting the Critique Right. *Political Studies* 64(4): 948–65.

Patapan, Haig. 2015. Drifting to New Worlds: On Politics and Science in Modern Biotechnology. In *Policy Legitimacy, Science and Political Authority: Knowledge and Action in Liberal Democracies,* edited by Michael Heazle and John Kane. London: Routledge, 165–84.

Patapan, Haig. 2021. *A Dangerous Passion: Leadership and the Question of Honor.* New York: SUNY Press.

Patapan, Haig and Yi Wang. 2018. The Hidden Ruler: Wang Huning and the Making of Contemporary China. *Journal of Contemporary China* 27(109): 47–60.

Perkin, Harold. 2007. History of Universities. In *International Handbook of Higher Education,* edited by James J. F. Forest and Philip G. Altbach. Dordrecht: Springer, 159–205.

Pesic, Peter. 1999. Wrestling with Proteus: Francis Bacon and the 'Torture' of Nature. *Isis* 90(1): 81–94.

Petras, James. 1989. Metamorphosis of Latin America's Intellectuals. *Economic and Political Weekly* 24(14): 719–22.

Pielke Jr, Roger A. 2007. *The Honest Broker: Making Sense of Science in Policy and Politics*. Cambridge: Cambridge University Press.

Pielke Jr, Roger and Roberta A. Klein. eds. 2010. The Rise and Fall of the President's Science Advisor. In *Presidential Science Advisors*. Dordrecht: Springer, 149–67.

Pineda, Dorany. 2021. Amanda Gorman Brings the Representation Debate to the Small World of Book Translation. *Los Angeles Times*, 22 March, <https://www.latimes.com/entertainment-arts/books/story/2021-03-22/amanda-gorman-hill-we-climb-translation-backlash-sparks-controversy> (last accessed 12 July 2022).

Plato. 1979. *Dialogue on Friendship: An Interpretation of the Lysis*. With a new translation by David Bolotin. Ithaca: Cornell University Press.

Plato. 1980. *The Laws of Plato*. Translated by Thomas L. Pangle. New York: Basic Books.

Plato. 1984a. *Apology of Socrates*. In *Four Texts on Socrates*. Translated and with an introduction by Thomas G. West and Grace Starry West. Ithaca: Cornell University Press.

Plato 1984b. *The Being of the Beautiful: Plato's Theaetetus, Sophist, and Statesman*. Translated by Seth Benardete. Chicago: University of Chicago Press.

Plato. 1989. *Timaeus, Critias, Cleitophon, Menexenus, Epistles*. Translated by Robert G. Bury. Cambridge: Harvard University Press.

Plato. 1991a. *Republic*. Translated by Allan Bloom. New York: Basic Books.

Plato. 1991b. *Ion*. Translated by Allan Bloom. In *The Roots of Political Philosophy*, edited by Thomas L. Pangle. Cornell: Cornell University Press, 356–70.

Plato. 1993. *Symposium*. Translated by Seth Benardete. Chicago: Chicago University Press.

Plato. 1998a. *Phaedrus*. Translated by James H. Nichols Jr. Ithaca: Cornell University Press.

Plato. 1998b. *Gorgias*. Translated by James H. Nichols Jr. Ithaca: Cornell University Press.

Plato. 2004. *Protagoras* and *Meno*. Translated by Robert C. Bartlett. Ithaca: Cornell University Press.

Plato. 2005. *Phaedrus*. Translated and with an introduction and notes by Christopher J. Rowe. London: Penguin Books.

Plato. 2009. *Phaedo*. Translated and edited by David Gallop. Oxford: Oxford University Press.

Plekhanov, Georgii. [1912] 2009. Art and Social Life. In *Russian and Soviet Views of Modern Western Art, 1890s to Mid-1930s*, edited by Ilia Dorontchenkov, translated by Charles Rougle. Berkeley: University of California Press, 132–3.

Popper, Karl R. [1945] 2012. *The Open Society and its Enemies*. London: Routledge.

Porter, W. H. 1943. The Sequel to Plato's First Visit to Sicily. *Hermathena* 61: 46–55.

Posner, Richard. 2003. Introduction. In *Public Intellectuals: A Study of Decline*, revised ed. Cambridge: Harvard University Press, 1–40.

Prior, Moody E. 1954. Bacon's Man of Science. *Journal of the History of Ideas* 15(3): 348–70.

Pusey, Michael. 2010. The Struggles of Public Intellectuals in Australia: What Do They Tell Us About Contemporary Australia and the Australian 'Political Public Sphere'? *Thesis Eleven* 101(1): 81–8.

Rabbås, Øyvind. 2010. Writing, Memory and Wisdom: The Critique of Writing in the *Phaedrus*. *Symbolae Osloenses* 84(1): 26–48.

Radaelli, Claudio M. 1999. *Technocracy in European Union*. London: Routledge.

Rahe, Paul A. 2003. The Idea of the Public Intellectual in the Age of the Enlightenment. In *The Public Intellectual: Between Philosophy and Politics*, edited by Arthur M. Melzer, Jerry Weinberger and M. Richard Zinman. Lanham: Rowman & Littlefield, 27–52.

Rasmussen, Chris. 2006. Ugly and Monstrous: Marxist Aesthetics. *James A. Rawley Graduate Conference in Humanities* 7: 1–14.

Rawlinson, Kevin. 2016. Cecil Rhodes Statue to Remain at Oxford After 'Overwhelming Support'. *The Guardian*, 29 January. <https://www.theguardian.com/education/2016/jan/28/cecil-rhodes-statue-will-not-be-removed--oxford-university> (last accessed 1 July 2022).

Redditt, Paul L. 2008. What is a Prophet? In *Introduction to the Prophets*. Grand Rapids: William B. Eerdmans, 1–18.

Reeve, C. D. C. 1988. *Philosopher-Kings: The Argument of Plato's Laws*. Indianapolis: Hackett Publishing.

Renneberg, Monika and Mark Walker, eds. 1994. *Science, Technology, and National Socialism*. Cambridge: Cambridge University Press.

Rhodes, R. A. W. and John Wanna. 2007. The Limits to Public Value, or Rescuing Responsible Government from the Platonic Guardians. *The Australian Journal of Public Administration* 66(4): 406–21.

Rickless, Samuel C. 2012. Should Philosophers Become Public Intellectuals? In *Global Academe: Engaging Intellectual Discourse*, edited by Silvia Nagy-Zekmi and Karyn Hollis. New York: Palgrave Macmillan, 151–62.

Riedweg, Christoph. 2005. *Pythagoras: His Life, Teaching, and Influence*. Ithaca: Cornell University Press.

Riker, William H. 1982. *Liberalism Against Populism*. Prospect Heights, IL: Waveland.

Rimon, Helena. 2013. Paradoxes of 'Free Floating' and Controversy of Betrayal: Intellectuals' Reflections on Themselves Against the Background of Terror. *Terrorism and Political Violence* 25(4): 531–49.

Robbins, Bruce. ed. 1990. Introduction. In *Intellectuals: Aesthetics, Politics, Academics*. Minneapolis: University of Minnesota Press, ix–xxvii.

Roberson, Michael. 2012. Nietzsche's Poet-Philosopher: Toward a Poetics of Response-ability, Possibility, and the Future. *Mosaic: A Journal for the Interdisciplinary Study of Literature* 45(1): 187–202.

Rohr, John A. 1988. Bureaucratic Morality in the United States. *International Science Political Review* 9(3): 167–78.

Rosemont Jr, Henry. 1997. Classical Confucian and Contemporary Feminist Perspectives on the Self: Some Parallels and Their Implications. In *Culture and Self: Philosophical and Religious Perspectives, East and West*, edited by Douglas Allen. Boulder: Westview Press, 63–82.

Rosen, Stanley. 1965. The Role of Eros in Plato's 'Republic'. *Review of Metaphysics* 18(3): 452–75.

Rosen, Stanley. 1993. *The Quarrel Between Philosophy and Poetry*. London: Routledge.

Rosen, Stanley. 2005. *Plato's Republic: A Study*. New Haven: Yale University Press.

Ross, George. 1990. Intellectuals against the Left: The Case of France. *Socialist Register* 26: 201–27.

Ross, Sydney. 1991. Scientist: The Story of a Word. In *Nineteenth-Century Attitudes: Men of Science*. Dordrecht: Springer Science, 1–39.

Rosser, Christian. 2018. Max Weber's Bequest for European Public Administration. In *The Palgrave Handbook of Public Administration and Management in Europe*, edited by Edoardo Ongaro and Sandras Van Thiel. London: Palgrave Macmillan, 1011–30.

Rothstein, Bo. 2019. Epistemic Democracy and the Quality of Government. *European Politics and Society* 20(1): 16–31.

Rousseau, Jean-Jacques. [1762] 1978. *On the Social Contract, with Geneva Manuscript and Political Economy*. Edited by Roger D. Masters and translated by Judith R. Masters. New York: St. Martin's Press.

Rubin, Burton. 1956. Plekhanov and Soviet Literary Criticism. *The American Slavic and East European Review* 15(4): 527–42.

Rubinson, Paul. 2011. 'Crucified on a Cross of Atoms': Scientists, Politics, and the Test Ban Treaty. *Diplomatic History* 35(2): 283–319.

Russell, Bertrand. 1939. The Role of the Intellectual in the Modern World. *American Journal of Sociology* 44(4): 491–8.

Sadri, Ahmad and Arthur J. Vidich. 1992. Max Weber's Sociology of Politics as a Sociology of Intellectuals. In *Max Weber's Sociology of Intellectuals*. New York: Oxford University Press, 69–104.

Said, Edward W. 1994. *Representations of the Intellectual: The 1993 Reith Lectures*. New York: Pantheon Books.

Said, Edward W. 2002. The Public Role of Writers and Intellectuals. In *The Public Intellectual*, edited by Helen Small. Oxford: Blackwell, 19–39.

Sarkissian, Hagop. 2010. Recent Approaches to Confucian Filial Morality. *Philosophy Compass* 5(9): 725–34.

Scheideler, Britta. 2002. The Scientist as Moral Authority: Albert Einstein Between Elitism and Democracy, 1914–1933. *Historical Studies in the Physical and Biological Sciences* 32(2): 319–46.

Schofield, Malcolm. 1999. *Saving the City: Philosopher-Kings and Other Classical Paradigms*. London: Routledge.

Schumpeter, Joseph A. 1942. The Sociology of the Intellectual. In *Capitalism, Socialism, and Democracy*. New York: Harper, 145–55.

Schwartzberg, Melissa. 2015. Epistemic Democracy and its Challenges. *Annual Review of Political Science* 18: 187–203.

Schweber, Silvan S. 2013. *In the Shadow of the Bomb: Oppenheimer, Bethe, and the Moral Responsibility of the Scientist*. Princeton: Princeton University Press.

Scott, John C. 2006. The Mission of the University: Medieval to Postmodern Transformations. *The Journal of Higher Education* 77(1): 1–39.

Scott, Kyle. 2009. A Platonic Critique of Codification. *Journal of Jurisprudence* 3(1): 159–76.

Scrivener, Michael Henry. 1982. *Radical Shelley: The Philosophical Anarchism and Utopian Thought of Percy Bysshe Shelley*. Princeton: Princeton University Press.

Segal, Joes. 2016. *Art and Politics: Between Purity and Propaganda*. Amsterdam: Amsterdam University Press.

Sending, Ole Jacob. 2015. *The Politics of Expertise: Competing for Authority in Global Governance*. Ann Arbor: University Michigan Press.

Shapin, Steven. 2008. *The Scientific Life: A Moral History of a Late Modern Vocation*. Chicago: University of Chicago Press.

Shapin, Steven. 2010. *Never Pure: Historical Studies of Science as if It Was Produced by People with Bodies, Situated in Time, Space, Culture, and Society, and Struggling for Credibility and Authority*. Baltimore: Johns Hopkins University Press.

Shaw, Carl K. Y. 1992. Hegel's Theory of Modern Bureaucracy. *The American Political Science Review* 86(2): 381–9.

Shelley, Percy Bysshe. 1840. A Defence of Poetry. In *Essays, Letters from Abroad, Translations and Fragments*. London: Edward Moxon.

Shih, Hu. 2013. The Natural Law in the Chinese Tradition. In *English Writings of Hu Shih*, edited by Chih-Ping Chou. Heidelberg: Springer, 217–34.

Shils, Edward. 1968. Intellectuals. In *International Encyclopedia of the Social Sciences*, edited by D. L. Sills and Robert K. Merton. New York: Macmillan, 399–415.

Shils, Edward. 1972. Intellectuals, Tradition, and the Traditions of Intellectuals: Some Preliminary Considerations. *Daedalus*, Intellectuals and Tradition, 101(2): 21–34.

Showstack Sassoon, Anne. 1981. Some Notes on Gramsci's Theory of the Intellectuals. *Politics* 1(1): 13–19.

Simon, H. A. (1947). *Administrative Behavior: A Study of Decision-Making Processes in Administrative Organization*. New York: Macmillan.

Simplicius. 2022. *On Aristotle Physics 1.1-2*. Translated by Stephen Mann. London: Bloomsbury.

Singer, Daniel J. 2019. Diversity, Not Randomness, Trumps Ability. *Philosophy of Science* 86(1): 178–91.

Singer, Irving. 1954. The Aesthetics of 'Art for Art's Sake'. *The Journal of Aesthetics and Art Criticism* 12(3): 343–59.

Small, Helen, ed. 2002. *The Public Intellectual*. Oxford: Blackwell.

Smith, Graham. 2009. *Democratic Innovations: Designing Institutions for Citizen Participation*. Cambridge: Cambridge University Press.

Smith, Steven B. 2016. *Modernity and its Discontents: Making and Unmaking the Bourgeois from Machiavelli to Bellow*. New Haven: Yale University Press.

Smyth, William Henry. 1919. 'Technocracy'– Ways and Means to Gain Industrial Democracy. *Industrial Management* 57(5): 385–9.

Sowell, Thomas. 2009. Intellect and Intellectuals. In *Intellectuals and Society*. New York: Basic Books, 1–9.

Stadter, Philip A. 1991. Pericles among the Intellectuals. *Illinois Classical Studies* 16(1–2): 111–24.

Stapleton, Julia. 1999. Political Thought, Elites, and the State in Modern Britain. *The Historical Journal* 42(1): 251–68.

Stapleton, Julia. 2000. Cultural Conservatism and the Public Intellectual in Britain, 1930–70. *The European Legacy: Toward New Paradigms* 5(6): 795–813.

Steele, Katie. 2012. The Scientist qua Policy Advisor Makes Value Judgments. *Philosophy of Science* 79(5): 893–904.

Steinberg, Charles Side. 1941. The Aesthetic Theory of St. Thomas Aquinas. *The Philosophical Review* 50(5): 483–97.

Steinberger, Peter J. 1989. Ruling: Guardians and Philosopher-Kings. *The American Political Science Review* 83(4): 1207–25.

Steptoe, Andrew, ed. 1998. *Genius and the Mind: Studies of Creativity and Temperament*. Oxford: Oxford University Press.

Strauss, Leo. 1978. *City and Man*. Chicago: University of Chicago Press.

Strauss, Leo. 1985. *Studies in Platonic Political Philosophy*. Chicago: University of Chicago Press.

Strickland, Donald A. 1968. *Scientists in Politics: The Atomic Scientists Movement, 1945–46.* Lafayette: Purdue University Studies.

Sun, Anna Xiao Dong. 2013. *Confucianism as a World Religion: Contested Histories and Contemporary Realities.* Princeton: Princeton University Press.

Surowiecki, James. 2004. *The Wisdom of Crowds.* New York: Doubleday.

Swift, Jonathan. [1726] 2005. *Gulliver's Travels.* Edited by Claude Rawson, with notes by Ian Higgins. Oxford: Oxford University Press.

Tănăsoiu, Cosmina. 2008. Intellectuals and Post-Communist Politics in Romania: An Analysis of Public Discourse, 1990–2000. *East European Politics & Societies* 22(1): 80–113.

Tertullian. 1985. Prescription Against Heretics. In *Ante-Nicene Fathers,* vol. 3, edited by Alexander Roberts, James Donaldson and A. Cleveland Coxe, and translated by Peter Holmes. Buffalo, New York: Christian Literature Publishing Company. Revised and edited for New Advent by Kevin Knight, <https://www.newadvent.org/fathers/0311.htm> (last accessed 12 July 2022).

Thiele, Leslie Paul. 1990. *Friedrich Nietzsche and the Politics of the Soul: A Study of Heroic Individualism.* Princeton: Princeton University Press.

Thorpe, Charles. 2002. Disciplining Experts: Scientific Authority and Liberal Democracy in the Oppenheimer Case. *Social Studies of Science* 32(4): 525–62.

Thucydides. 1982. *History of the Peloponnesian War.* Translated by Walter Blanco. New York: The Modern Library.

Tocqueville, Alexis de. 2000. *Democracy in America.* Translated and edited with introduction by Harvey C. Mansfield and Delba Winthrop. Chicago: University of Chicago Press.

Todorov, Tzvetan, Alina Clej, Lawrence D. Kritzman, Frances Ferguson, Howard Young, Patrick Saveau and Gerard Genette. 1997. The Genealogy of the Intellectual since the French Enlightenment. *PMLA* 112(5): 1121–8.

Tolstoy, Leo. [1899] 2011. *What is Art?* Translated by Aylmer Maude and G. Jones. Bristol: Bristol Classical Press.

Trompf, Garry W. 1977. Social Science in Historical Perspective. *Philosophy of the Social Sciences* 7(2): 113–38.

Tu, Wei-ming. 1972. Li as Process of Humanization. *Philosophy East and West* 22(2): 187–201.

Tucker, Mary Evelyn. 1998. Religious Dimensions of Confucianism: Cosmology and Cultivation. *Philosophy East and West* 48(1): 5–45.

Tuncel, Yunus. 2015. Why Do Poets Lie Too Much? Nietzsche, Poetry and the Different Voices of Zarathustra. *The Agonist* 8(1): 1–17.

Turner, Stephen P. 2013. *The Politics of Expertise.* New York: Routledge.

Ulam, Adam B. 1973. *Stalin: The Man and His Era.* London: Allen Lane.

Vibert, Frank. 2007. *The Rise of the Unelected: Democracy and the New Separation of Powers.* Cambridge: Cambridge University Press.

Viehoff, Daniel. 2016. Authority and Expertise. *Journal of Political Philosophy* 24(4): 406–26.

Volt, Marek. 2002. Controversy about the Traditional Theory in Aesthetic. *Journal of Comparative Literature and Aesthetics* 25(1–2): 123–33.

von Schomberg, René. 1993. Political Decision Making in Science and Technology: A Controversy About the Release of Genetically Engineered Organisms. *Technology in Society* 15(4): 371–81.

Vööbus, Arthur. 1951. The Origin of Monasticism in Mesopotamia. *Church History* 20(4): 27–37.

Waldron, Jeremy. 1995. The Wisdom of the Multitude: Some Reflections on Book III Chapter 11 of the Politics. *Political Theory* 23: 563–84.

Wang, Jessica. 1999. Competing Political Visions for Postwar Science Scientists and Science Legislation, 1945–1947. In *American Science in an Age of Anxiety: Scientists, Anticommunism, and the Cold War.* Chapel Hill: University of North Carolina Press, 10–43.

Wang, Jessica. 2002. Scientists and the Problem of the Public in Cold War America, 1945–1960. *Osiris*, Science and Civil Society, 17: 323–47.

Ward, Ann. 2020. *The Socratic Individual: Philosophy, Faith and Freedom in a Democratic Age.* Lanham: Lexington Books.

Weber, Max. 1978. *Economy and Society*, 2 vols. Edited by Guenther Roth and Claus Wittich. Berkeley: University of California Press.

Weinert, Friedel. 2005. *The Scientist as Philosopher: Philosophical Consequences of Great Scientific Discoveries.* Berlin: Springer-Verlag.

Weingart, Peter. 1982. The Scientific Power Elite – A Chimera; The De-Institutionalization and Politicization of Science. In *Scientific Establishments and Hierarchies*, edited by Norbert Elias, Herminio Martins and Richard Whitley. Dordrecht: Springer, 71–87.

Weingart, Peter. 1999. Scientific Expertise and Political Accountability: Paradoxes of Science in Politics. *Science and Public Policy* 26(3): 151–61.

Weintraub, E. Roy. 2002. *How Economics Became a Mathematical Science.* Durham: Duke University Press.

Weiss, Roslyn. 2006. *The Socratic Paradox and its Enemies.* Chicago: University of Chicago Press.

Weitz, Morris. 1956. The Role of Theory in Aesthetics. *Journal of Aesthetics and Art Criticism* 15(1): 27–35.

Wewinshon, Richard. 1958. *Prophets and Prediction.* London: Secker & Warburg.

Wheelwright, Philip. 1997. *The Presocratics.* Upper Saddle River, New Jersey: Prentice Hall.

White, Nichols P. 1979. *A Companion to Plato's Republic.* Oxford: Basil Blackwell.

Whitlock, Greg. 1953. Concealing the Misconduct of One's Own Father:

Confucius and Plato on a Question of Filial Piety. *Journal of Chinese Philosophy* 21(2): 113–37.

Williams, Bernard. 2002. *Truth and Truthfulness*. Princeton: Princeton University Press.

Williams, Malcolm. 2000. Where Did Science Come From? In *Science and Social Science: An Introduction*. London: Routledge, 8–27.

Wong, Benjamin. 2013. Political Meritocracy in Singapore: Lessons from PAP Government. In *The East Asian Challenge for Democracy: Political Meritocracy in Comparative Perspective*, edited by Daniel Bell and Chenyang Li. Cambridge: Cambridge University Press, 288–313.

Woodhead, Linda. 2004. *An Introduction to Christianity*. Cambridge: Cambridge University Press.

Wordsworth, William. [1798] 2013. *Lyrical Ballads: 1798 and 1802*. Edited by Fiona Stafford. Oxford: Oxford University Press.

Wordsworth, William. [1805] 1970. *The Prelude: Or, Growth of a Poet's Mind (Text of 1805)*. Edited and with introduction by Ernest de Selincourt. Oxford: Oxford University Press.

Wu, Duncan, ed. 2012. *Romanticism: An Anthology*, 4th ed. Oxford: Blackwell.

Wycherley, Richard E. 1959. The Garden of Epicurus. *Phoenix* 13(2): 73–7.

Yankelovich, Daniel. 2003. Winning Greater Influence for Science. *Issues in Science and Technology* 19(4): 7–11.

Yeats, William B. 1919. On Being Asked for a War Poem. In *The Wild Swans at Coole*. London: Macmillan.

Yong, Huang. 2007. Confucian Theology: Three Models. *Religion Compass* 1(4): 455–78.

Yu, Jiyuan. 2005. The Beginning of Ethics: Confucius and Socrates. *Asian Philosophy* 15(2): 173–89.

Yunis, Harvey. 2007. The Protreptic Rhetoric of the *Republic*. In *Cambridge Companion to Plato's Republic*, edited by Giovanni R. F. Ferrari. Cambridge: Cambridge University Press 1–26.

Zhao, Guoping. 2009. Two Notions of Transcendence: Confucian Man and Modern Subject. *Journal of Chinese Philosophy* 36(3): 391–407.

Znaniecki, Florian. [1940] 1968. *The Social Role of the Man of Knowledge*. New York: Harper Torchbooks.

Zuckert, Katherine. 1996. *Postmodern Platos*. Chicago: University of Chicago Press.

Index

Abelard, P., 38
ability, 12, 15, 16, 20, 21, 25, 43,
    58, 66, 75(n50), 76(n61), 93,
    97, 107, 108, 114, 117, 126,
    130(n48), 145, 154, 155, 160,
    162, 164, 172, 178, 180, 181,
    183, 185
Addison, J., 84
Adeimantus, 10, 11, 12, 17, 28
Adorno, T. W., 83
advisors, 5, 7, 11, 30, 42, 64,
    104–33
    and best regimes, 105–7
    danger of, 104, 109, 114, 115
    as hidden philosopher kings,
        104–33, 140, 171, 178
    institutionalisation, 124–7
    and princes, 107–15, 127
    scientific, 135, 139–41, 144, 148
Aesop, 2
aesthetics, 78, 79, 80, 82, 83–4, 86,
    100(n24)
    Marxist, 79, 80, 82–4, 88, 95, 96,
        100(n17)
    modern, 84, 86
Al-Farabi, A. N., 27, 35, 37
Alcibiades, 173
alienation, 67, 73(n26), 81, 83, 146
ambiguity, 41, 108, 115, 118, 146,
    154, 178, 185
ambition(s), 4, 5, 7, 8, 11, 15, 19, 22,

25, 28, 29, 30, 58, 59, 70, 86, 90,
    94, 98, 110, 119, 120, 121, 134,
    137, 139, 142, 148, 156, 157,
    160, 162, 169(n61), 171, 172,
    173, 175, 182, 189(n45)
Anaxagoras of Clazomenae, 23, 154
Anglicanism, 51
anti-intellectualism
    American, 75(n48)
    definition, 154
    democratic, 153–9
    see also Tocqueville
Apocalypse, 37, 42, 43
Apostles, 36, 37, 39, 40, 42, 43, 45,
    48, 55(n34)
Arendt, H., 26
aristocracy/ies, 60, 156, 157, 158
Aristophanes, 85, 144
Aristotle, 21, 27, 29, 37, 38, 88, 106,
    135, 147, 178, 184
    defence of democracy, 161–2
Aron, R., 68
Arrow Paradox, 18
art, 77–103
    capitalist, 81, 83, 94
    and Chinese communism, 82, 96
    Christian, 87, 95, 100(n30)
    definition, 78–9
    as entertainment commodity, 94–5
    Heroic approaches, 79, 80, 84, 86,
        88

art (*cont.*)
  Marxist perspectives, 80–4, 88
  and politics, 77, 79–84, 86, 94–9,
    99(*n*5)
  revolutionary, 81–4
  Romantic approaches, 79, 84–8
  Soviet, 81–2, 96
  theories, 78, 82, 95, 101(*n*44),
    102(*n*49)
  see also aesthetics
artist(s)
  and class, 81, 82, 83, 84, 97,
    100(*n*16)
  as creators, 6–7, 77–103
  critique of, 86–7, 94
  as geniuses, 77, 79, 84–8, 94
  as heroes, 82, 86, 91
  and identity, 80, 84
  patronage, 94
  as philosopher-kings, 5, 77, 79, 80,
    84, 87–94, 97–9, 171
  and politics, 11, 30, 77, 78, 79, 80,
    83, 84, 86, 97, 98
  as revolutionaries, 81–4, 95, 96–7,
    101(*n*31)
  worker-artist, 80–4
Athenian Stranger, 105, 127, 174,
  182, 183, 184, 188(*n*25)
Athenians, 3–4, 21
Athens, 8(*n*5), 21, 27, 38, 63, 154,
  173, 174, 175, 176, 177
authenticity, 69, 78, 131(*n*69)
authority
  of artists, 79, 90, 91, 97
  democratic, 127
  divine, 23
  of intellectuals, 58, 60, 61, 65, 66,
    171
  moral, 65, 66, 71
  papal, 40, 47, 48–9, 50, 52,
    56(*n*59)
  and philosophers, 28, 127, 152,
    154, 163, 175, 184, 189(*n*45)
  political, 6, 9, 46, 66, 79, 99, 139,
    144, 146, 173
  scientific, 135, 136, 138, 139, 141,
    144, 145, 146, 151(*n*47)
  spiritual, 40, 44, 47
  temporal, 47

autonomy, 60, 62, 70, 74(*n*29), 82,
  131(*n*69)
Averroes, 27, 37, 104

Bacon, F., 134, 135, 138, 141, 144,
  145
Baconian method, 136, 138
Baudelaire, C., 83
Bauman, Z., 64
Baumgarten, A. G., 78
belief, 10, 17, 38, 40, 142, 159
Bell, D., 143
Benda, J., 62, 66
benevolence, 7, 117, 130(*n*37),
  130(*n*42), 166
Benjamin, W., 83
Bernal, J. D., 69
Bernstein, E., 62
Biden, J., 96
Bishop of Rome, 44, 46, 47, 48
Boethius, 26, 37, 88, 178
Bogdanov, A., 81
Brecht, B., 83
British exceptionalism thesis, 69,
  75(*n*49)
Buddhism, 35
Bukharin, N., 81, 104
bureaucracy, 105, 124–7, 128,
  132(*n*84), 133(*n*96), 150(*n*29);
  see also Hegel, Weber
Burke, E., 68, 85
Byzantine Empire, 46, 51

Caesar, 39, 87
Callicles, 24, 25
Calvin, J., 51
capitalism, 72(*n*16), 81, 83, 143
Carlyle, T., 86
Cato the Elder, 26
Cave metaphor, 13, 14, 63,
  189(*n*45)
censorship, 21, 84, 96, 99, 103(*n*90),
  185
Cervantes, M., 97
Charlemagne (Charles I), 46
Charmides, 174
Chomsky, N., 57, 69
Christ, 6, 36, 38, 39, 40, 41, 42, 44,
  45, 46, 47, 48, 50, 87

Christian Church
  doctrinal contests, 47, 50
  separation of Church and state, 28,
    47
  struggle between popes, princes,
    emperors, 46–9
Christianity, 27–8, 35–56
Chrysippos, 18
Cicero, 37, 178
citizens, 14, 15, 16, 51, 63, 71, 117,
  153, 156, 157, 158, 165
clergy, 47, 49, 56(n59), 56(n61)
Coleridge, S. T., 85
Communism, 68, 83
Comte, A., 137, 142
Condorcet, N., 60, 137
Condorcet
  Jury Theorem, 164
  Paradox, 170(n68)
Confucianism
  conceptions of virtue, 117
  political thought, 115–28
  sage and political rule, 118–121
  scholar–officials and the sage king,
    115–27
  see also Confucius, meritocracy
Confucius
  comparison to Socrates, 115–6,
    121–4
  gods, 119, 121, 122–4
  education, 117, 118–9
  family, 117, 121, 122–4
  and the individual, 116–7, 121,
    122–4
  leadership, 119–20
  politics and philosophy, 7, 115,
    117, 118
  public service, 119
  and the sage king, 105, 116, 119,
    120, 121, 124
Constantine the Great, 45, 46, 47
constitutionalism, 8, 124, 174,
  187(n12)
contemplation, 13, 16, 18–26, 41, 63,
  144
Copernicus, N., 136
cosmology, 123, 136
cosmos, 11, 17, 18, 20, 22, 23, 28,
  33(n61), 38, 89

counsellors see advisors
courage, 12, 16, 17, 65, 91, 92, 105,
  106, 184
creativity, 79, 88, 96, 149(n16)
Critias, 174
cruelty, 3, 14, 17, 18, 52, 67, 71, 87,
  119, 182, 186
Crusades, 51, 56(n66)
Cubism, 97
Cultural Revolution, 82, 96

d'Alembert, J-B., 60
De Botton, A., 26
De Man, P., 68
de' Medici, L., 107
de Saint-Simon, H., 142
deliberation, 71, 90, 162, 165, 166,
  172
Delphi oracle, 43, 92, 123
democracy/ies, 7, 22, 24, 29, 55(n36),
  96, 103(n89), 139, 143, 147,
  149(n18), 151(n35), 152,
  152–70, 177, 103(n89), 167(n3)
  and anti-intellectualism, 153, 154,
    159, 75(n45)
  and the arts, 156, 157, 158, 159
  challenges to, 147, 153–6,
    170(n77)
  deliberative, 164–5, 170(n72),
    170(n76), 170(n77)
  epistemic, 147, 164, 165, 169(n65),
    170(n77)
  and equality, 24, 152, 154, 155,
    156–7, 159
  and experts, 169(n50)
  liberal, 71, 96, 151(n47)
  limitations, 162–3, 170(n76)
  and literature, 156, 157, 158–9
  modern, 29, 129(n21), 143, 147,
    153, 154, 156, 159, 160, 161,
    162, 163
  and philosopher kings, 29, 152,
    153, 154, 161, 162–3, 166
  and philosophy, 152–3, 159–63
  representative, 153, 160, 164
  and science, 143, 147, 157–8,
    159
  of the wise, 153, 166–7, 171
  see also Aristotle, Tocqueville

democratic
    institutions, 153, 155, 159, 160–1,
        165, 171
    politics, 143, 148, 160, 161, 165
    rule, 152, 153
    voting, 164, 168(n12), 170(n68)
Deng Xiaoping, 9
Descartes, R., 27, 53, 104, 136, 138,
    155
desires, 8, 12, 14, 15, 24, 25, 55(n48),
    99, 157, 158, 172, 175, 181
despair, 1, 3, 8, 120
Dewey, J., 78
dialectical materialism, 80–1, 83
Diderot, D., 60
dignity, 8, 29, 68, 104, 105, 111,
    127
Diocletian, 45
Diogenes the Cynic, 19, 26
Dion, 176, 177
Dionysius I, 104, 106, 176, 177
Dionysius II, 104, 106, 176–7
dissent, 64, 71
divine (the), 3, 18, 24, 25, 26, 36, 85,
    123, 131–2(n72), 132(n75)
divine right of kings, 28, 46
doubt(s), 1, 21, 53, 70, 111, 113,
    127, 140, 144, 145, 147, 159,
    169(n49)
doxa (belief, opinion), 10, 17
Dreyfus affair, 59, 72(n14)
Durkheim, E., 137

education, 7, 10, 14, 15, 16, 37, 61,
    82, 91, 111, 117, 118, 119, 162,
    176, 177
Einstein, A., 139, 145
elite(s), 62, 63, 69, 73(n17), 74(n29),
    76(n55), 96, 142, 147, 151(n48),
    167(n4), 169(n64)
elitism, 7, 167(n4)
Emotionalism, 78
Emperor Henry IV, 48, 104
Emperor Marcus Aurelius, 26, 178
Emperor Nero, 26, 45, 104
Emperor Qin, 2, 104
empiricism, 53, 137
enemy/enemies, 1, 3, 29, 38, 39, 40,
    82, 91, 162

Engels, F., 59, 80, 81, 82
Enlightenment, 53, 58, 59, 60, 68, 70,
    72(n16), 137, 146, 147
Epicurus, 20
Epimenides Paradox, 18
Epimetheus, 24
epistemology, 123, 141
epistocracy, 147, 151(n45), 167(n5)
equality, 24, 96, 130(n40), 152, 154,
    155, 156–7, 159
Erasmus, 106
ethics, 23, 37, 146
Etkind, A., 69
evil, 87, 91, 92, 109, 166
excellence, 17, 19, 24, 87, 89, 109,
    110, 112, 115, 116, 117, 118,
    122, 123, 124, 129(n34), 154,
    161, 172

faith, 27, 35, 36, 38, 39, 41, 43, 44,
    50, 52, 53, 53(n10)
faithfulness, 109, 110
fear, 3, 29, 110, 112, 127, 147, 154,
    177, 187
Feyerabend, P., 145
First World War, 142
flattery, 66, 110–11, 112, 113, 114,
    127, 129(n21), 170(n76)
followers, 42, 116, 182, 185
Formalism, 78, 96
fortune(s), 4, 66, 107, 158, 159, 173,
    185
Foucault, M., 57–8, 69, 143
Frankfurt School, 83
freedom, 4, 45, 59, 60, 96, 111, 161,
    167
French Revolution, 68
friendship, 40, 122, 166, 176,
    189(n45)

Galbraith, J. K., 143
Galileo 52, 136, 145
genius/geniuses, 7, 77, 79, 84–8, 94,
    97, 100(n21), 103(n93)
Gerasimov, A., 95
Giles of Rome, 42, 48, 106
Glaucon, 10–11, 24, 25, 28, 89, 175,
    181
glory, 61, 98, 177

gods (the), 4, 22, 23, 24, 28, 35, 45, 89, 91, 92, 93, 97, 99, 102(n69), 105, 119, 121, 122-4, 131(n72), 173, 181, 182, 185
Goethe, J. W., 86
good (the), 16, 25, 32(n39), 64, 87, 90, 92, 109, 110, 131(n72), 146, 178, 183
  common, 32(n39), 113, 119, 126, 134, 165
  public, 32(n39), 58, 64, 65, 127, 133(n96)
goodness, 11, 23, 91, 108, 109, 110, 116, 144, 145, 147, 172
Gorgias of Leontini, 21, 24, 25, 98
Gorky, M., 81
Gouldner, A., 143
Gramsci, A., 62

Habermas, J., 165
Hadot, P., 26
Halevi, J., 27
Han Fei, 2, 104
haoxue (love of learning), 119, 129(n33)
happiness, 1, 16, 17, 18, 19, 23, 25, 26, 28, 59, 117, 122, 180, 185
harmony, 15, 23, 115, 116, 117, 130(n37), 130(n42)
Havel, V., 57
Hayek, F., 68
heaven(s), 2, 39, 40, 43, 47, 98, 116, 123, 130(n40), 159, 175, 176
Hegel, G. W., 70, 89, 125, 126, 142
  conception of bureaucracy, 125-7
Heidegger, M., 68, 86
Heine, H., 86
Heraclitus of Ephesus, 20, 22, 64, 97
Herder, J. G., 85
hero/es, 22, 28, 86, 91
Herodotus, 23
Hesiod, 22, 91, 98
hierarchy/ies, 56(n59), 62, 116, 117, 122
Hippias of Ellis, 21
history (discipline), 60, 67, 78, 149(n12)
Hitchens, C., 57
Hobbes, T., 137, 141

Hofstadter, D., 67, 154
Hölderlin, F., 86
Homer, 22, 84, 91, 93, 98
honour, 16, 68, 108, 109, 110, 111, 128(n8)
Horkheimer, M., 83
Hu Jintao, 9
human
  endeavour, 11, 24, 121
  nature, 38, 86, 116-7, 130(n37), 130(n40)
humanity, 4, 5, 11, 17, 18, 23, 25, 26, 28, 30, 39, 60, 87, 110, 117, 130(n37), 130(n42), 144, 148
Hume, D., 68, 78, 137, 145
humility, 111, 129(n20)
Hundred Schools of Thought, 2
Huygens, C., 136

ideology/ies, 28, 70, 76(n55), 80, 81, 82, 95, 100(n16), 143, 145
imitation, 78, 80, 88, 90-1, 93, 102(n50), 102(n55)
impiety, 21, 174, 181
Impressionism, 94, 95
individualism, 60, 124, 131(n69), 169(n49)
individual(s), 11, 17, 19, 20, 26, 31(n7), 44, 46, 60, 63, 71, 85, 86, 88, 94, 95, 96, 101(n32), 105, 128, 135, 138, 167(n1), 170(n67), 170(n69), 173, 179, 182
  and the city, 12, 18, 21, 116, 122
  and Confucianism, 116, 117, 121, 122, 131(n69)
  and democracies, 155-9, 163, 164, 170(n76)
  heroic, 86, 101(n32)
  and Socrates, 121, 122
injustice, 4, 14, 18, 67, 91, 174
innovation(s), 7, 11, 19, 20, 24, 25, 27, 36, 41, 52, 53, 64, 65, 80, 90, 95, 97, 105, 136, 137, 138, 142, 145, 146, 147, 148, 154, 157, 159, 162, 171, 179, 180, 183, 184
integrity, 58, 64, 65, 66, 67, 84, 184
Intellectualism, 76(n58), 78

intellectual(s)
  challenges to, 58, 75(n46)
  and class, 60, 61–2, 74(n29)
  critiques of, 67–72
  and decline thesis, 69–72, 75(n49),
    75(n50), 76(n55)
  definition, 57–61, 70, 73(n22)
  and democracy, 71, 75(n45),
    167(n1)
  and the Enlightenment 58, 59, 60,
    70, 72(n16)
  and Marxism, 62–3
  and modern philosopher kings, 5,
    58, 61, 63–5, 66, 67, 69–72
  and modern state, 71, 73(n17)
  organic, 62, 74(n32), 100(n16)
  and political power, 58, 61–5, 67,
    74(n32)
  and politics, 11, 30, 58, 60, 61, 63,
    64, 67–8, 71
  and progress, 58, 60, 63, 64, 65
  public, 6, 57–76, 171
  and revolution, 62, 74(n29)
  and social media, 71
  and totalitarianism, 68–9,
    75(n45)
  traditional, 62, 71, 100(n16)
  as tragic heroes, 66–9
  typologies, 73(n27)
  and universities, 70, 71, 75(n50),
    76(n58)
  'vanguardist' role, 62, 65
intelligentsia, 59, 72(n12), 76(n55)
  technical, 62, 74(n29), 143
Intuitionism, 78
Ion, 92–3
Islam, 27, 35, 53(n3), 95

Jacoby, R., 59
Jewish thought, 34(n74), 36, 53(n2)
Jiang Zemin, 9
John the Baptist, 43
John of Paris, 48
John of Salisbury, 38, 106
Judaism, 27, 35
judgement, 7, 61, 65, 68, 108, 109,
    112, 120, 125, 126, 127, 139,
    152, 155, 159, 160, 162, 163,
    164, 166, 178, 184, 186, 187

political, 40, 51, 139, 172, 173,
    183
practical, 16–17, 126, 166
junzi (exemplary person), 118, 119,
    122, 130(n45), 130(n48)
just city, 4, 11, 19, 25, 30(n7),
    32(n42), 93, 174, 189(n45)
just war theory, 40
justice, 1, 2, 3, 4, 5, 7, 8, 11, 12, 13,
    16, 17, 18, 19, 23, 24, 25, 26,
    27, 28, 29, 30, 32(n39), 33(n45),
    39, 40, 43, 60, 61, 66, 85, 91, 92,
    93, 95, 106, 122, 124, 131(n72),
    154, 171, 172, 173, 174, 175,
    179, 181, 182, 185, 186, 187,
    189(n45)

kallipolis, 4, 10, 182
Kant, I., 27, 78, 85, 145, 165
Kautsky, K., 59, 62
Kepler, J., 136
Khmer Rouge, 3, 69
King Ahab, 43
King David, 43
King Ferdinand of Castile, 51
King Henry VIII, 104
King Philip IV (of France), 48, 49
King Phillip IV (of Spain), 77
King Victor Emanuel III, 52
King Zhang of Qin, 2
Klinias the Cretan, 105, 106
knowledge, 1, 12, 15, 16, 26, 36, 42,
    44, 45, 60, 73(n21), 89, 107,
    116, 126, 134, 135, 136, 139,
    140, 141, 143, 144, 145, 147,
    162, 166, 167(n3), 170(n77),
    172, 180
Kuhn, T., 145

law (the), 7, 30, 35, 36, 37, 47, 49,
    82, 129(n36), 161, 180, 181,
    182, 186, 187(n12), 189(n46);
    see also natural law, rule of
    law
laws, 2, 8, 15, 22, 23, 24, 49, 53(n1),
    86, 93, 95, 105, 119, 122, 125,
    136, 137, 138, 157, 160, 174,
    182, 183, 184, 189(n46)
leaders, 3, 9, 21, 51, 55(n34), 71, 117,

119, 143, 160, 166, 168(*n*11), 168(*n*12), 174, 182
and advisors, 98, 104, 107, 114, 119, 139, 148, 171
and philosopher kings, 28, 53, 98, 127
political, 28, 98, 104, 117, 119, 127, 139, 140, 148, 160, 173
revolutionary, 9–10
leadership, 9, 10, 119, 121, 130(*n*50)
legitimacy, 5, 20, 28, 58, 65, 67, 95, 138, 140, 144, 147, 162, 164, 165, 171
Leibniz, G. W., 104, 145
Lenin, V., 10, 62, 81, 178
Leon of Salamis, 173, 174
li (ritual propriety), 117, 119, 123, 132(*n*77)
Liar Paradox, 18
life
active, 18, 26
civic, 181, 182
contemplative, 3, 18, 26, 63, 135
examined, 122, 123
good, 11–12, 24, 186
of the mind, 14, 105, 153, 154, 155, 158, 159
philosophical, 26, 28, 121, 122
political, 3, 13, 17, 18, 25, 26, 39, 41, 67–8, 121, 144, 181
tyrannical, 11, 24, 189
unexamined, 115, 173
Lilla, M., 27, 68
Lindblom, C. E., 140
literature, 73(*n*20), 78, 82, 103(*n*89), 156, 157, 158, 159, 169(*n*49)
Locke, J. 27, 137, 145, 162, 178
love of learning, 115, 119, 121, 123, 129(*n*33)
loyalty, 106, 108, 117, 122, 130(*n*42), 184
Lukács, G., 62, 68, 83
Luther, M., 38, 50–1
Lutheranism, 51
Luxemburg, R., 62

Machiavelli, N., 7, 28, 52, 98, 105, 106–15, 124, 127
magnanimity 111, 129(*n*20)

Maimonides, 27, 36, 37
Manifesto of the Vienna Circle, 142
Mannheim, K., 61
Mao Zedong, 9, 10, 82, 96, 178
Marcuse, H., 83
Marshall, A., 137
Marsilius of Padua, 48–9
Marx, K., 28, 59, 62, 70, 80, 81, 82, 83, 94, 98, 146, 178
Marxism, 62, 63, 84
materialism, 25, 60, 80, 83, 137
mathematics, 73(*n*18), 135, 136, 137, 138, 144
Megillus the Spartan, 105–6
Melanchthon, P., 38
Melians, 3, 4, 8(*n*5)
meritocracy, 151(*n*36), 154, 167–8(*n*10)
metaphysics, 68, 123, 135, 136
Milesian School, 22
Mill, J. S., 85, 137
Milton, J., 85
mimesis (imitation of nature), 78, 80, 88, 90, 94, 95, 97, 98
miracles, 42, 44, 52
moderation, 12, 16, 28, 92, 162, 172
modernity, 7, 8, 52, 53, 63–4, 65, 68, 70, 76(*n*54), 78, 83, 88, 89, 95, 99, 146, 147
monastic tradition, 41
monasticism, 54(*n*26)
Montesquieu, C. L., 162, 178
morality, 7, 20, 22, 60, 85, 87, 146, 150(*n*29), 156
music, 77, 78, 83, 86, 87, 89, 91, 95, 96, 99, 101(*n*33), 103(*n*88), 119, 135, 144, 161
myth(s), 87, 93, 101(*n*34), 102(*n*68), 103(*n*86), 105, 122, 182, 188(*n*26)

National Socialism, 95
natural law, 116, 129(*n*36)
nature, 3, 5, 6, 10, 30, 130(*n*42), 166
and art/artists, 78, 85, 90, 101(*n*31)
concept, 23–4, 33(*n*61), 33(*n*62)
discovery, 22, 23
and Enlightenment critiques, 60

nature (*cont.*)
  importance in philosophy, 17–8,
    22, 25, 26, 28, 33(*n*59), 33(*n*60),
    116–7, 121, 130(*n*37), 135, 136,
    145, 190(*n*55)
  laws of, 138
  mechanistic conception of, 136
  and science, 145, 151(*n*39)
Nazism, 68
necessity, 5, 10, 67, 87, 90, 94, 109,
    112, 114, 161, 162
New Public Management, 127,
    133(*n*96)
Newton, I., 53, 136, 138
Nietzsche, F., 27, 86–7, 97, 98, 145
nihilism, 27, 70, 87
noble lies, 17, 32(*n*42), 91, 102(*n*69),
    103(*n*86)
nomos (laws, customs, conventions),
    23, 182
norms, 23, 24, 25, 34(*n*67), 89, 95,
    116, 117, 121, 126, 182
nous (mind), 23, 135

Oakeshott, M., 27
obedience, 40, 47, 173
oligarchy, 147, 173
ontology, 141
opinion(s), 10, 12, 14, 17, 59, 64,
    111, 112, 155, 156, 171, 178,
    179
Organicism, 78
Orphic rituals, 20

papacy, 40, 44–9, 50, 51, 52, 53
paradox, 9–30
  as action, 18–26
  as contemplation and action, 18–26
  definition, 18
  and philosopher kings *see*
    philosopher kings
parliament, 153, 160
parliamentarism, 124, 160
Parmenides of Elea, 18, 20, 23, 181
parrhesia (frankness), 111, 113, 114,
    129(*n*21)
Parsons, T., 61
passions, 15, 66–7, 85, 90,
    101–2(*n*47), 154

patriotism, 21, 110, 182
Paul (apostle), 40, 42, 43, 53(*n*6)
peace, 24, 26, 87, 117, 123, 134, 142,
    148, 185
Peace of Westphalia, 52
Peloponnesian War, 173
people (the), 152–70
  and democracy, 96, 152–70
  as philosopher kings, 5, 7, 152,
    153, 163–7
  sovereignty, 152, 162, 163–6,
    171–2
  wisdom, 30, 152, 153, 163–6,
    171–2
perfectability, 5, 8, 26, 156, 157, 159,
    171, 173, 186
Pericles, 21, 154
Persian Wars, 23
persuasion, 14, 106
Petrucci, P., 108–9, 113
philosopher kings
  and advisors, 104–33
  and artists, 88–93, 98–9
  and democracy, 29, 152, 153, 154,
    161, 162–3, 166
  hidden, 105–15, 124, 127, 128,
    139, 141, 144, 148, 171, 178
  and intellectuals, 69–72
  modern, 6, 7, 8, 19, 26–30, 36, 42,
    47, 49–52, 58, 63, 65, 66, 67,
    69, 70, 72, 79, 80, 84, 97, 98–9,
    127–8, 138, 139, 144, 145, 148,
    152, 163, 171–90
  paradox, 4, 5, 6, 8, 9–30, 30(*n*4),
    33(*n*45), 35, 58, 66, 67, 72, 77,
    79, 104, 105, 115, 116, 118, 121,
    124, 125, 127, 128, 134, 135,
    139, 144, 152, 153, 154, 163,
    167, 171, 173, 174, 175, 178,
    183, 185, 186
  pious, 6, 36, 41, 44, 46, 49–50,
    52–3
  and popes, 49–52
  and princes, 49–52
  promise, 4, 5, 6, 7, 8, 11, 17, 24–5,
    26, 28, 29, 35, 36, 58, 72, 79, 99,
    105, 128, 148, 152, 153, 167,
    171, 172, 173, 183, 185, 186
  and prophets, 35–44

and ruling, 13, 16–18, 104, 182
and scientists, 135–7, 141–3
see also advisors, artists, intellectuals, scientists
philosophical
 engagement, 179, 183
 method, 155, 157
 reflection(s), 7, 59, 63, 163, 180, 182, 184
 rulers, 6, 16, 175–7, 178
 speculation, 20, 53(*n*3), 124, 138, 180, 184
 writings, 6, 185
philosophy
 and contemplation, 63, 144
 and corruption, 18, 20, 173, 181
 Eastern, 138
 natural, 37, 138
 and poetry, 80, 88–98
 quarrel with poetry *see* Socrates
 see also democracy, politics, science, theology, writing
phronesis (prudence), 178, 188(*n*27)
phusis (nature), 22, 116, 135
physiologoi (enquirers into nature), 22, 23
piety, 4, 20, 22, 27, 28, 29, 35, 36, 38, 39, 41, 44, 46, 47, 50, 51, 52, 117, 120, 123, 130(*n*42), 173
pious king(s), 5, 6, 11, 36, 42, 46, 171
Plato, 4, 10, 11, 23, 24, 29, 37, 39, 80, 85, 88, 89, 97, 104, 105, 106, 127
 defence of philosophy, 28
 as philosopher king, 173–5
 reservations about politics, 174, 175–7
 and writing, 20, 179, 180, 182, 183
Platonic dialogue(s), 25, 28, 92, 174, 180–1, 182, 183, 184
Plekhanov, G., 82
Poe, A., 79
poetry, 17, 20, 78, 80, 83, 85–94, 98, 99, 101(*n*32), 101–2(*n*47), 102(*n*68), 103(*n*86), 103(*n*87), 116, 161
 quarrel with philosophy *see* Socrates

Romantic, 84–6, 100(*n*26), 101(*n*31)
 see also philosophy
Polemarchus, 39
politeia (regimes), 122
political
 agonism, 183
 ambition(s), 11, 25, 119, 121, 175, 189(*n*45)
 corruption, 10, 15, 16, 21, 60, 64, 65, 67, 141, 174
 philosophy, 26, 34(*n*75), 35, 53(*n*3), 86, 115, 183
 prosperity, 115, 116, 117
 rule, 8, 17, 63, 108, 112, 118–21, 139, 161, 182
politics
 and art *see* art
 democratic, 143, 148, 160, 161, 165
 and philosophy, 2, 3, 4, 5, 11–30, 35, 41, 44, 45, 50, 51, 61, 63–4, 65, 68, 94, 98, 115, 118, 121, 124, 127, 159, 173–4, 181, 182, 186
 and science *see* science
 and wisdom *see* wisdom
pope(s), 6, 35, 41, 44–9, 50, 51, 52, 53, 171
 as new philosopher kings, 49–52
 see also Christian Church
Popper, K., 29, 68
positivism, 137, 142
poverty, 40, 49, 50, 65, 87, 116
power
 political, 4, 9, 10, 14, 24, 43, 44, 58, 61, 64, 65, 121, 139, 186
 separation from truth, 61–5
 and wisdom *see* wisdom
praxis (practical action) 135, 178
prejudice, 64, 181
Presbyterianism, 51
pride, 29, 111, 129(*n*20), 177, 187
priest(s), 6, 36, 43, 45, 46, 65, 91
Prince Arjuna, 1
princes, 35–56
 and advisors, 105–115
 Christian, 36, 44–9, 50, 51, 52, 53
 and flatterers, 110–11

princes (cont.)
  as new philosopher kings, 48,
    49–52
  and the papacy, 44–9
  and secretaries, 110, 113, 114
progress, 5, 6, 7, 8, 26, 28, 58, 60, 63,
  64, 65, 67, 68, 70, 154, 156, 159,
  171, 173, 176, 184, 186
proletariat, 61, 62, 63, 81, 82, 84
Prometheus, 24
propaganda, 29, 96, 99(n6)
prophecy, 42, 43, 44, 55(n37),
  55(n49), 89
prophets, 6, 7, 27, 30, 35–56, 61, 65,
  80, 86, 88–9, 97, 98, 155, 171
  false, 7, 44, 52
Protagoras of Abdera, 21, 22, 23–4,
  25, 98, 145
Protestantism, 95
providence, 5, 11, 18, 23, 24, 26, 30,
  38, 89, 183
prudence, 5, 6, 28, 51, 108, 112, 114,
  120, 125, 127, 139, 161, 166,
  173, 178, 179, 183, 184, 187,
  189(n47)
public (the), 15, 20, 60, 65, 66, 67,
  71, 91, 92, 94, 138, 142, 155,
  156, 157, 159, 170(n77)
public sphere(s), 6, 74(n29), 76(n60),
  167(n1)
Pythagoras, 20, 23
Pythagoreans, 20

Qing Dynasty, 124
Queen Catherine de Medici, 52
Queen Christina of Sweden, 104
Queen Isabella I of Castile, 51
Queen Mariana, 77
quietism, 41, 42, 186

radical historicism, 60, 70
Ranyou, 119
rationality, 71, 143, 165
reason, 2, 3, 38, 59, 68, 123,
  129(n36), 165, 166
  human 23, 27, 52
Reformation, 38, 50–1, 56(n65)
  counter-reformation movements,
    51

regime(s), 10, 19, 24, 62, 68, 80, 95,
  96, 98, 105, 106, 107, 108, 121,
  122, 123, 152, 154, 162, 163,
  165, 175, 181, 182
  authoritarian, 72, 143
  political, 80, 121, 123
  technocratic, 143, 144
religion(s), 27, 35, 36, 41, 52,
  55(n52), 56(n57), 64, 98, 110,
  155, 169(n49)
  and art, 95
  and laws, 53(n1)
  and philosophy, 27, 28, 132(n77)
  and politics, 27, 37, 44
  revealed, 35, 39, 41, 44, 52, 53, 88
  see also Christianity, Confucianism
ren (benevolence), 117, 118, 123,
  130(n37), 130(n42)
respect, 110, 123, 130(n42), 138
responsibility/ies, 39, 57, 64, 69,
  75(n46), 117, 125, 150(n28),
  173, 182
revelation, 28, 53(n5), 88
rhetoric, 11, 17, 21, 22, 37, 107, 135,
  166, 181
rights
  individual, 53, 96
  liberal, 124
Rimbaud, A., 83
Rimon, H., 69
Roman Empire, 45, 46, 47, 48
Romantic Movement, 85
Rousseau, J-J., 27, 68, 70, 146, 164
rule of law, 174, 182
Russell, B., 18, 26

sacrifice, 16, 17, 32(n39), 36, 44, 45,
  67, 105, 126
Said, E., 57
Saint Augustine, 37, 38, 39, 40, 88,
  106
Saint Peter, 40, 41, 42, 46, 47
Saint Thomas Aquinas, 27, 38, 40,
  42, 88
salvation, 39, 50, 51, 186
Sartre, J-P., 68
Schiller, F., 85
Schlegal, F., 85
Schopenhauer, A., 87

Schrödinger, E., 137, 138
science
    challenge to piety, 52–3
    critiques/challenges, 135, 144–8
    decline, 144–8
    and democracy, 103(*n*89), 143,
        147, 155, 156, 157–8, 159,
        167(*n*1)
    and ethics/morality, 137, 146, 148,
        150(*n*28)
    and expertise, 71, 140, 141, 142,
        143, 147
    modern, 7, 136, 137, 141
    nature of, 149(*n*20)
    and philosophy, 7, 52, 87, 135,
        136, 137, 138–43, 144,
        149(*n*14)
    and politics, 134–5, 138–43,
        144, 145, 146, 147, 150(*n*26),
        150(*n*28), 151(*n*41), 151(*n*49)
    public benefit, 138
    and public policy, 134, 139, 140–1,
        142, 143, 150(*n*26)
    transformation, 135–6
scientific
    advice, 114, 140, 141, 150(*n*26)
    advisors, 139–41, 144, 148
    innovations, 136, 137, 138, 145,
        146, 147, 148
    insight/approach, 78, 80, 134, 137,
        145
    kings, 141–3, 144
    knowledge, 135, 139, 140, 141,
        150–1(*n*33)
    method(s), 53, 138, 145, 167(*n*1)
    movements, 150–1(*n*33)
    truths, 134, 139
scientist(s)
    as advisor(s), 135, 139–41, 144,
        148
    dangers, 146–7
    definition, 135–6
    and democracies, 147, 167(*n*1)
    as modern benefactor(s), 134–51
    natural, 20, 144
    as philosopher (kings), 5, 7, 11,
        135–8, 139, 141–3, 144, 145,
        147, 148, 171
    and politics, 11, 30, 59, 134,

138–9, 141, 143, 144, 145, 148,
    150(*n*26), 150(*n*28)
    and public policy, 139
    role, 60, 140, 141, 149(*n*21),
        149–50(*n*22), 150(*n*25)
Second World War, 140, 151(*n*35)
Shakespeare, 3, 84, 97
shandao (efficacious way), 119
Shelley, M., 146
Shelley, P. B., 85, 86, 98
shengren (sage), 118
shenren (efficacious people), 119
shi (scholar apprentice), 118, 130(*n*45)
Shils, E., 61
Simon, H., 140
Simonides, 91
slavery, 40, 176, 182
Smith, A., 137
social contract, 53, 182
Socrates, 5, 10, 24, 28, 43, 87, 95, 97,
    144, 176
    comparison to Confucius, 115–6,
        121–4
    critiques of writing, 20, 179–180
    defence of the law, 181–2
    defence of philosophy, 181–2
    execution, 21, 23, 154, 174, 181
    and the family, 122
    and the Gods, 123, 131–2(*n*72)
    ignorance, 115, 181, 183
    and paradoxical philosopher kings,
        6, 12–13, 16, 19, 25
    as philosopher king, 173–5
    and politics, 4, 11, 14, 16, 63, 115,
        121, 181
    quarrel between philosophy and
        poetry, 80, 88, 89–94, 98
Song Dynasty, 124
sophists, 6, 11, 15, 16, 19, 20, 21–2,
    23, 24, 25, 29, 43, 63, 80, 89, 98,
    99, 116, 122, 175, 189(*n*45)
sovereignty, 7, 47, 48, 147, 148, 152,
    153
Spartans, 3
speech, 10, 85, 96, 130(*n*42), 179
    persuasive, 24
Spencer, H., 137
Spinoza, B., 36, 52
Stalin, J., 10, 81, 104, 178

Stoicism, 53(*n*6)
Swift, J., 144, 166–7

Tang Dynasty, 124
techne (art of how to make things), 23, 33(*n*45), 97, 135
technocracy, 142, 143, 147, 150(*n*31), 151(*n*34), 151(*n*35), 151(*n*36), 151(*n*37), 167(*n*5)
  movement, 142–3
technocrat(s), 7, 142
technology, 143, 144, 146, 147
  communication, 59, 167(*n*1), 171
telos, 17
Tertullian, 27, 38, 42
Thales of Miletus, 17, 20, 22, 23
Thamos Ammon, 179
theology, 37, 38, 49, 53(*n*9), 92, 98, 116, 123, 132(*n*77), 135, 136, 149(n12), 182
  debates, 48, 68
  and philosophy, 27, 36, 39, 50, 51, 52, 54(*n*11)
  see also religion
Theuth, 179
Thirty Years' War, 52
Thrasymachus of Chalcedon, 11, 21, 24, 25
Thucydides, 3
tian (heaven), 116, 117, 120, 123, 130(*n*39), 132(*n*75)
Tocqueville, A., 68, 147, 153, 154–9
Tolstoy, L., 78
totalitarianism, 29
tradition, 64, 67, 72(*n*6), 158, 159
Trotsky, L., 81
trust, 4, 8(*n*8), 110, 155
truth(s), 1, 7, 12, 16, 17, 38, 44, 53, 57, 58, 61, 67, 82, 83, 86, 87, 90, 98, 105, 106, 110, 111, 112, 114, 115, 135, 145, 155–6, 157, 164, 179, 186
  to power, 58, 65, 72(*n*6)
  scientific, 134, 139
  separation from power, 61–5
truth-telling, 111, 113, 114
Two Swords theory, 41
tyranny, 24, 25, 91, 154, 168(*n*12), 175, 190(*n*56)

tyrant(s), 24, 89, 104, 105, 106, 122, 128(*n*13), 176, 177, 188(*n*25)

ubermensch (overman), 87, 88, 98
universalism, 89

values, 7, 69, 87, 88, 125, 150(*n*28), 168(*n*10)
Veblen, T., 142
Velázquez, D., 77
Velázquez, J. N., 77
vice(s), 12, 86, 90
Vienna Circle, 142, 150–1(*n*33)
Virgil, 85
virtue, 21, 30(*n*4), 37, 65, 90, 108, 111, 117, 124, 154, 161, 162, 169(*n*55), 172, 173, 178, 181, 183
virtues, 12, 17, 18, 24, 26, 30(*n*4), 39, 104, 117, 121, 123, 130(*n*37), 161, 166, 181
  Christian, 111
  democratic, 159
  theological, 38
Voltaire, F-M., 60
Voluntarism, 78

Wagner, W. R., 86, 87, 96
war(s), 1, 3, 14, 15, 17, 22, 23, 40, 52, 103(*n*84), 150(*n*22), 186
  religious, 51–2
wealth, 15, 16, 17, 65, 81, 98, 109, 110, 116, 134, 139, 140, 158, 181
Weber, M., 137
  conception of bureaucracy, 125, 126–7
  ethic of conviction/ethic of responsibility, 125
Whewell, W., 135, 136
William of Ockham, 42, 49
wisdom, 1, 2, 11, 12, 15, 16, 17, 21, 26, 27, 28, 29, 30, 32(*n*40), 38, 39, 43, 58, 79, 92, 108, 109, 110, 111, 115–6, 117, 123, 147, 160, 161, 164, 165
  and politics, 2, 9, 35, 121, 152, 153, 161, 162, 166, 171, 172, 178, 179, 181, 183, 186, 187

and power, 2–8, 19, 29–30, 35, 44,
    50, 52, 58, 61, 63, 65, 66, 104,
    105, 106, 114–5, 118, 121, 123,
    124, 127, 148, 153, 167, 171,
    172–4, 180, 186
Wordsworth, W., 85, 86
Wright Mill, C., 59
writing, 77, 82, 98, 180, 187(*n*12)
    ambiguity for philosopher kings,
        178–9
    dangers, 183–6, 188(*n*36)
    as defence of philosophy, 181–2,
        183
    limits, 20, 33(*n*52), 179–83,
        188(*n*33)
    and philosophy, 30, 97, 180,
        188(*n*28), 188(*n*35), 189(*n*46)
    and political power, 98–9,
        188(*n*26), 188(*n*38), 190(*n*56)
    as ruling, 7, 8, 177–86

Xenophanes, 23
Xenophon, 106
Xi Jinping, 9, 168(*n*10)
Xi Jinping Thought, 9
xin (trustworthiness), 117, 129(*n*33)

Yang Huo, 120
Yeats, W. B., 98

Zengxi, 116
Zeno of Elea, 18
Zeno's Arrow Paradox, 19
Zeus, 24, 78, 91
Zhdanov, A., 81, 96
zhi (wisdom), 115, 116, 117, 118,
    119, 120, 123
Zigong, 119, 120
Zilu, 115, 116, 119, 120, 123
Zola, É., 59, 72(*n*14), 94

EU representative:
Easy Access System Europe
Mustamäe tee 50, 10621 Tallinn, Estonia
Gpsr.requests@easproject.com

www.ingramcontent.com/pod-product-compliance
Lightning Source LLC
Chambersburg PA
CBHW071102280326
41928CB00051B/2727